THE
SELF-AWARE
PARENT

D0390652

THE SELF-AWARE PARENT

RESOLVING CONFLICT AND BUILDING A BETTER BOND WITH YOUR CHILD

Dr. Fran Walfish

palgrave
macmillan

THE SELF-AWARE PARENT
Copyright © Fran Walfish, 2010.
All rights reserved.

First published in 2010 by PALGRAVE MACMILLAN® in the United
States—a division of St. Martin's Press LLC, 175 Fifth Avenue, New York, NY
10010.

Where this book is distributed in the UK, Europe and the rest of the world,
this is by Palgrave Macmillan, a division of Macmillan Publishers Limited,
registered in England, company number 785998, of Houndmills, Basingstoke,
Hampshire RG21 6XS.

Palgrave Macmillan is the global academic imprint of the above companies and
has companies and representatives throughout the world.

Palgrave® and Macmillan® are registered trademarks in the United States, the
United Kingdom, Europe and other countries.

ISBN: 978-0-230-10256-9 paperback

Library of Congress Cataloging-in-Publication Data

Walfish, Fran.
    The self-aware parent / Fran Walfish.
        p.   cm.
    Includes index.
    ISBN 978-0-230-10256-9 (pbk.)
    1. Parenting.   2. Parent and child.   I. Title.
HQ755.83.W35   2010
649'.125—dc22

                                                    2010019159

A catalogue record of the book is available from the British Library.

Design by Letra Libre Inc.

First edition: December 2010

10 9 8 7 6 5 4 3 2 1

Printed in the United States of America.

In loving memory of my beloved first niece,
Jennifer Candace Rub
1972–2008

CONTENTS

ACKNOWLEDGMENTS

Special thanks to Mom and Dad, Betty and Cantor Hershel Walfish, who gave me everything, including life and love; Shelley, Steve (the most amazing exemplary dad I know), Carolyn, Barry, and Gary; Niesa and Mike; Emily, Ben, and Sam; Josh, David, Zev, and Alexa. You are each so very special to me!

Thanks also to Lisa Wysocky ("Top of the line. Thanks, Lisa!"); Luba Ostashevsky ("You're awesome!"); Courtney, Alan, Jen, Michelle, Ayesha, Laura, and the gang at Palgrave Macmillan; Trina and Adam Venit ("Without you, nothing"); Mel Berger, Collin Reno, Justin Ongert, Amir Shakhalili, and all the guys at William Morris Endeavor Entertainment; and Eric Myers, Keith Fleer, Tracy Brennan, Jaime Bergman, David Boreanaz, Tom Parziale, Katey Sagal, Fred Toczek, Kathy Walker, Michael McDonald, Deborah Raffin, Alexandra Guzman, MFT, Anna Maria Alberghetti, Pilar Guzman at *Cookie* magazine, Diane Debrovner at *Parents* magazine, Audrey Kolina at *The Today Show*, and Del Bigtree.

Thank you to Saul L. Brown, M.D.; Aviva D. Biederman, M.D.; Helen Reid, L.C.S.W.; Wendy Mogel, Ph.D.; Jan David, M.A.; Jane Rosenberg, M.A.; Stephen Holden; Michele Colluci; Tony Origlio; Kip Vanderbilt; Metuka Benjamin; Dr. Sheryl Cohen; Ron Nagel, M.D.; Lori Annes, Ph.D.; Leslie Lobell and the Can-Do-Kids Gang; Irene Wongpec; Elaine Leader, Ph.D.; Carey Simon at Parenting Teens Resource Network; Debra Delshad Banks; JoAnn Scrivner; Heather Hire; Natalie and Emma at Decisive Flow; and Larry Daniels.

And also to Bruce M. Ramer, Madeline Ramer, Ann Ramer, Neal Ramer, Tira Ramer, Joe Mannis, Neal Hersh, Diana and Charals Haagen,

Mario the "Tailor" Gonzalez, Sam Emerson, Stanley Diller, Stanley Black, Jona Goldrich, Phil Blazer, Ryo Tsukioka, and Laura Ornest.

To my patients: every child, parent, and family who has come to me for help, thank you for the privilege of your trust and for teaching me every moment to moment.

FOREWORD

There is much to be said about the parent/child relationship and how family members relate to each other. How parents relate to one another when their children begin, for example, to walk or talk says a lot not only about the marriage, but also about how the parents were raised.

I call the study of how families and parents interact with each other, their expectations, and a child's interactions with his or her family from the earliest weeks the "dynamic of family systems." As director of the Department of Psychiatry at Cedars-Sinai Medical Center I spent much of my career fascinated by this dynamic. Over the years I have seen the study of psychiatry and psychology change from focusing on the individual only, to focusing at least in some degree on the family unit. I am very glad to see our profession moving in this direction.

Every child falls into some kind of family system that is headed either by biological parents or other family elders. The more a therapist understands how a family, including grandparents, siblings, and even aunts and uncles, functions, the more helpful a therapist can be. The actions and behaviors of everyone in the dynamic will ultimately affect the child.

In the course of my more than fifty-year career I have mentored, counseled, and advised many therapists from the earliest days of their professional involvement. Dr. Fran Walfish is one of them. I was not surprised to learn she was writing a book for parents because she is one who early on comprehended the concept of how families function psychologically. Throughout her career I have observed her warm, caring enthusiasm while working with hundreds of parents, children, and families.

Dr. Fran is a very energetic person and is appropriately expressive as she interacts with her patients in a therapeutic situation. She is forthcoming and outgoing while at the same time an intelligent, close listener. To parents she offers a positive direction based on psychologic understanding.

Of particular importance is Dr. Fran's ability to recognize the differing value systems of families and parents. She takes note and does not come in with the preconceived stereotypical ideas that tend to box people into rigid beliefs and even behaviors. Instead, she ferrets out what is flexible in the family interactions and helps parents create a strong family foundation.

Dr. Fran offers a great deal in this book. Basically, she is writing about parents and for parents. Much has been written about psychotherapy for children, but help for children requires involvement to some degree from each family member, beginning with the parents.

My hope is that everyone who reads *The Self-Aware Parent* does so with an open mind. Dr. Walfish is an excellent therapist. She is an enthusiastic, vital person who cares. Her ideas and experience can be of value to all who are open to them.

Saul L. Brown, M.D.
Emeritus Director, Department of Psychiatry,
Cedars-Sinai Medical Center
Emeritus Clinical Professor, Psychiatry,
U.C.L.A. School of Medicine
Emeritus Faculty, Southern California
Institute for Psychoanalysis

THE
SELF-AWARE
PARENT

INTRODUCTION

When I was ten years old, all the young mothers on my Southern California block brought their babies to visit my mom, and invariably, each child ended up in my arms. Both the mothers and I realized early on that babies relaxed and fell asleep when I was holding them. I felt like I had been gifted with a special connection to babies and their moms and I knew without a doubt very early on in my life that I was here to help them.

I began my journey, as many young girls do, by babysitting. Then, when I was thirteen, I made a thousand dollars one summer as a camp counselor. You may not know this, but back in the 1960s a thousand dollars was a lot of money! I realized during that time that I specifically loved kids ages three to six. I loved their energy and their inquisitiveness, but also their honest assessment of situations.

I graduated from high school when I was sixteen, and life, as it sometimes does, opened a clear pathway for me. One of my friends was a speech therapist in the child psychiatry department at Cedars-Sinai Medical Center in Los Angeles, one of the premier teaching hospitals and medical centers in the country. On this day she called me in a panic, because a lot of the staff was out sick. She had a room full of emotionally troubled kids and wanted to know if I could come in and be another body in the room, a babysitter.

Intrigued by my friend's request, I went in to the hospital and tried to make a difference. The kids and I (because I was interacting with them) were observed through one-way glass by some of the leading mental health experts in the nation.

I can't tell you how thrilled I was at the end of the day when I was offered an internship. This was beyond my wildest dreams. Way beyond. But at the same time, I was frightened. I didn't know what to do with kids who didn't do as you asked, who weren't polite, who didn't communicate easily. This was all uncharted territory for me, so I did what a lot of people do. I ran. I stayed away for two weeks, during which time I sat at home and thought about the offer and the possibility that I could learn to impact those kids enough to help them communicate and improve their lives. Remember that by now I was just seventeen. I knew this was a life-changing opportunity, but how life-changing, I could not possibly realize.

When I returned I embarked upon a year-long, unpaid internship, and on my eighteenth birthday, I was hired by the hospital. I spent the next seven years at Cedars-Sinai, groomed by leading psychiatrists and psychologists. I also earned a Bachelor of Arts degree in child psychology and early childhood education. It is a rare occasion when we find the perfect environment, but for me, this was it. I blossomed and flourished.

After eight years, however, I realized I had gained enough confidence in myself to let other people know that I could sing. Singing had been an escape for me for many years and I loved the way music could make me feel, and the emotions it could bring. While I was still at Cedars-Sinai, I began doing showcases in the Los Angeles area in the evenings. At first I was afraid no one would show up, but, to my eternal surprise, all the shrinks I worked with during the day showed up at my showcases at night. I guess music was an escape for them, too. Soon I was bombarded with offers. I recorded four songs for A&M Records and toured the nation with acts such as Joan Rivers and Rodney Dangerfield.

Making the decision to leave the security of Cedars-Sinai for a "no promises" career on the road was not only difficult, it was agonizing. But I eventually realized that this was an opportunity that was not likely to come my way again, and it also offered me the chance to see a different side of life. And, I can tell you this: I learned far more about psychopathology in show business than I ever learned in school or at the hospital. Despite the waiting between gigs, I loved my time on the road. I mean, I really loved it.

In 1993, however, I began to search for something that had deeper meaning, and I knew I had to return to the career that had meant so much to me earlier in my life. I went back to school and got all my degrees in a five-year period. I was committed! I earned a Doctorate in Clinical Psychology and a license as a Marriage and Family Therapist. Since then I have become Chair of the Board of The Early Childhood Parenting Center, which was founded at Cedars-Sinai Medical Center forty years ago.

To earn my license and degree I had to complete a required three thousand hours of supervised internship. This I did at my old friend Cedars-Sinai and also in private practice and at a private school in Beverly Hills. There, I was a school psychologist, and it was just eight hundred kids, their parents . . . and me.

I opened my own private practice in 1995 in the 90210 zip code of Beverly Hills and was flooded with referrals from pediatricians, K–12 schools, and preschools, mostly for children ages two to six. I say this with awe and wonder because although I have since worked with and come to adore all ages, this was the age group that I had initially bonded with when I was still a teen working as a counselor at summer camp. And, this was the age group I specialized in for my degree in early childhood education. Since then, the average age of kids I see in my practice has risen to between ten and twelve, although I see many patients that are much older or younger than that. In some instances I see just the parents.

You might think that parents and kids who ride up the elevator to my office with the likes of Lindsay Lohan, Jennifer Aniston, Paris Hilton, and others on their way to visit exclusive clothiers and jewelers in my building would have issues that are unlike any issue that you and your kids could possibly have, but that's not true. Just like your kids, the kids I see yearn for more quality family time with their parents. They struggle with sibling rivalry, self-esteem, separation anxiety, divorce, acting out, and a host of other problems that you and your children might also struggle with.

Today I help parents balance work and family, and I assist divorced parents as they try to work together for the benefit of their children. I teach parents to tune in to the emotional needs of their children and to function in a strong and healthy manner instead of being ripped apart by guilt. I assist parents and teachers in determining the cause of acting out behavior in school and serve as a point person for parent and child so that we all are on the same page. And, I assess learning differences so children can be referred to the correct specialist.

When I first made the decision to travel this path I thought I would miss singing, miss the road, miss show business. But that has not been the case. I get so much gratification from giving to kids and their parents. This is so real, so meaningful, that I cannot imagine doing anything else.

My work is so invigorating for me because life and growth happens right in front of my eyes. I get to see it when I introduce into someone's life the ability to make change. So many parents walk in to my office feeling hopeless, but by the time they leave an hour or two later, they can see a light at the end of the tunnel. What could be better than that?

No longer satisfied with limiting myself to my Beverly Hills office, I wrote *The Self-Aware Parent* to help parents everywhere tackle the enormous challenge of raising children. Old-fashioned, traditional psychiatry treats the child alone. All of my training and experience has taught me to view parents as partners. I believe you, the parent, have the single most powerful influence on your children. I want to "share the gospel" so that you and your children will forge amazing relationships and develop into healthy human beings—and not need psychotherapy treatment.

I have found that all of my training in traditional psychotherapy recommends that treatment go at a slow pace to allow parents to take information in and process it. But what I have realized through the years is that kids grow rapidly and they do not have time for parents to catch up. We have to get to the meat of the issues quickly or the child will have wallowed too long without help.

The Self-Aware Parent is intended to give you the tools and courage to examine yourself, so you can help your child. It will also help you evaluate methods you want to pass along from the parenting you received, and those you want to replace with other supportive and attuned parenting strategies. The stories and case studies presented here are intended to dramatize and illuminate the issues raised; names and identifying details have been changed.

Parenting is a journey, a process. So is learning about yourself and your life. I can't tell you how proud and honored I am to travel alongside you as you embark on this adventure.

Very Truly Yours,

Dr. Fran
October 2010

CHAPTER ONE

THE IMPORTANCE OF KNOWING YOURSELF AS A PARENT

O ften, in the heat of the moment, parents say or do things they do not mean. I'm sure this is true with you, because it is true of all parents for the simple reason that parents are not perfect. In my practice, I have found that when emotions heat up, we all tend to repeat behaviors that were done to us when we were children. So, if we had a dad who tended to hit, that's what we also do. If we had a mom who screamed, that's our tendency. We don't mean to, but because it was programmed into us as very small children, that reaction has become our automatic response.

That is why understanding who you are, as a person and as a parent, is so important. Understanding yourself gives you choices, and when you choose to respond in a specific way, rather than respond automatically, situations more often than not resolve themselves favorably.

Understanding yourself and learning new responses to the buttons your child pushes can stop generations of learned behavior. For example, if you feel unsure, chances are that your parent, grandparent, great-grandparent, and the mother or father who came before them also felt unsure. What a gift it will be to your children for you to wrestle with that feeling and replace it with confidence and strength.

THE PROOF IS IN THE RESEARCH

Research supports the fact that a child who was parented negatively has a high likelihood of parenting her own child in the same manner. It doesn't matter if the adverse parenting was physical, verbal, sexual, neglectful, or just plain inconsistent, generation after generation passes down these damaging behaviors.

A 2009 study looked at data from three generations of Oregon families. It shows that "positive parenting" (which includes factors such as showing warmth, monitoring children's activities, being involved, and practicing consistent discipline) not only has a positive impact on adolescents, but it also has a positive impact on the way they will eventually choose to parent their own children.

In the first study of its kind, David Kerr, assistant professor of psychology at Oregon State University, project director Deborah Capaldi, and co-authors Katherine Pears and Lee Owen of the Eugene-based Oregon Social Learning Center examined surveys from 206 boys who were considered at risk for juvenile delinquency. The boys, then in elementary school, were interviewed and observed, as were their parents.

Starting in 1984, researchers met with the boys every year from the time they were nine years old until they were thirty-three. That is twenty-four years of observation! Additionally, as the boys grew up and started their own families, their partners and children began participating in the study as well.

Kerr writes, "what we find is that negative parenting, such as hostility and lack of follow-through, leads to negative parenting in the next generation not through observation, but by allowing problem behavior to take hold in adolescence. For instance, if you try to control your child with anger and threats, he learns to deal in this way with peers, teachers, and eventually his own children. If you do not track where your child is, others will take over your job of teaching him about the world. But those lessons may involve delinquency and a lifestyle that is not compatible with becoming a positive parent."[1]

While this study followed children from adolescence, in my practice I see these same behavioral trends long before children hit puberty. Children as young as four model behavior; for example, if a parent uses anger and threats when dealing with their child, then their child will use anger and threats when dealing with others.

The study shows that children who experienced high levels of negative parenting were more likely to be antisocial and delinquent as adolescents. Boys who had these characteristics in adolescence were more likely to grow up to be inconsistent and ineffective parents, and to have children with challenging behaviors.

"We knew that these negative pathways can be very strong," Kerr writes. "What surprised us is how strong positive parenting pathways are as well."

Researchers found that children who had parents who monitored behavior, employed consistent rules, and showed warmth and affection were more likely to have close relationships with their peers, be more engaged in school, and have better self-esteem.

"So part of what good parenting does is not only protect you against negative behaviors but instill positive connections with others during adolescence that then impact how you relate with your partner and your own child as an adult," Kerr writes. "This research shows that when we think about the value of prevention, we should consider an even wider lens than is typical. We see now that changes in parenting can have an effect not just on children but even on grandchildren."

THE CULTURAL DIVIDE

In addition to the many parents I see who were born here in America, I see a diverse group of parents who have immigrated to the United States from the Middle East, Eastern Europe, Latin America—virtually every continent on Earth. In treating these families, it is clear that some are not aware that parenting is cultural. For example, in some countries it is normal for parents to slap their children. In other countries it is normal for a woman to stay in the home and not go out in public unless she is chaperoned. When these parents come to the United States they have a choice to make: Do we want to keep this cultural parenting style, or should we adopt a style that is closer to what is normal here in America? It is a difficult, life-changing decision that must involve both parents if it is to be successful.

Cultural Divide: A Case Study

When Susan, Lily's mom, first showed up in my office, it was evident that she hailed from a strictly traditional European family. Her father was the undeniable head of the household and his decisions were always final. In addition to being strict, he was highly critical. He loved his family, but because his father had been critical with him, this was how he related to his own children.

Susan's mother, on the other hand, was very much the proper lady. She was an elegant and respected member of her community and was quite preoccupied with how she—and her family—looked and dressed. She experienced her husband and children as extensions of herself and reflections on her identity as mother and wife. Susan eventually realized that her mother cared too much about others' opinions, but that realization came long after our first meeting. Years, actually.

Combined, Susan's parents were so concerned with being perfect that they forgot one element that is critical in raising happy children: feelings. In this family there was absolutely no room for feelings. Not surprisingly, Susan married a man who was much like her father. He was strict, with high expectations of Susan and their young daughter, Lily. As a result, Susan felt that she could never live up to what was expected of her. She never felt "good enough."

When Lily was little more than a toddler, she began to pick at her food. Susan, of course, with her expectations of being the perfect mother, would demand that Lily eat, but Lily would refuse. At school Lily showed some real talent in art. One evening, Susan, hoping to validate herself by showing her talented daughter off to others, asked Lily to show one of her drawings to guests in their home. Lily, of course, clammed up and refused.

Like many children of parents who make demands, Lily was shy. In addition to being a picky eater, Lily developed separation anxiety. She didn't want to leave her mother to go to school or to a friend's house. From Lily's perspective, she was overloaded with the same high expectations that her grandfather had put on her mother. Susan and her husband were passing the parenting style along to the next generation.

Susan and her husband reacted to Lily's shyness by pushing her even harder. Unfortunately, pushing is exactly the way to get a child "stuck." And that's where Lily and her parents were when she and Susan landed in my office, stuck in a vicious cycle of rigid expectations and resulting shyness and constriction.

Susan and I worked first on the feelings she had when Lily would not perform. "I'm embarrassed," Susan cried. "I am a failure as a mother. What is wrong with me?" Over time, I helped Susan see Lily for who she is, gifts, flaws, and all. Then I helped them both flourish by giving Susan verbal scripts she could use to help Lily. For example, when Lily refused to show her artwork to her teacher, Susan said, "I see you're not ready to show your artwork to your teacher, but I'm so happy you could show it to Mommy. I am sure that one day soon, you'll be ready to show it to your teacher. I know she will like it as much as I do."

Sure enough, a few days later, Lily showed her artwork to her teacher. Susan and her husband incorporated similar scripts into other areas of Lily's life and Lily is now eating well and enjoying spending time at friends' houses. Once the pressure was off and her feelings were validated, Lily could blossom like the true flower she has always been.

A GOLDEN GIFT

Parents like Susan's, who are so very strict and demanding, do themselves a disservice because they cut themselves off emotionally from their children. A child finds it comforting and reassuring when a parent acknowledges, validates, and talks about feelings. But these parents are not at all in touch with either their feelings or the feelings of their child. They are way too emotionally cut off, and the result is that their kids grow up anxious.

Surprisingly, the reason that rigid and demanding parents do not stop to deal with feelings is because they are scared. These parents did not have an available parent to help them identify and understand their feelings.

Therefore, they did not have a mellow place within their families that helped them calm down when overcome with strong feelings. Now, the fear in these parents is that they may be overwhelmed by powerful emotions and left to deal with them alone. They fear drowning in their own feelings without a supportive person to rescue them.

While you may not be overly strict or put demands on your child, you may be scared. Or, you may be overwhelmed, frustrated, tired, anxious, or feeling any number of other emotions. This book is a gentle invitation to explore your feelings and fears. It is a place for learning and understanding, for acceptance and love. The result is the precious gift of a better parent to your child. And, how wonderful it will be when you see your children raising happy and healthy children of their own.

WHEN IT COMES TO BEHAVIOR, THERE IS ALWAYS A REASON

While most of you who are reading this book will not have parents who are rigidly strict or emotionless, you may have thought about how you were parented and what different choices you can make now that you are in the driver's seat with your own kids. For example, your dad might have spent too many hours at work, or your mom might have been self-absorbed and distant. I know that my own parents had unique personalities and parenting styles that affect me to this day.

One Sunday morning when I was a little girl of about seven my dad was working, so my mom was washing the car by herself. In the process of rinsing the car, Mom accidentally and unknowingly got water on the brakes. It's harder to do that now, as cars are built to stricter standards, but when I was a child, it wasn't an uncommon thing to have happen.

After she dried the car, Mom got cleaned up and took my sister (who was nine) and me for a day of fun. But before we could go too far, we needed to get gas. Mom stopped at a busy and popular intersection, filled up, and we headed out only to find that the brakes were so wet, they did not work. Mom began pumping the brakes, to no avail. The car would not slow down. Even worse, the car began accelerating. As you can imagine, we were all terrified. But Mom's reaction was to go into a complete hysterical panic. "We're all going to die," she screamed. "Help us! Somebody help us!" This was seconds before she steered the car into a curb and we came, safely, to a stop.

As a result of this episode and my mother's reactions to it, I felt very vulnerable and for years had a tendency to panic in situations of crisis. I looked to my tall, grown-up mother as my rock. She always took care of me, and when she screamed, "We're all going to die!" I believed her. I really did. All children look to their parents as a barometer to see if they can get through disaster. I truly did, in that moment, believe my mother. And my sister apparently did, too, as we both echoed her cries. All three of us were screaming and crying, but looking back, I think my mom was crying the hardest. The biggest surprise of the whole event was when we bumped up against the curb and I realized that we weren't actually going to die. That's how much I believed my mother, and your child is no different.

You know, the experience did not cause me to doubt my mom until I was much older. Then, I was able to see her reaction as part of a pattern. Every parent is allowed a mistake (or two or three!). But when a parent's actions and reactions become a pattern, it affects their child's personality. A son or daughter will not worry too much about a parent's outburst or failing, but when the same outburst or failure is repeated, it causes the child to feel both doubt and worry.

It is important for you to know that all kids want to give their parents more chances. They love you and want you to succeed. Let's say you tell your eight-year-old son that after he finishes his homework, you'll both go to the park. But the homework takes too long and now you have to make dinner; there is no time for the park. You might feel your son will not trust you because you did not deliver on your word. Please know that this one time, it's okay. Two or three times: no.

It is expected that you will make mistakes in parenting your children. After all, you are only human. And no one has perfect models in their parents. I hope that in reading *The Self-Aware Parent* you will become aware of patterns in your parenting, as well as in the parenting you received. My goal is to create awareness of your own internal feelings and processes, so that instead of reacting automatically, you can evaluate which of your reactions are best for your child.

This brings me back to my mother. I love her dearly and we all have our plusses and minuses, but her overreaction was part of a pattern. Much later, I was able to separate the incident into two parts: One, my mom was far more frightened than I was, and, two, her panic was a reaction to her fright. Because she passed on her heightened reactions to me, even now, if a child is hurt, I have to check myself to be sure I do not overreact, that I am not smothering. My mom communicated to me in a time of crisis that she was not in control, and because of that I try to be sure I am always communicating that I am in control. I have a choice in my actions and re-actions, but I have to remember to stop, think, and choose how I will respond and behave.

While it is reassuring to a child to know that his or her parent is capable, we have to be sure not to go so far that we expect too much from our children. This happens far more often than you might think.

Selective Mutism: A Case Study

Both Cindy and her husband, Jim, had brilliant minds. Both were business advisors who excelled in math and reasoning, but definitely not in feelings and emotions. Cindy and Jim were also very nice people who loved their three-and-a-half-year-old daughter, Jenna, but didn't have a clue how to tune in to her.

Jenna was sent to me because she refused to be toilet trained. Jenna's frequent urination "accidents" were her way of releasing anxiety that she held throughout the day. Additionally, Jenna refused to speak in public, a condition called "selective mutism." Children diagnosed with selective mutism have normal verbal skills but choose not to talk in social settings such as school. There is some evidence that the disorder starts in preschool, is more common in girls, and is seen in all social strata.[2] Jenna was both female and preschool age; when you factor in the pressure from her emotionally distant parents, she was unfortunately a prime candidate for selective mutism.

Both Jim and Cindy were scared. Jim especially so, and he also was anti-therapy. This couple didn't know what was going on with their daughter and were even less sure what to do about it. Lack of knowledge breeds fear, and my job was to educate them enough so that they were no longer too scared to make changes.

The first time I met Jenna I could see that she was anxious. Her anxiety manifested in selective mutism because she was afraid to let go and show her emotions. Not speaking, which may have grown out of her fear and shyness, had become one way she could stay in control. This little girl was not yet four and already she was relating to others the same way her parents related to her—with control.

Jenna had learned that she could refuse to wear clothing or cooperate on any level, including walking alongside her mother. The root cause, of course, was the lack of attunement, or the failure to identify and express emotion, at home. With Jim not participating, I sat with Cindy and Jenna on the floor of my office amid a pile of toys and games, and Cindy and I talked about power struggles. The toys and games were an important part of my plan to help this family. They were there so Jenna could focus on something other than our conversation—if she chose—and so she would not become even more anxious. Jenna was made aware that she could chime in at any time, but at this point, she chose not to.

Cindy told me that Jenna spoke loud and clear at home, but never in public. I asked her how she felt when Jenna wouldn't wear an outfit, wouldn't speak, or dug her heels into the ground. Cindy expressed her frustration and fear very eloquently. Then, in front of Jenna, I gave Cindy phrases she could use and demonstrated them with Jenna.

Over time, Cindy saw Jenna slowly release her rigid hold and we both watched her barriers fall. I thought it was very interesting that when Jenna finally spoke her first words to me they were complaints about her mother. I immediately validated her feelings and worked with mom and daughter so Cindy could say things such as, "I know you are mad at Mommy. You wanted to wear the blue shirt and I wanted you to wear the pink one. But the blue shirt is in the laundry. You can wear it tomorrow, after it is washed."

I gave Cindy 100 percent of my support and empathy as we walked step-by-step through Jenna's opposition. As a therapist, I can't always accurately predict who will have a window of openness for change and who won't, but I can say that the more open you are the further you'll go. While Cindy was generally not open, driven by frustration, she was open enough to consider change.

I gently worked on Cindy's openness and continually asked her open-ended questions such as, "How do you feel when Jenna tries to control you by ignoring you?" Cindy finally realized she felt angry and impotent, and then came to the important realization that she was acting just as her mother had acted with her. Then she began to cry. She told me how she felt her mother had misunderstood her. Finally I could tell her that was how Jenna felt about her.

Cindy and Jenna stayed in therapy for about a year. Jim did come every few months, just to see what was going on. He didn't want to be involved in the therapy, but he also did not put the brakes on Cindy and Jenna's involvement, and for that I am grateful. He also successfully used the phrases Cindy took home with her and enjoyed watching his daughter emerge from her shell.

NOT WORTH FIGHTING OVER

By the way, there are two areas you should never fight with your child about: what goes in and what comes out. In other words, your child must be the boss of his or her own body. Some parents inadvertently get caught in a power-struggle with their child about eating or toileting. Don't do it! You will lose every battle. One more thing . . . don't fight about what your child wears. Orange checks and pink plaid together are fine as long as your child feels beautiful.

WHAT TO EXPECT

This book explores the importance of being self-aware. In the following chapters we will talk about a number of parenting styles. You should know that it is rare for a parent to fall specifically within just one style. Instead, most parents find elements of themselves in several styles. This is important for you to know because in chapter 15, after you have learned all about the parenting styles I most commonly see, you will have the opportunity to find your own style, or styles, as the case may be. Then you can go back and re-read those sections that most specifically relate to you.

DR. FRAN'S TOP TIPS CHAPTER ONE

- Understand how and in what ways you are similar to your parents.
- Examine yourself so as not to automatically repeat mistakes your parents made.
- Be aware of your feelings, moment to moment.
- Slow down your reactions. Reflect before speaking or taking action.
- Speed up your internal thinking process. First think, "How do I feel?" Then think, "How is my child feeling?"
- Expand the scope of options for how you can deal with your child.
- Self-evaluate so that you can make good, educated choices about how to raise happy, emotionally thriving children with good self-esteem.
- Self-awareness is comforting and leads to calm parenting.

CHAPTER TWO

SEPARATING YOUR CHILD FROM YOU

My young friend Abby is a beautiful, fun-loving six-year-old girl, but she was not invited to a classmate's recent birthday party. Granted, only a select few were invited, as the parents of the birthday child wanted to keep the celebration small. When Abby's mom, Leigh, found out that her daughter was not invited, she was visibly devastated.

The funny thing is that Abby initially didn't care that she was not invited; she was not a close friend of the girl who was having the birthday. But, because her mom made such a big deal about it, Abby began to place blame onto other people for being excluded. She learned from her mother's behavior and reaction that it was everyone else's fault that she was not invited. In reality there was no blame to place. The party was small and Abby was not a close friend.

Because Leigh could not separate *her* feelings from those of her daughter, she is what I think of as an enmeshed parent. And, like many children of enmeshed parents, Abby began to play the victim. To take it a step further, Leigh, like many enmeshed parents, could not fully separate her own identity from Abby's. Whatever Leigh thinks and feels, she assumes that Abby also thinks and feels.

While dads can become enmeshed, the typical enmeshed parent is, like Leigh, more often a mom. In many cases the mom (or dad) projects unresolved issues from their own childhood onto his or her child. So when Abby was not invited to the party, *Leigh* felt hurt, pain, and rejection because she was left out as a child.

A good example of this is an enmeshed father I know named Scott, whose own father abandoned the family when Scott was three years old. Because Scott suffered by growing up with the loss, and because he also longed for a father, he projected that onto his firstborn son, Isaac. As Isaac grew, Scott could not say no, set boundaries, or give him appropriate consequences. Scott was afraid that if he did, Isaac would become angry with him, reject him, and leave—just as his father did.

Like Scott, the typical enmeshed parent periodically experiences feelings of emotional loneliness or emptiness but dodges the uncomfortable feeling by filling up with an overdose of a too-close relationship with his or her son or daughter.

As you can see, the enmeshed parent is not a great kind of parent to be, especially because children of this type of parent have a high risk of experiencing separation anxiety. This is because enmeshed parents are unable to contain their own anxieties and worries within themselves. Unconsciously, these parents *use* their child as a container into which they spew their own uncomfortable feelings. Then, enmeshed parents become dependent on their child for relief of these unwanted feelings. This is the opposite of the way it is supposed to be. You need to be the sounding board for your child, not the other way around. You need to be sturdy enough to hear and hold all of your child's unwanted feelings. And, you need to demonstrate, by example, your ability to bear unwanted emotions. It is good to teach your child that hard feelings are temporary, that though the feelings might be big, they will not stay forever.

The child of an enmeshed parent also reads subtle cues from their parent about behavior expectations, and the expectation is usually that the kid should stay close. In most cases, either by the onset or the end of adolescence, the child works out the parent's need to keep them nearby. However, these children can evolve into adults with two possible options: They either become enmeshed parents themselves, or they rebel.

One of the messages children often get from an enmeshed parent is that they don't have to own up to personal responsibility. This is because the enmeshed parent constantly steps in to help, fix, rescue, or excuse their son or daughter. An example of this is when a young girl gets a poor grade because she didn't study for the exam. The mom blames the teacher for giving too tough a test. But I ask you, if this parent always helps her child out, always runs interference, how will the girl ever learn important lessons?

When children of enmeshed parents grow up they often tell me they suffer from too much worry. This is because they were subjected over and over to an enmeshed mom or dad who worried when they were separated. The child then grows up to worry about separation, too. Often, they feel panic or hysteria when stressed with simple tasks of self-reliance, such as washing their clothes or picking up their room. These children were taught dependency, not independence or autonomy. As adults, they are not equipped with the necessary coping skills for frustration, disappointment, and scary situations.

Kids of enmeshed parents also often have trouble in their adult relationships because the enmeshed parent has given the child no opportunity for a true disconnect, which is required to move forward in healthy adult relationships. In a very subtle, unspoken, unknowing way, the enmeshed parent communicates to her child that the parent will suffer greatly if the child separates. The child invariably buys in to this distorted belief.

And, it gets worse. I hate to tell you but if there is no separation, children of enmeshed parents usually partner as adults with spouses who cannot understand the over-attachment between their spouse and his or her parent. The partner then becomes critical and distant. If they have a child, the partner's critique, together with the spouse's enmeshed history with their own parents, can give the spouse even more reason emotionally to hold on tighter to a child, and the child becomes a substitute companion. Often these moms or dads talk too much to their children by sharing adult issues that should only be shared with their partners.

A GOOD THING

In this context, a healthy disconnect is a good, positive goal. This disconnect does not mean that the child and parent are on bad terms or that they do not operate as a close family unit. Instead, it means a mom or dad can embrace a child's normal milestones, praise every increment toward a child's autonomy, and understand that even though their son or daughter may still be tiny, he or she is a unique person separate from Mom and Dad. Even tiny people have their own separate thoughts, feelings, and ideas.

By the time a child grows up, it is critically important that he or she have a reasonable separation from his or her parents. A child's worry about her parent should not intrude on normal functioning.

Take the example of the good daughter, Joan, whose parents argued and fought most of her childhood. Belinda, Joan's enmeshed mother, turned to Joan for comfort every time her husband yelled at her. To Joan's eye, her mother was the victim of a harsh, screaming husband. When Joan left her parents' house to live with her new husband, David, her mother still phoned Joan every day for comfort and validation. This behavior quickly began to interfere with and sour Joan's relationship with David.

This is just one example of why enmeshed parents need to take the blinders off and open their eyes, because they put so many of their issues onto their children. I understand that it is a challenge to let go of your child, because once you take your blinders off, you will need to deal with a lot of uncomfortable feelings. And you will have to do this on your own, without your child as your partner. To the enmeshed parent this can be very scary.

HELP FOR ENMESHED PARENTS

In therapy, I serve myself up to be the enmeshed parent's partner and provide a safety net. That way the enmeshed parent doesn't fall too far down as we help separate and free the child. In the first chapter we discussed the tiny bit of openness that is so important in affecting change. Once you find that tiny thread of openness, here are a few things for you to consider.

1. RECOGNIZE THE ISSUE

This is by far the hardest part. One of the biggest problems I see is that enmeshed parents deal with a certain amount of high anxiety all the time. On occasion, I have made the mistake of trying too soon to separate the "glued together" mom and child, and the family bolted from treatment. I have wondered so many times what happened to those children.

The art of separation is exactly that—an art. The therapist must tread slowly, cautiously, and delicately if success is to be achieved. Please give yourself the same guidelines. If you are an enmeshed parent, allow yourself time to separate incrementally. Don't beat yourself up if you can't handle it cold turkey. This is hard to do!

2. ENMESHED PARENT SELF-TEST

Here is an exercise to try to see if you are an enmeshed parent. First, turn up the volume on registering your own anxiety level. Take an opportunity when you are feeling super anxious, worried, or upset about something that has nothing to do with your child. Now hold the feeling. That means feel it and do nothing—especially do not tell your child. If your anxiety escalates and goes through the roof, and if you feel like you want to jump out of your skin, you are an enmeshed parent.

Your challenge now is to work on holding your uncomfortable feelings, learning to self-soothe, and creating a self-dialogue that calms yourself down. This is a process that you can do on your own or with a therapist. Absolutely do not depend on your child for help in mastering this. Also know that mastery of the above task leads to emotional maturity in you, and that's a very good thing.

3. DO YOU SMOTHER?

Many enmeshed parents also worry and think obsessively. They do not see that too much "love" can actually be counter-productive for their children. (I put "love" in quotation marks because this continual stepping in to rescue a child is not love. It is fostering dependency with enmeshment.) Too much love that smothers does not allow a child to think clearly and solve issues and problems on his own. It does not teach him to stand up for himself, or that there are consequences for every action he takes.

For example, if your child has a fight with a classmate, ask her how she thinks she might deal with it. If she complains that she was given too much homework, ask what *her* plan is for tackling the dilemma. Be a compassionate listener and direct her to figure out solutions for herself.

The key thing is to recognize the difference between self and child and fight the urge to project or over-protect. It is hard to get through to an enmeshed parent. As I mentioned earlier, too many parents become scared and angry and pull out of therapy before any headway can be made. Hopefully this is not you.

4. TAKE A HARD, PAINFUL LOOK AT YOURSELF

If you are an enmeshed parent, own up to it. This is a good thing. Admitting a problem goes a long way toward curing it. And understanding that smothering your child is actually hurtful, rather than helpful, is a real breakthrough. So please be honest. If you are not sure, ask yourself if this kind of parent is you, or a part of you. Remember that most parents do not fall completely into one category or another. Most moms and dads have elements of several parenting styles.

5. DECIDE YOU ARE READY TO TAKE ANOTHER TRACK

It is very hard to say, "I alone am not enough." That's why it is critical that an enmeshed parent partner up. With somebody. If a spouse or the other parent is not available, then find a grandparent, aunt, uncle, neighbor, cousin, or clergyman. Find someone who can help balance you and the kind of help you offer your child.

Even if a spouse is willing and able, many enmeshed parents do not allow them to share in the responsibility of raising their children. The enmeshed parent often thinks the spouse or other parent cannot handle the child as well or as sensitively as they can. Sometimes the enmeshed parent complains that their spouse is too harsh. They do not understand that this "harshness" actually holds the line and sets important boundaries for the young son or daughter. Sometimes the spouse holds the line with anger, which is why the enmeshed parent calls it harsh. Truth be told, the spouse usually *is* angry at the enmeshed parent for inadvertently blocking or diminishing his or her authority as the other parent.

This all, of course, is harder for single parents, but not for the reason you might think. Very often a single parent has a single child. Without meaning to, the parent uses the child for company and this takes the child into the area of companion and peer. This does not serve your child well for several reasons. The child needs to be encouraged to develop his or her own social circle of same-age friends. It is important for a child to feel that he belongs to a group at school. By the same token, the single parent needs a life that includes friends outside of their son or daughter. Also, many only children of a single parent carry an unspoken burden of responsibility for pleasing or entertaining the parent. You may not realize it, but that's too much pressure for a child.

Here's a great example. A very nice mom came to see me a while ago. Her name was Rose and she had just gone through a very rough divorce. Rose was having a lot of trouble with her only child, a teenaged daughter named Katie. The good news about Rose was that she recognized that she was the cause of the problem. Rose had been letting Katie witness her own emotional fallout from the divorce and had begun confiding in her. Rose came to me off and on for the better part of a year, and whenever she began to slip backward into relating with her daughter as a peer, I busted her for it.

Eventually Rose learned to be aware of this on her own. If she hadn't, she would have become an enmeshed parent, projecting her thoughts and ideas about her ex, Katie's father, onto her daughter. This could easily have happened, even though Rose had not been enmeshed with Katie before the divorce.

6. GET HELP

If you find that you are an enmeshed parent or have elements of enmeshment in your parenting style, know that it is extremely hard to separate from your child without help. You need support from someone who can see the situation with a clear eye, who will tell you how it really is, and who has the knowledge to point you in the right direction. This is especially true because old habits are usually solidly set and it is particularly easy to fall back into entwinement.

THE ENMESHED PARENT-CHILD RELATIONSHIP

Many enmeshed parents also become hysterical during times of crisis or when under stress. The trigger might be as simple as a trash can blowing out onto the street during a windy day, but the parent somehow communicates to the child that the situation will surely turn into a disaster. Usually, this communication involves the tone, pitch, and facial expression of panic.

That also is an unfair pressure to place on a child. These strong reactions that fall somewhere on the spectrum of hysteria are based in fear. The enmeshed mom or dad can be perceived as rigid if someone, such as a spouse, tries to inject reality by saying, "Nothing terrible happened; no need to panic." An enmeshed parent, in fact, holds rigidly tight to the belief that danger lurks at any time and one is not safe in the world. Therefore, they merge with their child. The parent feels unsafe and believes her child needs her so she can be safe.

You also need to know that enmeshed parents generally raise enmeshed children. These kids sense how their mom or dad "needs" them to function. It is as if the enmeshed parent is on a seesaw with his child. There is a certain balance that they reach that makes the seesaw go back and forth with very little propulsion from either side. That's when the tangle of enmeshment takes on a life of its own.

When the enmeshed parents try to separate, their children frequently resist, powerfully, because their children's feeling is that if the separation occurs, then the parents will go down. If the parent goes down, then so will the child. The child then becomes so anxious about separating that there is no mellow place in the equation. It is a vicious circle that never produces any state of calm in either parent or child.

At some point in either adolescence or early adulthood, many children of enmeshed parents feel angry at the parent when the parent says or does something to imply their child should "take care" of them emotionally. When a child expresses anger directly at an enmeshed parent, the mom or dad often shows visible signs of collapsing. Perhaps it is with tears or defensive retorts like, "I was only trying to help," or statements like, "You hurt my feelings." Then the child is usually overcome with feelings of guilt.

This becomes another vicious circle. So here, in another elaborate way, an enmeshed parent keeps his or her child attached, and the child keeps coming back in the hope that "this time it will be different." It rarely is.

Help from Scripts: A Case Study

In my practice, I see far more enmeshed parents than you might think. One of my patients, Sarah, was the wife of a clergyman. Sarah was married at eighteen, but before her marriage, she was emotionally dependent on her parents. Over time, Sarah's husband, Brad, became a leader in his field. Brad also was quite a demanding person. In fact, as a grown man, he wasn't too much different from Sarah's father.

Brad's relentless, driven quest for leadership in his career, and his highly critical nature, created difficulties in the marriage, so Sarah became enmeshed with her children to satisfy her emotional needs. In doing so, Sarah projected all of her adult insecurities and worries onto her children, and when her oldest child, Andy, reached school age, he worried terribly that his mom couldn't manage at home without him. He developed what initially was a classic case of separation anxiety, but, by the time I saw him, had escalated into a swimming phobia. At the pool, Andy couldn't let go of the rail; he was afraid he would drown. It doesn't take a genius here to see the strong parallel between letting go of the railing on the pool and letting go of Mom.

I began helping Andy by including Sarah in our sessions. Then, as he got more comfortable, Sarah began sitting in the parent waiting area for short periods of time. Once Andy realized both he and his mom were functioning well apart from each other, we increased the time Sarah spent in the waiting room until eventually Andy spent his entire session apart from his mom. This, by the way, did not happen overnight. Separation is definitely a gradual process.

I also included Andy's father, Brad, in a few sessions. I would like to have included him more, but he was busy so I was thrilled with any kind of involvement and support. This was especially important because it showed Andy that even though his dad was not as involved as we all would have liked, he could be accessed as an alternative parent and source of support. Brad had the potential to be an effective father, but unfortunately, we do not live in an ideal world. As therapy continued, Brad was still chasing his career, but he was at least a little more involved at home.

The next step was to encourage Sarah to accept play dates on Andy's behalf. One of the biggest problems children of enmeshed parents have is that they do not want to leave their mom (or dad) to play with other kids. Even at birthday parties, these kids stick pretty close to their parent and do not fully engage with individual children or socialize in groups. I encouraged Sarah to go to the play dates with Andy, but to plop herself in a visible corner where he could see her. I also asked Sarah to encourage Andy to come and go between her and the children as often as he liked. But, when he came to her, she was to greet him, then see if he didn't want to go back and play with the other kids. After a few trial runs, Andy was doing considerably better on his play dates.

Birthday parties were a little harder for Andy. In larger group situations, Andy stuck closer to his mom. I suggested that in this setting Sarah not direct Andy to join the other children, but wait and allow Andy to move away from her at his own tempo based on his comfort level. Sarah was always positioned in the same place and as he felt more comfortable, he could move away from her and explore the environment, then return by his own choice. This way he didn't get the message from Sarah that she wanted him to stay close, nor did he get the message that she was pushing him away before he was ready.

It is important for the enmeshed parent to empower their children in peer interactions. For example, most children of enmeshed parents do not know how to advocate for themselves. If they get into a scuffle at school or if they are teased, they do not know how to handle it. And why would they? Mom or dad has always come to the rescue. Part of childhood is learning these important social skills so you can function as an adult. The enmeshed parent, in an effort to provide loving support and their idea of security, prevents their son or daughter from learning these important lessons.

In Sarah's case, I armed her with scripts that she could give to Andy to use whenever he encountered a difficult situation. If a friend became argumentative, rather than having Andy run to Sarah, he could say, "Hey, that's not a friendly way to talk." These words tell the other child that Andy recognizes that the child is not being a good friend to him. This contrasted with Andy's previous way of dealing with life: He presented a "poor, pitiful me" attitude and either ran to his mom or sat down and cried.

A second script might be something like, "You've hurt my feelings. You don't seem like the kind of kid who would do that on purpose. Are you?" This puts the responsibility of the action on the other child, not Andy, because Andy is in effect saying, "It's *you* who is being mean. It's not *me* who deserves this." And let me tell you, to get this kind of thought process going in a child of an enmeshed parent is a giant step in the right direction.

LONG-TERM EFFECTS

We've talked about the anxiety children of enmeshed parents have, but you either might not realize the devastating long-term effects the anxiety can have, or you are saying, "Well, my child doesn't have anxiety." All I can say is that he probably doesn't. But you owe it to yourself and to your family to read the next few paragraphs with extra attention.

In 2001, a multi-site National Institute of Mental Health (NIMH) study of treatments for anxiety disorders in children and adolescents found that anxiety disorders affect an estimated 13 percent of children and adolescents during any given six-month period.[1] This makes anxiety disorders the most common class of psychiatric disorders for our youngest generations. What is especially interesting, though, is that the study found, among other things, that the disorders often go unrecognized and untreated.

Signs of anxiety disorders in children include excessive worrying about ordinary activities (such as going to school or summer camp, taking a test, or performing in sports). Physical symptoms can include palpitations, sweating, trembling, stomach ache, or headache. The child might also avoid situations perceived to be sources of anxiety, and social withdrawal can result. A diagnosis of anxiety occurs when symptoms cause extreme distress and interfere with the child's usual activities.

The end result is that anxiety disorders can cause significant suffering and functional impairment in children. Some children even are affected into adulthood. I know that this is not what you want for your child.

A MEASURABLE OBJECTIVE

The ultimate goal for both the child and the enmeshed parent is for each to define his- or herself without the other. Many enmeshed parents find that they have no other role identification except as a parent, so they need to ask, "Who am I separate and beyond being my child's parent?"

This is hard because so many people lose their own identity inside a marriage or a family that they forget that they used to be a wonderful artist, a strong speaker, or a whiz at math. We all have wonderful gifts, but the enmeshed parent often has forgotten what theirs are, or they married young, straight out of their parents' home, and never before explored their own identity.

As far as the child is concerned, it is important that each child of an enmeshed parent thrive, and this means encouraging them to explore his or her strengths on their own, and empowering them to get past their weaknesses. If your son shows an interest in bicycle riding, encourage his father to teach him how to ride a two-wheeler. Your impulse will be to teach him yourself for fear that he may fall and his dad won't be as quick to catch him as you may be.

Trust your spouse to do a "good-enough" job and help yourself let go of being the "only one" or the "best one" to do the job. Once your son is proficient in bike riding, he can share that activity with his father. Then you can introduce the idea to your son that bike riding is especially fun when you ride with a classmate or friend. This is your supportive way of separating from your enmeshment, and praising every increment in your son toward his separateness and autonomy. Good for you!

It is also not unusual for children of an enmeshed parent to be afraid to speak to adults, even those they see regularly, such as a teacher. One patient, Ricky, thought his homework was too hard. He didn't understand it. Typically, enmeshed parents will do the homework with or for their children, which accomplishes nothing. First of all, the child doesn't fully learn the lesson the homework is supposed to teach, and second, it further deepens the circle of enmeshment because the child learns he can turn to the parent to bail him out of just about anything. He never learns to do anything on his own, or to ask his teacher for help.

But, in this case, Ricky had a smart mom. Sharon used to be very enmeshed, but she was learning a better way. So, instead of doing Ricky's homework for him, as she used to do by standing over Ricky's shoulder and actually writing the answers on the paper, she said, "I know you think this homework is too hard and that you don't understand it, so tomorrow morning, before school starts, why don't you ask your teacher for help during free play. It is much better for you to do that than do it wrong."

This is a great script because it accomplishes several things. One, it validates Ricky's teacher by putting Sharon's stamp of approval on her. This gives Ricky confidence that it is the right way to approach the situation. And two, saying these words tells Ricky that while he has to do this on his own, Sharon is not completely abandoning him. She has provided a viable plan.

DOING IT RIGHT

Giving children the tools to become self-reliant is the biggest gift we can give them, and I have to tell you about a mom and daughter that I know, Zelda and Diane. Diane is Zelda's adult daughter. In fact, Diane is now a grandmother who praises her mother, along with Zelda's parents, for giving her the ability to be a great mom and grandma.

You see, Zelda loved Diane with all her heart, but she was not an enmeshed parent. Many of you might think you can't loosen the strings and still love your children with everything you have, but that's not true. You not only can, that is your goal. I think Zelda and Diane's story will show you why.

Zelda was the daughter of a high-level, highly respected politician. This, of course, was many, many years ago and she went to college in an age when women just didn't do that. Eventually Zelda married and had two children, Diane and her younger brother, David.

Zelda loved and adored her children, but instead of holding them too closely, she praised their separation and growing every step of the way. When David took out the trash, she'd greet him on his return with a hug, and say, "You are a *wonderful* helper!" When Diane learned her first ballet positions, Zelda exclaimed, "I've never seen such grace!" Zelda never said the words falsely; she believed every one of them.

So often we think positive, wonderful things about our children but for whatever reason, we do not say them. *Say* them. *Tell* them. Frequently. Your children need to be reminded every day how superb their accomplishments are—especially the accomplishments that occur without your involvement.

As Zelda's children got older she loved them even more, but she did not hold on to them. Many enmeshed parents are not supportive of the girl- or boyfriends of their children. Zelda praised each one. She found the good in each friend and played that up not only to her children, but also to the friend. Diane met her husband when they both were ten and they've now been married for forty years. How many mothers support a childhood romance? Zelda did because she praised the good in both of them, and acknowledged and reminded them of their strengths. Because of this, Diane and her future husband never pushed the boundaries of their relationship past what was age appropriate. They didn't want to disappoint Zelda. The important distinction here is that their decisions about their relationship were their choice, not Zelda's command.

As the years passed, Zelda praised every increment of her children's separation from her, and just as with Diane's childhood friendship with her husband, the praise and the healthy separation only brought her children closer to her. The old saying, "if you let a bird go and it flies back to you, it's yours," is so true.

When Diane was in her early twenties she was offered a fabulous career opportunity . . . in another country. Instead of saying things such as, "But will you come home for Thanksgiving?" "Will I see you for your birthday?" and "How will you survive amongst all those strangers?" Zelda helped push Diane out of the nest. She helped her daughter fly by encouraging the move and by being excited with Diane about all the wonderful things she would see and do on this new adventure.

Think of two people gently bouncing on a mattress; that's the kind of rhythmically synchronized relationship Zelda and Diane had. Rather than the earlier seesaw example that took on a negative life of its own, together Zelda and Diane were loving, affectionate, and supportive. They rarely fought, and were very warm toward each other. Never was Zelda clingy or overprotective, but Diane never doubted that Zelda did support her and was securely there for her. And you know, Diane has the same relationship with her daughter that Zelda had with her.

Zelda passed away recently, a grand lady well into her eighties. And what a legacy she left her family, for I know that Diane's daughter is already relating to her children in the same loving, supportive, healthy relationship style that she experienced from her mother and grandmother.

I love telling people about Zelda and Diane because don't they have what we all want? For our children to be happy, healthy, productive people? But your children will only get there if you allow them to learn lessons on their own. Yes, that means some heartbreak early on in life. If your daughter isn't invited to the party, well, that's part of life. A great parent will not rush to "fix" the situation but instead will help her through it. That parent can be you.

DR. FRAN'S TOP TIPS CHAPTER TWO

- Embark on a new path of hard, honest, looking within.
- Cut yourself some slack by giving *you* permission to not be consistently successful at the beginning.
- Separate your own feelings from those of your child's.
- Praise every increment in your child's moving away from you. This includes making her own choices, decisions, and even disagreeing with your ideas.
- If this process is too painful or difficult to bear alone, enlist the help of your partner/spouse, or another trusted adult, to engage your child in the separation process.
- Expect your anxiety to rise as you let your child go. Part of the reason you need your child close is to avoid feeling your own anxiety. Be brave and own it.
- Get supportive help for yourself. Choose people close to you that you trust and feel safe with to talk about your feelings. It is too hard to do this alone. You may feel more comfortable talking with a clergyman or counselor. Build your support system as best you can.

CHAPTER THREE

MANAGING YOUR PARENTAL WORRIES AND CONCERNS

One of my patients recently gave me what I consider the ultimate compliment. She said she appreciated my being a "real person." In today's world, traditional therapy teaches therapists not to disclose anything personal about themselves; the therapist is supposed to be a blank slate so the patient can project his or her thoughts, feelings, behaviors, and emotions onto the therapist (this is called transference). But, having done time sitting in that "other" chair myself, I found it helps to know that the person you are talking with has some inkling of what you are going through, above and beyond their clinical training.

I mention this so you understand that I am a person who has a tendency to worry. I want to do the best I can for my patients, so I worry about them and wonder if I am doing enough. The same goes for my family and friends, and in that way, I am like all worried parents. Fortunately, my knowledge and training lets me know where the line is between normal, healthy concern and unnecessary worry.

While all parents worry about their children, there are several kinds of worried parents that go overboard. The first is the parent who worries excessively about germs and doesn't allow his or her child the freedom to play outside, play at friends' homes, or participate in any rough-and-tumble activity. This parent is far too overprotective.

The second type of worried parent focuses on grades and academic performance, becoming excessively anxious regarding tests. This kind of worry not only puts a great deal of pressure on a child, but also pushes them to become anxious themselves. This child believes that simply because the parent is worried, there must be a reason, even if there isn't a problem with their academic performance. In some cases, the child ends up rebelling.

The third type of worried parent worries about sports and athletic performance, and sometimes drills his child over and over and over, or schedules many private coaching sessions. This much extra attention gives the child a subtle cue that he is "less than" what is expected and "needs more." These repetitive drills also let the child know the great importance sports performance holds for his parent. Sports then become either an avenue for pleasing the parent and winning approval, or an avenue for rebelling by refusing to participate.

THE DEVASTATING EFFECTS OF WORRY

In addition to the fact that worry is not productive, it can actually be physically harmful. A study published in the January 2006 issue of *Psychophysiology* found that large rises in blood pressure during times of mental stress, including worry, are associated with higher levels of activity in areas of the brain associated with negative emotions and physical responses. This may include fingernail biting, chewing on one's own shirt sleeve, or, in extreme cases, pulling out one's own hair and eyelashes (trichotillomania). The research also suggests that excessive rises in blood pressure due to worry and stress may place you at a greater risk for heart disease.[1]

Additionally, dermatologists now know that worry-related stress can cause both acne and hair loss.[2] Basically, stress causes your body's cortisol levels to increase. One of the symptoms is an increase in oil production, which causes acne. Stress and worry also cause our bodies to pull resources from "unnecessary" areas and direct them to more important body functions. As far as our body is concerned, hair is not a necessity. Hence the hair loss. These anxiety-induced symptoms can create a vicious loop, causing you even more anxiety, which will make the symptoms worse.

If heart disease, acne, and baldness aren't enough, research also suggests that stress may activate immune cells in your skin and result in inflammatory skin disease.[3] Normally, our skin provides our first defense to infection, serving not only as a physical barrier but also as a site for white blood cells to attack invading pathogens. During times of worry and stress, however, the immune cells in the skin can overreact, and inflammatory skin diseases such as atopic dermatitis and psoriasis can occur.

David Brown, an epidemiologist at the Centers for Disease Control and Prevention in Atlanta, and his colleagues ran a survey of more than seventeen thousand adults. They found that people who had been exposed to six or more traumatic childhood experiences (such as a divorce, a move across country, the death of a close family member, a loved one's major illness, et cetera) before the age of eighteen were twice as likely to die prematurely as those who hadn't suffered such experiences. [4]

On average, study participants who reported worry from six or more traumatic childhood experiences died at age sixty. People with little or no major childhood stress or worry lived, on average, to age seventy-nine.

Brown said that children who are confronted with stressors that negatively affect their neurodevelopment experience health problems and diseases throughout their life. As a consequence, these stressors may cause them to die younger.

While not everyone will have six major childhood stressors, the study suggests that any accumulation of stressors can cause premature death. Let's say you (or your children) experienced just a few traumatic childhood events. While you may not have as many years trimmed from your life as those who experienced numerous stressful incidents, compared to people who experienced no stressors, your life may still be shortened by a few years. Moreover, the study found that two-thirds of study participants reported at least one stressful childhood experience. Just think of the number of lives that may have been shortened!

Evidence also suggests that prolonged worry and stress take a toll on the adult body, too. In particular, psychological stress affects molecules that play a key role in cellular aging and, possibly, disease development.

In a study published in *Proceedings of the National Academy of Sciences,* a team led by researchers at the University of California, San Francisco, determined that chronic worry had a significant impact on telomeres.[5] Telomeres are DNA-protein complexes that cap the ends of chromosomes and promote genetic stability. The results of the study, which involved fifty-eight moms of either healthy or chronically ill children, were dramatic. In one of the study's key findings, the duration of stressful care giving was critical: the more years of stressful and worrisome care giving, the shorter the length of the telomeres. This means that cells stop dividing earlier, which speeds up aging. In fact, in the most stunning result, the telomeres of women with the highest perceived psychological stress had undergone the equivalent of approximately ten years of additional aging, compared with the women who had the lowest perception of being stressed.

The findings suggest a cellular mechanism for how worry and stress may cause premature onset of disease, as they appear to have the potential to shorten the life of immune cells.

Now, it's not as if my waiting room is full of bald, itchy, pimply, coronary patients. But the point here is that the stress that long-term worry puts on your body can affect not only the quality of your life, but also the length of your life. To be the best parent you can be, you need to be as calm and healthy as you possibly can, and a big part of this is not being overly worried about your child.

Yes, there are times when you should be worried, even need to be worried, but worry is never productive unless you can develop an action plan that will change whatever you are worried about in a positive way. This next story about two patients, Nancy and Sam, shows how effective an action plan can be.

A Very Worried Mom: A Case Study

Nancy was the detail-oriented mother of a ten-year-old boy who had significant allergies to dust, trees, pollen, and other similar substances, often resulting in mild asthma. Because there was a crisis with Sam's allergies and asthma when he was very young that required a hospital stay, Nancy worried about Sam all the time. She overprotected him by excessively cleaning his room, wrapping his bedding and furniture in plastic, and continually spraying disinfectant. When Sam got a cold, she worried about catastrophic possibilities to the point that it impaired the functioning of the entire family. In short, Nancy overreacted to the situation. Yes, Sam has allergies. Yes, Sam needs some special care because of them. But Nancy's worrying overshadowed everything Sam did.

In one instance Sam was invited to a mid-summer swimming party that began at four o'clock. Nancy allowed him to go only if he absolutely got out of the pool at five, when the weather began to marginally cool. To avoid feeling as if he were under a spotlight and being ridiculed by the other boys, Sam defied his mother's direction and stayed in the pool long after five o'clock. When the host's mother later told Nancy, there was wrath to pay.

While Nancy had reason to be concerned, the way she micromanaged Sam and his environment communicated to him that there must be something terribly wrong with him. Plus, Sam felt gypped that he could not enjoy life in the same way that other boys his age could. He also picked up on his mother's worry and began worrying himself, becoming tentative and withdrawn, and eventually angry. When Sam's anger became an issue, they both came to my office.

Nancy at first glance appeared to be relaxed and open, but inside there was a rigidity that was hard to break through. Often there is not a lot that I—or anyone—can do to convince a parent to loosen the tight hold they have on the fear that controls them. It was as if Nancy's fear was a ball of string, and whenever I unraveled it, trying to find ways to calm her worries, Nancy was there, holding on with white knuckles. It was a vicious circle.

Because Nancy had experienced crisis with Sam's health in the past, there was not much I could do to convince her to treat her child normally. But there were things I could teach her that would help.

For Sam to begin to feel like a regular kid, Nancy had to find ways to stretch her own tolerance for worry and get used to sometimes living with a higher level of anxiety. In the instance of the swimming party, instead of demanding that Sam come out of the pool after just one hour, I mentioned that she could provide Sam with a nice, thick, warm towel, and ask the supervising parent to keep an eye on him. In cases such as this, the mom is always more worried than the kid. Nancy tried this at Sam's next swimming party, and though it raised Nancy's personal anxiety, it removed anxiety from Sam. Sam just needed to go and have a good time, which he did.

You have probably figured out that my task here was as much to help Nancy as it was to help Sam. For Sam to thrive, Nancy needed to learn different responses to her rising anxiety. Rather than projecting her worry and anxiety onto Sam, I taught Nancy to have a dialogue with herself. You can practice this technique, too, and you do not need a therapist to guide you.

First, Nancy needed to find out what most often triggered her anxiety. Then she needed to create an internal dialogue to reassure herself that she had prepared Sam as well as he could possibly be prepared.

A few things Nancy and I came up with for her to tell herself were:

1. "It's not really that chilly out, and if it becomes colder, Sam knows what to do."
2. "I know Sam knows how to take good care of himself and I have taught him well."
3. "There's not that much dust in his room. It's okay for me to vacuum once a day, rather than twice a day."
4. "I know my anxiety is high right now, but in reality nothing happened. Sam is fine."

Having a plan in place gave Nancy something positive she could do when she began to over-worry, and over time her anxiety began to lessen. Now, instead of tossing and turning one sleepless night after the other, Nancy can reassure herself that she has done everything that needs to be done to take care of Sam. In doing this she reminds herself that she can't control the unknown.

THE ISSUE OF CONTROL

Control is a common way for some people to try to manage elevated levels of anxiety. This usually begins in early childhood, between the ages of two and four. If you had, for example, parents who constantly argued in front of you and your siblings, or parents who kept their distance and left you to flounder and "figure it out for yourself," your anxiety level probably increased beyond what you were capable of managing. In my office I occasionally see a three- or four-year-old child line up toys in patterns or draw a picture with color and design in supremely organized fashion, which is a sure sign of their anxiety, and resulting need for order and control.

In the Dr. Fran dictionary, I define anxiety as fear. You probably know a "control freak." It could be a friend, another parent, or your boss, and it is good to understand that these are not mean or bad people—they are people who are afraid. Trying to control their environment and the people around them is their way of dealing with the fear. No one ever taught them that you cannot control people. Your environment, yes. People, no. So instead of trying to control everything in their child's world, moms like Nancy must trust that they did everything they could . . . and then let go.

I also taught Nancy that it was okay to get flustered, and to occasionally allow herself strong reaction to her fears, but that it was not okay to put them on her child. After all, she loved Sam dearly and his history left legitimate cause for some concern. Over time, however, Nancy learned to bear the discomfort of worry. She understood that her worry was putting too much pressure on her wonderful little boy, and that became her motivation for change.

MY OWN SELF-TALK

I mentioned earlier in this chapter that I have a tendency to worry, so I could well relate to Nancy's feelings whenever I think about my two adorable nephews to whom I am extremely attached. When these two boys went through the fallout of their parents' turbulent divorce I had to take a step back from my own worrying. When I spent time with the boys during that period I could see that they were suffering; their family unit was being ripped apart and they were struggling.

During that time I had to do my own self-soothing self-talk each night after I returned home from a visit with the boys. In doing this I found that some of my dialogue was very similar to that of Nancy's and of other parents whom I work with. But my talks with myself also turned to action. It went from, "Will the boys be okay?" to "How can I help?"

I got through the first question by reminding myself that 49 percent of families across the country divorce[6] and a whopping 67 to 70 percent of families in Los Angeles County divorce.[7] Not great statistics in general, but for my purposes it reassured me that my nephews were not alone in this. Other boys (and girls) landed on their feet after their families divorced, so it was quite possible that my nephews would, too.

For the second question, "How can I help?" I came up with a short list that was very specific to my situation, and to me. While you may be going through a divorce, or have family members who are, your situation is unique to your family, and your self-talk and action plans will reflect this. I offer mine only as an example of the kind of talk and action that could be helpful.

First I told myself to get hold of my worry so that any planned action would not intrude unduly on the boys' parents. Everyone involved knew I was willing and able to help if needed. And I learned long ago that you can't help others if they don't want to be helped.

Second, I knew as a therapist that if I didn't manage my own anxiety that it would spill onto the boys. If the boys knew how worried I was it would make them think there was true cause for worry. I did not want to project that onto them at all. Plus, I realized that only by keeping my own worries at a manageable level would I have the attention and focus necessary to help the boys with their worries.

And last, I reminded myself that you cannot worry about things you cannot control. There was no possible way that I could control anything that was going on in my brother's divorce. So why spend all of my energy worrying about it? No worry of mine would change anything. I had to forfeit control. All I could do was support my nephews as best as I could.

My support took the form of being an available aunt to the boys. I provided comic relief, took them to the movies, and generally tried to provide a break for them. They just needed to have some fun. But through it all, they knew they could talk to me. About anything. And they did.

I am sure that you want to be the best, most supportive and available parent to your children. We have that in common: this desire to help our families. Sometimes, however, our desire to help backfires, as it did with the following family.

The Pressure of Grades: A Case Study

Paul and Catherine's daughter Hillary was finishing elementary school and her middle school exams were looming. Paul, who had long worried about the influence of Hillary's friends, now began to worry day and night about her grades. Would they be good enough to land her in the top classes in the top schools in the area?

In California, if you want your son or daughter to go to a private middle school, your child has to take a very tough sixth-grade exam called the Independent School Entrance Exam (ISEE). The ISEE is similar to the SAT that is given for collegiate admission, and is the major deciding factor in determining if your child is accepted by any private middle school, and—because different schools have different standards—if accepted, by which school. Paul was adamant that Hillary be accepted into advanced placement and honors classes at the best schools. He not only sent Hillary to test prep classes, he also hired a private tutor for her twice weekly. Paul's obsession with academic performance put a lot of pressure on Hillary, and instead of excelling at school her grades began to slip. Then she began acting out. Soon the three of them were in my office.

Paul was a lawyer, and a fine one at that. Both he and Catherine, a homemaker who took care of their four children, were approaching middle age, and anyone looking in on this family would say they had done very well. For Paul, however, that wasn't good enough.

It just took one session for Paul to acknowledge that the reason he was so worried about Hillary's grades and her academic performance was that he felt no one had pushed or encouraged him in the same area. While he had gone to a very good law school, it wasn't Harvard or Yale. Now, in his middle years, he felt that if he had attended either of those schools he would be much farther along in his career. Rather than being a good lawyer, he could have been a "great" one who brought home much more money than he did. He would have been able to provide more for his family. In essence, Paul's one big regret in life was that he did not have a parent who pushed him hard enough. He wanted to be sure he did not make the same mistake with his children.

All four of Paul and Catherine's kids were bright, and until Hillary began having meltdowns, all functioned very well. It was obvious that these parents loved their children very much, but what Paul failed to understand, and what you might not realize about your children, is that his goals for them and their goals for themselves were very different. Several of the kids were extremely motivated. Hillary was not one of them. She did well in school but had no burning desire to have a high-profile career or earn a million dollars a year. That wasn't who she was, but because her dad was so wrapped up in his own dreams for his children, he failed to see that.

In one instance, instead of allowing Hillary to perform on a sixth-grade cheerleading squad, he said, "How will that look on your high school transcript?" Instead of taking pride in her already good grades, he said, "That won't get you into Harvard or Yale, or even Brown or Stanford. You have to do better." Because of his own expectations, his life's mission had become to save his kids from mediocrity.

Hearing all of this, I wasn't all that surprised when, the first time I saw Hillary in my office, she collapsed under the pressure to the point where she threw herself on the floor and cried. My job, then, was to loosen her dad's ropes so he could let Hillary be who she was. The amazing thing here is that Hillary did just fine without all the pressure. She was a nice, polite, engaging girl with lots of friends who willingly did her chores at home, studied regularly, and got, by most standards, wonderful grades. Her mostly As, some Bs, and one C would have been cause for joy in most households. But sadly, not this one.

You probably know a parent like Paul, one who means well but is so wrapped up in his own expectations that he forgets who his son or daughter is, steamrolling over their dreams and their unique abilities. And like Paul, the parent that you know is probably very nice. The problem with Paul was that because of his own experience and his own regrets, he could see no other way and refused to talk in a constructive manner.

So, on to Plan B. Because I could not get through to Paul, I instead met with Hillary to help her understand why her dad was the way he was. She needed to know that all of this was about his life's dreams and regrets. None of it was really about her. I also worked with Hillary's mom, Catherine, and taught her how to be a buffer for Hillary and her dad.

For example, when Paul yelled at Hillary for taking a break from studying to phone a girlfriend, I told Catherine to go to Hillary's bedroom and just listen as Hillary blew off steam about how hard her Dad is on her. I taught Catherine to talk reflectively ("I hear how hurt and angry you feel when Dad comes down so hard. I know that's difficult.") without trying to fix the problem or disrespect Paul.

Interestingly enough, we found that Catherine had her own "pockets of rigidity," and the couple began coming to me to help them learn to help each other with this, and to deliver more balance to their family. And, once her parents loosened up and took the pressure off, guess what? Hillary got into a great private middle school and is doing fine. In the end, she did it on her terms, because she wanted to.

BALANCING WORRY WITH REASON

One common denominator worried parents have is that in loving and caring for their children, they tend to go overboard. These parents often become fixated on one element of their child's life, usually an area of weakness or perceived weakness, and put an extraordinary amount of pressure on their child to reach unreasonable expectations. If you are a worried parent, or think you might be, how do you tell the difference between encouragement and pressure, between reasonable and unreasonable expectations? How do you know when enough is enough?

First, take a hard look at yourself:

1.   Are you having trouble falling asleep or staying asleep because of worried thoughts about your child?
2.   Do those worries creep into your mental space during daytime hours?
3.   Do you find that you and your child wind up pushing against one another over your expectations?
4.   Are there times when you feel rapid heart palpitations or have difficulty in taking a deep breath when thinking about your child?

Notice when you have these feelings and ask yourself, "What am I afraid of right now?" Your goal is to use these symptoms of anxiety and worry as a learning opportunity to look within and raise your self-awareness. The more you know about your own fears, the freer you are to make better choices for your child.

The Sports Dad: A Case Study

While we've talked about two different kinds of worried parents, we can't forget the parent who worries too much about athletics. One dad who comes to mind is Richard, once a bright athletic star who, a number of years ago, was significantly disabled in a life-threatening car accident.

Since Richard was no longer able to perform, he transferred all of his goals onto his ten-year-old son, Marcus. While I can't be sure of the extent of the athletic ability that Richard had, if it was anything like Marcus's, it was significant. By the time I met him, Marcus was already a superstar in several sports, including soccer, football, and basketball. He was well-built, fit, and had a wonderful smile.

The problem, as you may have guessed, was that because Richard worried so much about Marcus's future he went overboard in pushing athletics on him. Since Richard did not have the same earning capability he had before the accident, he wanted to be sure that Marcus would be able to provide for himself. And he saw the easiest path toward this goal as a major league sports deal. Excellence in sports became so important to Richard that he drove Marcus in every imaginable way. He hired personal train-ers, sports coaches, and fitness instructors to enhance Marcus's significant natural ability.

Until just before they started coming to my office Richard and Marcus worked well as a team: Marcus practicing moves and drills, and Richard finding the right opportunities for Marcus to shine. Richard's efforts paid off and Marcus was able to join district travel teams that competed against the best athletes from other states. Both Richard and Marcus knew that to be included in this level of competition when Marcus was just ten was a real honor.

Marcus attracted a lot of attention on and off the field, but once you got to know him, it was apparent that much of his ath-letic drive came from his desire to please his dad's passionate, un-fulfilled dreams. Marcus's ability in sports was a way to get closer to his father.

Just before I started to see Marcus and his dad, Marcus began to believe his dad's repeated spiel that if he didn't have sports, he had nothing. He also began to see the added trainers as a sign that he didn't measure up, and that he needed more help just to be equal with the other star athletes. You can imagine how that af-fected Marcus's self-esteem, and because he felt he didn't measure up, he began to focus so much on sports that he neglected his ac-ademics. Added to the mix was the fact that Marcus already had attentional focus issues, so when his teachers pressured him to study harder, he began to act out. Marcus also used his prowess in sports as a platform to brag to his friends, whose numbers soon dwindled down to a mere one or two.

Situations like this, if left alone, usually end up in one of two ways. One: Marcus could become a somewhat depressed teenager and adult. Two: He could rebel by turning his anger against his father, and this path could lead to drinking, drugs, and other dangerous behaviors. Obviously neither of these situa-tions is good.

When I first saw Marcus he had a powerful anger toward his dad and said over and over that his dad was too strict. In talking to Richard I agreed that, yes, he had set a lot of rules. The problem with these rules, though, was not that there were too many, but that they were based in Richard's history with his own father and set out of his extreme worry for Marcus's future. There was little consequence if the rules were broken, and this, of course, taught Marcus that rules did not mean much. When his teachers told him he had to work harder in school, it meant nothing to Marcus because, at home, rules were broken all the time.

You might ask where Marcus's mom was in all this, and that is a great question. Sharon was a full-time working mom—a nice person, but she was emotionally distant and incapable of providing rules or structure. Once upon a time in the 1970s Sharon was a hippie who was anti-establishment and anti-rules. Much of that carried into her current life and this, combined with the problems he was having with his dad, gave Marcus the sense that he was "king of the family."

Because Sharon was so busy and unavailable, I worked with Richard to lighten up on the rules, and also to follow through on the rules that he kept. He had to learn to turn empty threats into true consequences. This did not happen overnight. It actually was quite a slow process, but inch by inch, step by step, we got there.

Marcus is now in an academically rigorous private school and on the honor roll. Recently, he got straight As and one B. He now has lots of friends, because I taught him to cool it on the bragging and to develop curiosity about the interests and accomplishments of his peers. Marcus is now invited to classmates' parties and he attends all school activities. He just needed the follow-through on his dad's former empty threats to go along with his father's wonderful support and interest. I was also able to help Marcus's mom to truly "be" with him when they were together, even if it was for short periods of time.

If you are a worried parent, do not expect yourself to stop worrying overnight. It takes time. You have to release your hold on your anxiety slowly and develop a new comfort level before you can release more. It is a process, and a slow one at that. You will need a lot of support along the way, but remember that together, through this book, you and I will get there.

DR. FRAN'S TOP TIPS CHAPTER THREE

- Try as honestly as you can to separate which of your worries are your own and which are your child's.
- Determine if there is a legitimate reason to panic or worry, or if you are reacting before anything has gone wrong.
- Do not project your fears and worries onto your child.
- See your child as who he or she is. If she isn't a math whiz, help her shine with other skills.
- Create an inner dialogue to calm and settle yourself.
- Deal with your own worries before you deal with your child, or your child will likely absorb them.
- Find support in someone non-judgmental whom you trust. It helps tremendously to feel that your husband, friend, clergyman, or counselor understands you.
- Expect to have success in slow increments. Know that you may have a few failures mixed in with your successes. That's how it goes. Accept it and accept yourself in the process.

CHAPTER FOUR

THE HELICOPTER PARENT

The helicopter parent is an interesting hybrid. Partly enmeshed, partly worried, and constantly assisting, this parent pays too close attention to his or her child's experiences and problems. The term helicopter parent was first used in the 1990 book *Parenting with Love and Logic: Teaching Children Responsibility* by Foster W. Cline, M.D., and Jim Fay,[1] and it caught on. Helicopter parents hover closely and are rarely out of reach, whether their children need them or not.

A similar term, "lawnmower parents" describes moms and dads who try to mow down obstacles before they can stump their child. This can include interfering at the workplaces of adult children who have graduated from college and are living on their own. "Black Hawk" parents can even behave unethically, for example, writing their children's college admission essays, or falsifying references on job applications.

You might be surprised at the lengths hovering parents go to. Some parents of college students call their children every morning to wake them up for class, or complain to their child's professors about grades. But helicopter parents are not limited to parents of older children. It can start when the kids are in elementary school. Typically, this style of parenting becomes a vicious circle. If the behavior pattern is not broken (which can be very hard to do) the child then models the behavior and helicopters around their own children. Before you know it there are several generations of helicopters all bumping into each other. I can't tell you what a mess that is!

UNDERSTANDING THE DIFFERENCES

As you can see, the helicopter parent is a close cousin to parents profiled in chapters 2 and 3, but this style of parenting is different enough from both the enmeshed parent and the worried parent to have a chapter all its own. Helicopter parents:

1. are not fully enmeshed. Unlike enmeshed parents, helicopter parents *can* separate their feelings from those of their child.
2. are not overcome by worry to the point that they can't tolerate being separated and apart from their child.
3. do hover over their child in fear that their son or daughter will not succeed without their ever-present shadow.
4. are well-meaning but neglect to do a full job of letting their child succeed or fail on his or her own merits.
5. know they can function well without their child but are worried about their child's ability to function without them. This is truly the defining point. This is not just a case of the parent thinking they can do a "better" job at something than their child can. It goes much deeper.

As the child grows up, their problems become increasingly apparent: These kids are not adequately prepared for self-sufficiency and crumble when pressed to do things for themselves. It's not that children of helicopter parents don't want to do the dishes in the frat house or wash their own clothes, it's that they *can't*. They have never been taught, or if they have, have never actually had to do the task by themselves. These kids also don't know how to eat nutritious meals because someone else has always cooked for them. Someone else has always picked up their clothes, watered the plants, done the shopping, and checked the air in the tires on their car. These kids have weak life skills or no life skills at all. And it's all because their loving, well-meaning parents have always done things for them instead of challenging them to do it themselves.

If only helicopter parents could see that allowing their children to make mistakes is part of life. So what if their daughter has an overdraft at the bank? Maybe it will teach her to balance her checkbook. And watch out for the helicopter parent who covers that overdraft: It belongs to her daughter. Let her handle it so she learns to cope with life.

WHO BECOMES A HELICOPTER PARENT?

Anyone can become a helicopter parent, but typically it is a mom or dad who realizes, either on a conscious or subconscious level, that they missed teaching their child some of the basics in skill development. The mom or dad knows there is a gap in the child's preparation for life and isn't sure how to fix the problem.

One of the peculiarities about helicopter parents is that while parents may begin helicoptering early, the effects are not visible until their children are about twelve. Around age twelve, middle school children are asked for more. This is when teachers—and leaders of extracurricular activities such as Boy and Girl Scouts and sports coaches—expect kids to show initiative and accomplish things without being asked or told. This is when children of helicopter parents begin to rely even more heavily on others, because they, themselves, are not capable of following through on such demands.

You know, it really is okay to hover some over your child when he or she is younger. For example, you wouldn't expect your seven- or eight-year-old son to go to the movies unsupervised with a group of friends. But that is something you might expect with a twelve-year-old boy.

There is another thing to consider. Some moms hover because they instinctively know something is wrong with their child. These "hovering" moms are often the first to realize that their young son or daughter is not marking normal developmental milestones, particularly during the first four years, when children are growing rapidly. Hovering moms are most challenged by their children's behavior beginning when they are eighteen months and resolving at four years of age. This is the time when children must claim themselves as separate beings from their moms.

As an example, a mom might notice her daughter is slow to sit on her own, to walk or talk, or she doesn't achieve and sustain eye contact the way we would expect for her age. That mom knows something the professionals haven't figured out yet and feels compelled to hover. This hovering mom is acting out of great worry and protectiveness (and sometimes despair) because she *knows* something is wrong. This heartbreaking hovering is very different from the kind of hovering that helicopter parents do.

The Mom Who Couldn't Let Go: A Case Study

My patient Natalie was a seventh grader who was having extreme difficulty adjusting in her first weeks at a new private school. Those of you who have switched schools yourself know how hard this can be. In fact, a study published in *The Journal of the American Medical Association* reported that 23 percent of children who switch schools frequently were likely to fail a grade, while just 12 percent of children who stayed in the same school failed.[2] The study analyzed more than nine thousand six- to seventeen-year-olds and also suggested that behavior issues can increase with frequent life changes such as a new school. Children who changed schools more frequently were also 77 percent more likely to have four or more behavioral problems.

This study is a few years old, but Paul Newacheck, who is a professor of health policy and pediatrics at the University of California, San Francisco, and one of the study's authors, says he expects the results would be similar if the study was conducted today.[3]

This was, in fact, the second school change for Natalie. She moved after the fourth grade and repeated the fourth grade at her new school. Her second switch in schools, the switch we were dealing with now, was far more traumatic. It is good to know that any move to a new school could be just as life changing for your own son or daughter. Even if you figure out a way to adjust to a new school, the above statistics show that your child, like Natalie, might not. Natalie just couldn't fit in with the other girls, was not making friends, and felt isolated and alone, particularly at lunchtime, when all the other kids enjoyed eating in small groups.

Her mom, Gloria, was a hovering, stay-at-home mom with rigid tendencies. She hurt for her daughter and wanted to do everything she could to ease the transition. Thinking she was helping, Gloria found reasons to "sneak" onto campus to bring Natalie a sweater or add something to her lunch. Gloria did this because she was not at all sure that Natalie could adapt on her own. Like other hovering moms, Gloria subconsciously knew something had been missed in teaching Natalie life skills. I think we all know someone like Gloria.

Natalie's response to her mom's increased presence at school was to count on the daily visits. At the time this was all happening, neither Natalie nor Gloria realized that Gloria's hovering behavior was crippling any progress Natalie might have made on her own to fit in. In fact, Gloria was actually keeping Natalie "stuck" as an outsider because rather than reach out to the other kids, Natalie relied on her mom to be there to provide moral support. As a result, she kept herself withdrawn, and instead of thinking about how she could initiate conversation and engage a few of her classmates, Natalie sat alone on a bench in the hall and waited for her mom.

To make matters worse, Natalie developed the habit of texting Gloria throughout the day. The desperate messages she sent were all to the effect of: "When can you come?" "When will I see you?" "When will you bring my lunch?" For her part, Gloria just wanted to be a good mom. She thought she was being loving and supportive by immediately answering each of the messages. After all, isn't that what good moms do? But after a time, Gloria realized the texting was getting out of hand. She was so overwhelmed with the volume of text messages and the phone calls that were coming in from Natalie during the day that she realized a change had to be made.

I brought Natalie and her parents, Gloria and Bill, into my office and told Natalie in front of her parents that she no longer could call her mom during the day. And just in case she thought that meant it gave her free license to contact her dad, I clarified that as well. I did allow Natalie to text her mom up to twice a day, with the understanding that Gloria was not going to reply. If Natalie did not adhere to those limits, then her phone would be taken away.

You might think that I am a tough, heartless person to set such strict rules. On the contrary, I am viewed among my colleagues as being a warm and fuzzy psychotherapist. But, as you will see, it was in Natalie's best interests. If the texting had been during optional recreation, a vacation day, or a weekend, the rules could have been relaxed. But it happened at school, where there are mandatory attendance laws. Natalie had to be there, so it follows that she had to learn how to fit in. That was her job, and until now she had been delegating that responsibility to her hovering mom, and Gloria had encouraged it. Going to school is a child's work, and children need to do three things in their work: learn, make friends, and have fun! They need to do that without their parents and that's exactly where Natalie tripped up.

The previous summer, Natalie's parents had sent her to a popular two-week sleep-away camp. But as soon as Natalie left, she began texting and calling her parents, sobbing that she wanted to come home. Natalie's mom and dad decided this was a growth experience and that she should stay. Maybe with the help and support of camp counselors she would adjust. But she did not. In addition to crying day and night, Natalie stopped eating and sleeping. Other kids tried to help her, to no avail. She was really suffering, and the suffering and the separation prevented Natalie from doing her job of learning, making friends, and having fun.

I urged Natalie's parents to bring her home. It was clear she was not ready for this kind of separation. But her parents did not take my advice, and Natalie suffered tremendously. The camp staff eventually decided it was too traumatic for Natalie to speak to her parents on the phone, because she hurt even more after talking with them. The staff also decided that Natalie could speak with me, her psychotherapist, once a day. This compromise allowed Natalie to get through the two weeks.

When she returned home, Natalie's anger toward her parents was huge. It took many sessions and weeks of dialogue between Natalie and her parents before they could work out their complicated feelings. Natalie's anger was second to her feeling of abandonment by parents who, maybe like you, didn't truly understand the impact of this trauma.

This brings us to the difficulties in Natalie's new school. To help Natalie learn to do her job, I suggested that regular attendance in school was required and needed to be enforced. Natalie was not in any danger and her parents and I felt it was reasonable to expect her to handle the separation for seven hours a day.

It was a real eye opener for the entire family to realize that rigid and hovering Gloria had unwittingly been sabotaging Natalie's efforts to fit in. Every time Gloria stepped in firmly with her good intentions, it fostered a dependency and taught Natalie that she didn't need to make an effort; mom would take care of everything. Natalie came to obsessively think, anticipate, and expect her mother's pop-in visits to campus. Natalie's excessive text messaging was a symptom of the overwhelming invasion of Mom into her mind, and she became obsessed with thoughts that she couldn't make it through the day without a visit from her mother.

To make our plan work, the entire family had to agree to it. At first, Natalie cried. She hated the boundaries that had been imposed on her. She also had a lot of resistance and anger toward me for thinking of the idea, and toward her parents for considering it. And there was a lot of resistance from her parents as well. They thought it was too strict. They all did agree to try, however, and after a short week things began to improve. Natalie admitted in our next weekly meeting that although she hated my idea, it was the right thing to not allow phone calling to her mom during school hours. Natalie said that, left on her own, she never would have stopped. She was actually grateful!

It wasn't too long after this that Natalie and Gloria learned a four-day overnight class trip was coming up. This was an annual trip for seventh graders and was designed to help students bond at the beginning of the year. It was a perfect opportunity for Natalie, but she refused to go. And, in all honesty, I felt it really was too much for her. Her anxiety was sky-high and while both she and Gloria had shown improvement, we had just started with the new rules and both still had a long road to travel.

I suggested that Gloria and Bill not force Natalie to go. Since they had disregarded my advice the previous summer regarding camp and it turned into a disaster, they were now open to my suggestions. This was great progress! We learned there was an option for the few seventh graders who, for various reasons, could not go: They could attend special classes and field trips during those four days. This particular year there were six students, including Natalie, who stayed behind. The entire situation was a blessing in disguise as Natalie bonded wonderfully with the other five kids, and she was settling in well when her other classmates returned. She now had five friends!

As an added benefit, Gloria relaxed more than any of us ever expected when she realized she could quit hovering. To be honest, when I first met this family I wasn't sure how much improvement could happen—there was so much resistance from both Natalie and her parents. Gloria had a rigid belief that she knew what was best for her daughter and had great difficulty taking my guidance. Only at very specific times when Gloria felt at a complete loss could she openly use my suggestions. Now they have all graduated from therapy.

The lesson here is not to force your child to separate if you have not done your job and given them wings. Sometimes hovering parents have to backtrack and teach a life skill that they missed the first time around. Like a lot of things, it can be harder to do at this later date, but it is very important that each child learn how to take care of him- or herself physically, emotionally, financially, and socially. Helicopter parenting sometimes prevents learning those skills, which, as you will see in a case study later in this chapter, can create a lot of difficulties.

PREVENTING THE HELICOPTER SYNDROME

It is pretty clear that even though helicopter parents are well-meaning, they actually do their sons and daughters a huge disservice. To that end, here are a few ideas that will help prevent you from becoming one of these parents. Or, if you recognize that you or your spouse already are a helicopter parent, the following ideas will help break the pattern and minimize the damage:

1. Teach your child beginning as young as age four that they are responsible for chores beyond dressing themselves,

brushing their teeth, and eating at mealtimes. These are given expectations, and even kindergartners can make an honest attempt at making their beds before school, helping take the trash out, picking up clothes, and putting wet towels in the hamper. These are not chores, by the way, that should be rewarded with a sticker or cash. These are real-life self-reliance tasks that everyone has to learn to do for themselves. No special rewards should be given here other than a lot of verbal praise.

2. Praise your children from a very early age with statements that promote a strong sense of self-esteem and independence. Rather than saying "good job," which fosters dependency on pleasing Mom and Dad, you can say, "My girl is growing up. You must be so proud of yourself!" "That's a good feeling you've got inside yourself!" Then your child can say, "Doing jobs makes me feel good about myself because they show me how much I am growing."

3. Allow yourself to feel the discomfort of knowing your child is wrestling with challenge. Maybe he is even struggling. But don't jump in quickly to smooth things over. Let him do his best to figure it out on his own. He will come to you if he needs help.

Hovering from Afar: A Case Study

Ken is a high-level CPA who worried that he and his wife, Lisa, had not prepared their son Jonathan properly for college. Ken worried excessively that Jonathan would not be able to handle his finances, clean his room, or do his laundry. And, while Ken took a tiny piece of the responsibility for this turn of events, he put most of the blame on his wife. In reality, while the majority of helicopter parents are indeed moms, this time it was the dad who was hovering. Mom may have hovered early on, but at some point Ken took over the reins on this one.

Intentionally or not, Jonathan chose a college far away from home, but Ken took every opportunity he could to fly out to the school to check on him. To his dismay, on the second or third visit Ken found that his fears were coming true. While Jonathan didn't have any problems with dorm living, his roommate did, and with good reason. He had valid complaints about Jonathan's mess, about how he kept the lights on all the time, about the smell of his dirty clothes.

Jonathan was not holding up his end of the bargain as a roommate because he was never taught proper self-custodial skills, meaning that he never learned to take care of himself, because his parents hovered. Before too many weeks went by Ken flew in to convince the dorm supervisor to give Jonathan a warning, rather than taking stronger action. Ken then began to complete a job he and Lisa should have taught Jonathan in elementary school.

Like a lot of children of helicopter parents, Jonathan was functioning under a social umbrella. His reaction was typical of helicopter kids. "I'm fine," he said. "Get off my back." Like Jonathan, other children of helicopter parents do not see their inability to deal with the everyday tasks of life as a problem. And it's not, to them, because they have been taught that eventually someone else will step in and take care of everything. A word of caution here: The older the child gets, the harder these life skills are to teach because the adult child, or nearly adult child, can no longer see the value in them.

As an example, I reap satisfaction and self-esteem from changing my own linens and cleaning, dusting, and mopping. These skills remind me that I am self-sufficient and do not need to rely on others for these self-care tasks. It's a drag, but you know, it feels good to finish a task or chore that no one wants to do. And when it's done, I feel a stronger sense of self because *I did it for me.* This is the value I want you to teach your children. It will keep them grounded where they belong.

Without this grounding, helicopter kids are conditioned to think other people will do things for them. In an unusual way, these kids are crippled. When parents like Ken and Lisa fail to teach responsibility and boundaries, children like Jonathan feel helpless and reliant on others. You can say to these children, "No one wants to grow up doing taxes or laundry or bills, but those are things we all have to do. I don't like it, but I do them." But whether your child will listen depends on their basic temperament and openness. If the child's temperament is willful, he may rebel against such a message from his parents.

You and I know that it is your job as a parent to prepare your children to be self-reliant, and as I said earlier in this chapter, that can start as young as age four. If you need to teach self-reliance when your child is a teenager, the job becomes very different. Rather than a few formative years of irresponsibility and entitlement to break through, you now have to combat almost two decades of learned dependence.

On my recommendation, Ken flew once again to the school and set up a meeting with Jonathan, the dorm supervisor, and himself. Together, they came up with rules that Jonathan had to follow. One was that the dorm supervisor was to come in every day to do a room check, so Jonathan's stuff didn't pile up. If the dorm supervisor found that Jonathan kept his school papers neatly on his side of the room, kept his laundry done, and kept his clothes folded and put away, then Jonathan would have free time and the freedom to go off campus in the evening. If not, he would lose the privilege of using his car.

That was a shocker for Jonathan, a boy who had grown up with a certain sense of privilege in his lackadaisical attitude about necessary daily tasks. But before Ken left, I armed him with a script that would give Jonathan no way out. I told Ken to say, "Your mom and I love you very much and we want to give you the privilege of using a car while you are here at college. Our only expectations are that you attend all classes, keep a C or above grade average, and that you keep your room clean. If those conditions are met, then we are happy to pay for your car. If not, we'll have to take the car away."

Fortunately, Jonathan was at a college that was willing to work with Ken and Jonathan, and with the ultimatum in place, Jonathan straightened up and did his part. Once that happened, Ken realized that he did not need to hover over Jonathan. Ken relaxed and the helicoptering disappeared.

As I mentioned earlier in this chapter, helicoptering can begin when a child is as young as four, although the repercussions aren't seen until much later. This is what happened with Jonathan and what could happen with Pamela and Hal's four-year-old daughter, Alice, and their nine-year-old son, Sebastian. Hal is a neat, clean, and organized person, and he complains to Pamela about the children leaving their wet, dirty towels on the bathroom floor. He has also tripped over used or dirty clothing that they leave on the bathroom floor before taking their bath or shower.

Instead of teaching and training the children to pick up their belongings and put them in the hamper, Pamela does it for them. She helicopters the house before bedtime and picks up after her children. By doing this, she is teaching them to depend on someone else to do the unpleasant daily tasks that are required for self-reliance. This includes making your own bed and school lunch, doing homework, walking the dog, and, in later years, doing one's own laundry, paying bills on time, and even preparing your annual taxes. If Pamela doesn't stop, her children will end up just like Jonathan.

ARE YOU A HELICOPTER PARENT?

It's sometimes hard to know if you are a helicopter parent, especially if your children are still quite small. A way to tell is to be brutally honest and openly ask yourself:

1. Are you doing this for your child? Or for you?
2. Are you hovering because you intuitively know your child has a kind of limitation, for example, weak fine motor skills or some other limitation?

Additionally, these need to be questions you ask yourself not just once, but regularly and often.

Out of love, helicopter parents often make life too easy for their children. This is often because helicopter parents had hard times themselves when they were younger. They want to spare their children the same hardships they had to face. So another question has to be:

3. Because of my hard times, am I overcompensating with my child?

Often these parents are working too hard to protect their children from facing disappointments and struggles.

Many helicopter parents are also very involved in their children's activities. They are room mothers, PTA presidents, scout leaders, and t-ball and soccer coaches. They think they are doing it for their child, but very often that is not the case. Frequently, the over-involvement is so the parent keeps a close eye and ear on their child.

I would be remiss if I failed to mention there is a tiny percentage of the global population that has entitled and trained privilege in their children because they are in a very wealthy financial bracket. Kids who are raised with multiple nannies and housekeepers often are taught that someone else will do the undesirable jobs. It is very important for these parents to teach their children the value of self-reliance, especially so the children do not collapse when they leave the encapsulated world they grew up in. This usually occurs when going off to college.

Not all help is helicopting. If you have extensive knowledge in a specific area, know that it is okay to become involved. If you are an Eagle Scout, go ahead and be a Boy Scout leader. You have much to offer all the boys in the group. If you were a champion soccer player in high school, coach your daughter's soccer team. You can add value to the team's experience that other parents cannot. But don't do it all. Let your child learn to fly without you.

THE IMPORTANCE OF BREAKING THE CYCLE

We've talked before about how easy it is to pick up actions and behaviors we experienced in how our parents related to us, and pass them along to our children. Our sons and daughters, then, pass the relating style on to their children. In this way, four generations or more can easily be impacted by the parenting style of one or two people. Mind boggling if you think about it.

It is also important to know that numerous recent studies have found that in Western countries, such as the United States, when parents step in to help older children too quickly, the children suffer. *Current Directions in Psychological Science,* a journal of the Association for Psychological Science, reported in 2009 that a review of the effects of parental control (or over-involved parenting) in the United States and China indicated that meddling by parents can have negative effects on the psychological development of children, although the effects may not be uniform.[4] The review was done by several noted psychologists, including Eva Pomerantz from the University of Illinois, Champaign-Urbana and Qian Wang of The Chinese University of Hong Kong.

The take-away message from the research is that too much parental interference will damage a child's psychological development. Their studies found that parental over-involvement makes children and young adults feel as if they lack control over their lives. This is particularly pronounced in the United States, where independence is emphasized.

In the United States, when children go through adolescence, parents tend to decrease their assistance and control more than Chinese parents do. Children in the United States expect this decrease, and therefore, their psychological functioning may be dependent on the extent to which parents decrease their involvement. This includes the decisions parents make for their children and also stepping in too soon when the son or daughter fails to follow through on tasks.

In addition, the negative effects of this style of parenting with regard to children's academics may be stronger in the United States than in East Asia. In East Asian countries, there is a strong moral aspect associated with learning, and education has a greater financial impact than in the United States. For these reasons, when it comes to academics, East Asian children may be more accepting of excessive parental involvement than children in the United States are.

While researchers have thought that certain aspects of East Asian culture may make children more accepting of their parents' intrusive behavior, Pomerantz and Wang conclude their report by noting, "Recommendations that parents limit their intrusiveness in children's lives are likely to be useful both in the [United States] and in East Asia."

You know, even though the term "helicopter parent" was coined a few short decades ago, the style of parenting is not new. In fact, it was more than a hundred years ago when, in 1899, General Douglas MacArthur's mom, Pinky, went with him to West Point. She even moved into an apartment near the campus and spied on him with a telescope to make sure he was studying. I am sure that none of you would go quite that far!

Dr. Patricia Somers is an associate professor of higher education at the University of Texas at Austin and spent more than a year studying parents of college-age kids, parents just like Douglas MacArthur's mom. To gather data, Somers and fellow researchers interviewed public university and college administrators, faculty, admissions staff, and counselors. She says they found that the helicopter style of parenting reaches all income levels, all races and ethnicities. There are even, she says, helicopter grandparents![5]

According to Somers, many universities have started to educate helicopter parents and wean students. There are separate orientations for parents and students, newsletters that offer tips for gradually disengaging, and policies that keep university staff from discussing an issue with a parent—unless the student brings it up first.

Dr. Steve Pastyrnak, pediatric psychologist at Spectrum Health's Helen DeVos Children's Hospital, adds that some helicopter parents are overcorrecting the way their parents raised them. He has said that parents need to understand that making mistakes can actually build a child's self-esteem. Parents should realize it's okay for kids to fail, if that teaches them how to do things better the next time around.[6]

FINDING BALANCE

This is not to say that you shouldn't have any involvement in your children's lives. Of course you should! As your children grow older there will be times when you see them going terribly off-track, and you will need to step in with a strong presence. You also need to be a solid sounding board and a trusted guide for your growing kids. Regular conversation is important, too. Your child needs to know she can talk to you and get your advice whenever she needs to.

What I am saying is you need to find the right balance between intrusion and ignoring a situation. Those are the far left and right ends of the spectrum. You need to find the healthy balance that is closer to the center. You may find that healthy balance lands you somewhere different on the spectrum for each child, and it may work best if you accommodate the balance to fit the needs of each individual child. Each of your children is a uniquely separate person, and you will find that you relate differently to each one.

The questions I gave you earlier in the chapter will help you find the right mix for you and your child. Please also keep in mind these four elements:

1. Your motivation. Why are you stepping in? Is it for you or for your child?
2. The consequences. Will your child's decision or behavior affect anyone's safety? If so, then you do need to step in.
3. The cost. Could your child's decision or action cost you financially more than you can afford? If so, then it's time to sit down for a heart to heart.
4. The blessings. Make a list of the good things that can come from you stepping back and giving your child the option to do the right thing. You might just be surprised at how long this list gets!

DR. FRAN'S TOP TIPS CHAPTER FOUR

- Commit to the belief that obstacles and disappointments in your child's life are opportunities to grow.
- Do not try to sweep away, avoid, or protect your child from wrestling with a challenge on her own.
- Be brutally honest with yourself to own what *your* feelings are rather than those of your child's.
- We cannot shield our children from hurdles. The best we can do is give our children coping skills to deal with all that will come their way.
- Each time you feel the impulse to "do" something that is your child's responsibility, ask, "By trying to make my child's life experience easier *now,* will it set him up for *later* disappointments?"
- Model self-sufficiency. Don't shirk household duties by putting them off and letting things pile up. Show your child that you can pitch in, even when you don't want to.
- Recognize that each individual—including your child—has his or her own style and tempo. If you think you can "do it better" than your son, you're in trouble because the impulse

will always be there urging you to take over. Own up to it. Then, cool it!

- If your child falls, allow her to handle both the fall and the struggle to find a solution. Don't rush in to fix anything. She may surprise you with good judgment and intuition.
- Praise every increment toward your child's independence and let him know you take pride, as should he, in his growing outward into the world.

CHAPTER FIVE

DEALING WITH YOUR PARENTAL DOUBT

Unlike the parents we've discussed so far, who forge ahead with clear, albeit misguided, agendas, the unsure parent is filled with self-doubt and has great difficulty making decisions. Even simple things such as deciding whether to have pasta or meatloaf for dinner can put this parent over the edge. Forget big decisions: which car to buy, whether or not to change jobs, if it is better to stay put in an apartment or buy a home. Doubting parents will waffle forever. This category includes parents who recognize they do not want to use the unsure parenting model their own parents set but are clueless about what other model to use. And it also includes parents who, regardless of the style of parenting they received, have doubts about everything.

The difficulty with unsure parents is that their children grow up doubtful, without the confidence to make their own decisions, and without the ability to advocate for themselves. Remember that our children learn from our actions and behavior, so if we model "uncertainty" to them, that's what they will learn.

Keep in mind, however, that if a child's personality develops as unsure, it is not 100 percent due to the uncertainty of the parent. Personality is related to the innate temperament of the child. For example, if a baby is born with a calm, mellow temperament, she will most probably grow into a person with less insecurity and hesitation than a baby who is born with an anxious temperament. This calm baby is also less likely to activate her mother's unsureness and indecisiveness, just as a calm mother will be less likely to feed her baby's anxiety. Because of her accepting nature, the calm baby communicates to her mom that she is effective, and this validates the mother's role and overcomes her doubt.

CHARACTERISTICS OF AN UNSURE PARENT

Unsure parents are easy to spot because unsureness permeates their being. Everything from a mom's body language to a dad's speech pattern can present a wavering effect, as if the parent can't figure out which side of a line to step on. Some specific characteristics of an unsure mom or dad are that the parent:

1. continually vacillates back and forth in a "should I or shouldn't I" pattern, and doesn't realize that many of the decisions that need to be made are not crucial.
2. tortures him- or herself with indecisiveness and cannot bear the thought of making the wrong decision.
3. is filled with self-disgust about his or her doubt.
4. often makes final decisions abruptly, rather than thoughtfully. These abrupt decisions frequently turn out to be poor decisions.
5. realizes they are caught in a vicious circle and want, badly, to do the right thing.
6. can't tolerate the repercussions of people being angry with them about a poor decision.

If this is you, or if you know someone like this, understand that the possibility for change exists. While it can be a difficult process, I know that the last thing an unsure parent wants is for their child to endure the same agony that they go through.

The Importance of Parenting Models: A Case Study

Victoria and Sanford had two adorable children: Warren, who was nine, and Bailey, who was six. Both of the parents wanted to do the best they could for their children, but each unknowingly carried "baggage" from their own family history.

In Victoria's case, her mom was critical, harsh, overprotective, and anxious. Anytime Victoria's mom set boundaries, her words and tone had a sharp edge. The interactions between Victoria and her mom were loving, but the love always came with yelling and screaming. Her mom would say things such as, "Don't you know better?" Or, "What are you doing?" And, "What are you doing to yourself?" Add a harsh tone and crank up the volume and you get an idea of what Victoria dealt with in her formative years.

This environment not only gave Victoria a mixed message about what love is, but over time, her mother's words and tone eroded any confidence that Victoria might have had. It also left Victoria with loads of self-doubt, and she second-guessed every decision she made.

As you can see, Victoria did not have a baseline for healthy parenting. Her saving grace was that she was an intelligent, kind-hearted, well-intended person who wanted to make a difference as a mother with her children. On her own, she decided she did not want to repeat her mom's model. Victoria wanted to be a patient, loving, milk-and-cookies kind of mom. And even before she showed up for counseling, she was all of that and more.

Victoria gave her all to her kids. She served wonderful home-cooked meals, was on the PTA, and did her time as room mother. She organized play dates and nurtured her children well. Where she fell down was in disciplining her children. You and I know that every child needs boundaries, and to her credit, Victoria did say all the right things. But she wavered and was indecisive when it came to setting limits.

It didn't help that her husband, Sanford, came from a much more unstable background than she did. His mom had been diagnosed as a sociopath and had actually attacked family members. This diagnosis, by the way, is more common than you might think. Harvard psychologist Dr. Martha Stout, author of *The Sociopath Next Door*, reveals that up to 4 percent of people—or one in twenty-five—possess no conscience, feel no guilt, and are, therefore, sociopaths.[1]

Sanford's mother had no conscience and was ice cold, distant, and self-serving. Sanford did choose well, though. Victoria was his mother's direct opposite. Sanford was a brilliant man, but he was also just as controlling as Victoria's mom. To top it off, he was a perfectionist whom no one could please. In this aspect, Victoria also balanced her weaknesses, as Sanford was well-equipped to make all the decisions that she could not, including decisions about their finances. Victoria didn't even have a checking account.

I realize this is a lot of back story, but it is important because Victoria and Sanford's older child, Warren, was having a lot of difficulty. Warren was being mean and disrespectful toward his mom. Warren also felt a lot of resentment and anger toward his sister, Bailey, because he felt his mom favored her. Due to these factors, Warren was in danger of falling into a depression.

Childhood depression is not the norm, but it is also more common than you might think. A National Institute of Mental Health study of nine- to seventeen-year-olds found depression in more than 6 percent of children in that age range in any given six-month period.[2] That is roughly one child in every classroom across the United States. In addition, they found the onset of depression is occurring earlier in life today than in the past. A separate study found that early-onset depression often persists, recurs, and continues into adulthood, and indicates that depression in youth may also predict more severe illness in adult life.[3] Long story short, Warren really needed his mom to set hard and fast rules and follow through with consequences. But as an unsure parent, this was hard for her to do.

To help them, I demonstrated to Victoria how she could set limits with Warren. For example, when Warren was hostile and demeaning to his mom, I intruded by asking him to speak to his mother in a respectful tone. You might think that Victoria was appreciative here, but not so much. Instead, she became nervous that I might be "upsetting" Warren. She became quite angry with me over this, as well as my attempts to get her to ask Warren to treat her with respect.

This is not unusual. When people are taken out of their comfort zone, a typical reaction is to lash back. And I have to say that Victoria was very uncomfortable making any kind of intrusion on Warren.

Because Victoria was so resistant at first, Warren and I talked between the two of us about his feelings. He blew hot and cold and was quite guarded and defensive, so I became his voice. For example, I'd say things to him such as, "If I had a mom and dad like you do, I'd be pretty mad about it." Or, "I know it's hard to talk about how you really feel when you are so angry." I used these specific words because Warren needed permission from an adult (in this case me) to express his anger at his parents. Eventually he opened up and we began to make progress.

I then asked Victoria to spend an afternoon once or twice a week doing something after school with Warren, just the two of them. It was up to her to decide on the activity and the flow of their time spent together. She chose going for ice cream, which I thought was great. But, because Warren was so hateful to her during these outings, she stopped after just a few times. For the most part, he gave her the silent treatment. They'd sit in the ice cream store and he would have tunnel vision with his cherished treat and completely ignore his mother. I really wish she had stuck it out, but Victoria could not decide what to do when Warren would not speak. So, I gave her a few guidelines that would help her in other attempts at bonding with Warren:

1. Rather than expect Warren to engage in reciprocal conversation, she should begin by describing out loud the experience they were having. For example, she could talk about the cold, sweet, chocolaty flavor of the ice cream they were having at home and say, "This is sooooo good!"
2. Victoria should also tell Warren how much she enjoys being with him, without his dad or his sister. "I love times when it is just us!"
3. If Warren expresses his anger to Victoria she should say, "I am so glad you feel open enough to tell me about your angry feelings. I'm the kind of mom who wants to hear it straight to my face."

These ideas not only helped Victoria begin to make good decisions, they gave her a plan and scripts she could pull out of her back pocket. Over time, as she became more decisive and clearer in her expectations, Warren improved. He became more respectful to her and began making new friends at school. And the really great news is that there were no more worries of Warren falling into a depression. His anger and unhappiness went away in direct proportion to his mother's ability to be responsive and sure about her decisions.

THE IMPORTANCE OF ERIKSON'S PSYCHO-SOCIAL STAGES OF DEVELOPMENT

Parents begin making decisions for and about their children just as soon as their sons and daughters are born. These decisions mainly include when to hold, bathe, feed, and play with their new bundles of joy. Most important, these early decisions help parents learn to confidently and accurately read cues given by their infants. Erik Erikson, a leading psychiatrist, developed the Psycho-Social Stages of Development in 1956.[4] His work demonstrated how very early in life a baby really does need his or her parent to be decisive and sure.

Erikson was born in 1902 in Germany, and his father abandoned him before birth. Raised by his Jewish mother, Erikson was teased at temple school because he was tall, blonde, and blue-eyed, and at grammar school because of his Jewish heritage. Later, after studying psychoanalysis with Anna Freud, he taught at Harvard Medical School. Erikson used his challenging childhood experiences and extensive knowledge of cultural, environmental, and social influences to develop his theories.

Erikson's theory helps us understand a human's psychological and emotional development over the course of a lifetime. Erikson categorized eight stages of development from infancy to late adulthood in which a person confronts, and hopefully masters, new challenges. And, just like other areas that require you to build on a previously mastered task (think math or spelling), if a stage is not successfully completed, it may reappear as a problem in the future. Our focus here is on Erikson's first stage, Hope: Trust vs. Mistrust.

This first stage occurs between birth and one year of age and is the most fundamental stage in life. It centers around a baby's basic needs being met by his or her parents. We all know that infants depend on their parents (especially the mother) for food and comfort. We should understand, then, that a child's understanding of the world comes from their interactions with their parents. For instance, if new parents expose their baby to security, consistency, and affection, the baby's view of the world will be one of trust. Should the parents fail to provide any of the above, and also fail to meet the child's basic need for consistent, immediate responses, mistrust will result. It is the parents' challenge and task to determine what the baby's immediate need is, whether it is food, a diaper change, comfort, or simply a matter of company.

Now here's the important part. Parents and caregivers who are inconsistent or unsure plant feelings of mistrust in the children they care for. And, if children are unable to develop trust during this early developmental stage, they may grow to fear their inconsistent world, possibly resulting in anxiety and heightened insecurities and, in extreme cases, a sense of hopelessness.

This is why parents must respond to their babies with confidence, clarity, and decisiveness. This way their children will grow up trusting and secure.

CURRENT RESEARCH AGREES

Erikson is not the only one who has done research on this issue. A recent Ohio State University study also provides interesting insights about adults who chronically doubt their judgments.[5] Herbert Mirels, the primary author of the study and a professor of psychology at Ohio State University, says his study shows that people who are dubious about their judgment are highly vulnerable. "They see every important decision they make as a trial in which they are likely to find themselves deficient, or to be found deficient by others."

As a result, self-doubters put off making important decisions and often ask others for advice. Such passivity lessens their anxiety in the short term, but in the long run it contributes to feelings of uncertainty.

To help study the unsure, Mirels and his colleagues developed the Judgmental Self-Doubt Scale, a questionnaire that measures the extent to which a person experiences doubt about his or her own judgment. Researchers used the questionnaire in several related studies. Participants in the studies were both college students and people from the general population, so it was a good, average sampling of people everywhere. The results are quite interesting. People who scored high on the scale tended to see decision making as an arduous activity. They reported that they changed their minds often, and when they finally made a decision, they were concerned that it was the wrong one.

Mirels noted that people who are chronically unsure tend not to enjoy tasks that require effortful thinking and, as a result, try to avoid it. Additionally, researchers found that:

1. self-doubters did not differ from others in their level of intellectual ability.
2. people who scored high on self-doubt also had low self-esteem, chronic anxiety, higher levels of depression, and a tendency to procrastinate.
3. self-doubt is related to steep emotional ups and downs. Students with high scores on judgmental self-doubt reported having more mood swings than those with low scores.
4. people with high scores in judgmental self-doubt also reported feeling they have little control over their lives.

According to Mirels, these results suggest that people who are unsure are less centered and react especially strongly to both positive and negative events.

Concurring with Erikson, Mirels said he believes that a sense of either confidence or doubt in one's judgment is formed early on, when children first begin detecting the reactions of their parents to the decisions they make. The present research suggests that if doubt takes root, it is likely to adversely affect many aspects of a person's life. "Self doubters tend to have a wide range of negative dispositions and self conceptions," Mirels said. "They are prone to hesitation and vacillation and probably are less efficient and accomplish less than more confident people."

IT'S OKAY TO ASK FOR HELP

If you are having trouble reading your child's cues, take heart—it does not mean you are a bad parent. If a mom's mother misread her cues when she was an infant, then the mom has no unconscious baseline for accurate reading. In other words, she, through no fault of her own, has poor "instincts." A new mom might also be too tense or nervous to accurately interpret her son or daughter's cues. Or, she might receive conflicting information from well-meaning friends and family members. But help is available! Understanding your child's cues can be learned in an infant/mom group or in therapy with an infant/child specialist.

It can be hard for parents to admit that they don't know how to respond to their children's needs. Audrey is a friend of mine from high school who automatically put a bottle in her baby's mouth every time her baby cried. But more often than not, the baby, an adorable little girl named Emma, wasn't crying because she was hungry. Usually Emma was crying because she just wanted to be held, or because she had gas.

It was hard for me to watch from afar as my well-intended friend fed Emma every time she didn't know what to do. Unfortunately, I had to watch from afar because Audrey had no interest in suggestions from others. As a child, Audrey was always unsure, as was her mother. But Audrey tried to mask her self-doubt by shooing away any help from family or friends. She felt she should automatically know what to do for Emma—after all, she was Emma's mom. Her instincts should tell her what to do. Unfortunately, it doesn't always work that way.

Feeding Emma became Audrey's automatic response for everything. I think you can guess the long-term effects of that. Yes, Emma wasn't much out of the toddler stage when she developed a compulsive eating disorder. The disorder is rooted in the fact that when Emma felt a pang of need, Audrey never learned to stop, slow down, and explore what the need was. Instead, she automatically shoved food into Emma's mouth. It wasn't that Audrey always thought Emma was hungry; it was that Audrey's anxiety refused to allow her to explore other options. The result is that compulsive eating has plagued Emma all her life, even now that she has graduated from college and is out on her own. Emma struggles every day with food and eating, and the root cause is because Audrey was unsure.

It is sad that Audrey did not realize that help was available. Now, more than ever, there are places and specialists who offer help to moms (and dads) who want to better understand their baby's needs. If you feel that you and your child could benefit, please ask your pediatrician for a referral.

HOW TO GAIN CONFIDENCE

Everyone is indecisive sometimes. We all have decisions that we mull over for weeks or months. But that is much different than the chronic, every-day unsureness I am talking about here.

You must understand that to evolve from doubt to confidence takes a very long time. It also takes steady, conscious work, and the best results are seen when you have a trusted partner, therapist, pastor, or friend who can help. If you are an unsure parent, the most important thing you can do is develop strategies that will help you become more confident. Here are a few ideas:

1. HAVE AN HONEST SITDOWN
Have a conversation with your partner and tell him (or her) that you are ready to share more of the responsibility for decision making. If you think you are, more than likely you are right on. But, if you and your partner are not on the same page, then call in a trusted neutral third party, such as a therapist or pastor, who can weigh the issues for each of you.

2. TAKE MORE CHANCES IN DECISION MAKING
When you are ready to make firm choices, know that some of your deci-sions will be right and some will not. This means you must be willing to take the risk of both success and failure in your decision making. Know that you will have both. The results of some decisions may even be told around the dinner table for years to come, but that's okay. It can be hard to take that first, decisive step, but I know you can do it.

3. EXPECT YOUR ANXIETY TO TEMPORARILY RISE
Know that your anxiety will elevate when you first embark on this coura-geous task, and understand that it won't be like this forever. Your anxiety will go back down in direct proportion to the new confidence that you feel.

4. START SMALL

It's best to begin with little decisions—which cereal to buy, or whether to go to the post office first or the library—and work your way up. Only when you can comfortably make firm decisions about small things should you take it up a notch: which music teacher to choose, which summer camp is best for your child, whether you should vacation in June or July. By going slowly and seeing the results of your good decisions, you will build confidence in your abilities.

5. INFORM YOURSELF

Good decisions are informed decisions. To that end, you must take on the responsibility of getting all the information you need to make a decision yourself, rather than rely on other people to provide information to you. For example, if you are thinking about taking your children to a movie, instead of calling a friend or your husband to discuss whether or not the film is appropriate, look up the reviews yourself. Check out several reviews and when you have a variety of viewpoints, make up your own mind.

6. STICK TO YOUR GUNS

When you make a decision, for better or worse, stay with it. Your children need to understand that your decisions are final. This gives them firm boundaries and a sense of secure well-being. You can still be a smiling milk-and-cookies mom; you'll just be a clear one.

7. TRY THERAPY

If change is difficult for you, seek out a skilled therapist who can hold your hand as you progress. A trained, caring professional can often allow you to lean on them in such a way that it neither allows you to fall or inhibits your ability to grow. Sometimes well-meaning friends or partners will allow you to lean too heavily on them. In these cases it is rare that you will make any advancement or evolvement in your efforts to be more sure.

8. DON'T BEAT YOURSELF UP

Create a benign self-observation—one in which you do not judge yourself harshly. The best way to do this is first to acknowledge that you are hard on yourself. Then, make a behavioral intrusion in your thinking. Every time you notice yourself thinking a self-deprecating thought, interrupt it. Gently think, "There I go again." Interrupt the negative thoughts each time. If you know you are working hard to make change for the better, then that's the best you can do. If you look at your history of decision making over a period of weeks, or months, you will most likely see a higher number of good decisions than bad ones. This will give you the confidence to work even harder!

WHEN ALL IS SAID AND DONE

I hope unsure parents do not feel I am being too harsh on them. Parents of this nature often are more sensitive and easily feel criticized. Yes, I am pushing you toward better parenting. But if someone doesn't give you that gentle nudge, then you, dear unsure parent, will never see change. Remember that this book is here as a resource for you. So read carefully and you will not fall. I have confidence in you!

DR. FRAN'S TOP TIPS CHAPTER FIVE

- Identify yourself and acknowledge that you are an unsure parent.
- Partner with a non-judgmental, supportive, understanding person.
- Know that you will have successes and failures.
- Expect your anxiety to temporarily rise as you take risks in decision making.
- Become informed before you make a decision. Do the research and find information on your own.
- Start small. Once you have mastered little decisions, you can grow from there.
- Once committed to a decision, stick to it. Do not give in to the temptation to waffle.
- Praise yourself for your courage. This is not easy, and you are brave to take this on.

CHAPTER SIX

THE SPAGHETTI PARENT

LEARNING THE VALUE OF SAYING NO

Spaghetti parenting potentially has a greater negative influence on children than any other style of parenting we've discussed so far. Children of spaghetti parents tend to have problems that are severe and can include negative behaviors such as insolence, disrespect, and even addiction to drugs and alcohol. If you think you might be a spaghetti parent, or know someone who is, please pay special attention to this chapter.

So just who are spaghetti parents? Simply put, they are moms and dads who absolutely cannot say no to their children. They are like the good grandma who spoils her grandchildren by letting them do as they please and then sends them home for discipline, boundaries, and real life. But when you are the spaghetti parent, this is real life. There is no one else to set boundaries and discipline your child. It is all up to you.

Children of spaghetti parents know that when their parents set boundaries, they can get mom or dad to loosen the rules with a just little wheedling. These children learn very early on that parents cave in quickly and are easily swayed. Over time, the children demand more and more and the behavior becomes worse and worse. Then, before the parents really realize what is happening, they find themselves in a world of chaos and pain.

Spaghetti parents experience a lot of internal conflict over saying no. The spaghetti parent knows he or she should hold fast to their word, but still quickly loses any backbone they might have had when it comes to holding the line with their child. This is because the spaghetti parent is afraid that if they say no, their son or daughter will no longer like them, or will be mad at them. But that is part of parenting. Your kids are not always going to like you and they will frequently be mad at you. The sooner you get comfortable with this, the better your parenting will be.

Typically, what happens is spaghetti parents give their children too much slack. They throw out miles and miles of rope, but when their little boy or girl gets to a certain point in their misbehavior, then the mom or dad tries to jerk the rope back and blows up in anger when the child does not comply. The problem is that neither the child nor the parent knows exactly where that point is, so when it is reached, it hits everyone by surprise.

I believe most parents are well-meaning, and the spaghetti parent is no different. This mom or dad truly wants to do the right thing but is absolutely clueless. He or she cannot grasp the basic concepts of boundaries and discipline and is easily overwhelmed by his or her child's behavior. The good news is that this kind of well-meaning parent is often open to guidance and can be willing to listen to a therapist's suggestions.

Wavering Boundaries: A Case Study

When talking about spaghetti parents, George and Rosetta and their fourteen-year-old son, Stephen, come to mind. When George was just two, his father left the country, abandoning George and his mom. George was raised without knowing his birth father at all. His mom eventually remarried a very kind man, but George always knew that his biological father, his "real" father, had left him. As he grew older, George came to the conclusion that the worst thing a father could do to a child was leave. In George's mind absolutely nothing could be more damaging. While George knew what a father shouldn't do, he had not learned what a father should do. It all got mixed up in his mind and George came to the conclusion that he should smile and say yes to Stephen. All the time.

The result in this case was that Stephen began drinking and staying out past curfew. In cases like this I have a rule. If, after half a dozen or so sessions, it is clear that a well-meaning spaghetti parent cannot put into practice my suggestions for holding firm boundaries, and if their son or daughter is as out of control as Stephen was, I sometimes suggest placing the child in a therapeutic boarding school.

You may think a boarding school a bit extreme. But consider Stephen's situation carefully. He quickly went from a sullen, lonely, fourteen-year-old who was having difficulty in school to a completely out-of-control fifteen-year-old.

I should also mention that Stephen had mild learning difficulties. Because of his difficulty in learning, Stephen was socially isolated. He had no friends and was bullied for not matching up with the other kids academically. Stephen hated school... and most people.

To compensate for the tough time Stephen was having, George over-indulged him with computers, games, and electronics. If it was a new state-of-the-art gadget, Stephen had it. George also gave his son way too much freedom and did little in the way of monitoring his activities.

As a result, Stephen began pushing for limits, dressing in a punk style and emulating rappers. Stephen, at some point, decided that if the good kids weren't going to accept him, then he would model the bullying behavior that had been done to him by some of his other classmates. Lo and behold, the bullies embraced him. Soon after that Stephen began getting in trouble at school and the rest is history.

George and Rosetta, obviously, were in a panic. While Rosetta was not a super strong mom, her instincts were better than those of her husband. She knew they had to take immediate steps. George, however, remained as well-meaning and as clueless as ever. Because of what his own father had done, it was very hard for me to get George to see that indulging Stephen in gifts, gadgets, and freedom was causing the problem. Believe me, I tried, but George continued to openly disagree with me.

Eventually George admitted that he could understand my point. Still, he was unable to effect change in his parenting. I felt a great deal of empathy for George. He was terribly stuck. Each week he would come into my office and state, "Dr. Fran, I didn't do one thing you told me to."

If a child is, like Stephen, stealing, drinking, drugging, and skipping school at age fifteen, and if his parents cannot control him, what are his chances for success at twenty, or thirty? Someone needs to halt the behavior, and if the parents can't do it, then a boarding school might be able to. While very expensive, many of these schools have an excellent success rate.

At first, George and Rosetta were not at all excited about the idea of sending their son away to school. George, in particular, was adamantly against it because he saw this as a repetition of his own father's abandonment. George felt if he sent Stephen to boarding school, that it would be akin to forsaking him. It took Stephen being arrested for theft and the threat of a long period of time in juvenile jail for George to wake up and really see what was happening. That the police echoed what I had been saying for two years also helped.

Stephen's parents first sent him to a six-week summer boot camp, followed by a year at a therapeutic boarding school. I just wish it could have happened much sooner. By this time, Stephen was a senior in high school and was allowed just one year in the therapeutic program. It would have been so much better if Stephen could have benefited from three years at the therapeutic school. I was grateful, however, that he at least got one year, and you know what? It helped. A lot!

A BETTER ALTERNATIVE

I am so very glad that Stephen was able to get the help he needed, but also saddened that these drastic measures were necessary. If George and Rosetta had intervened earlier and set and kept appropriate boundaries, Stephen would never have spiraled so far out of control.

You may know parents like George and Rosetta. You may even find elements of them in yourself. But unlike George and Rosetta, I know you will be more successfully effective at holding the line for your kids. I know *you* will listen. Here are a few ideas that will help prevent your child from walking the same path that Stephen did:

1. Know that indulging your child in gifts and gadgets is not the way to motivate them to listen better or to comply.
2. Determine which privileges have the most meaning to your child. Then offer the privileges as "earnings" for complying with expected behavior (for example, not getting in trouble at school, getting passing grades, being kind and courteous to classmates, et cetera).
3. If your child breaks one of your pre-set and discussed expectations, he loses all of his most meaningful privileges for a short time. This is non-negotiable.
4. Consequences should sting bitterly for a *short* time so as to motivate your child to try again. If the consequence is too long, he will think why should I even try? I already lost my cell phone for three weeks, I'll just keep messing up!

SUPPORTIVE FACTS

Studies confirm that children benefit from clear boundaries. A 1998 study by Lee Shumow, Deborah Lowe Vandell, and Jill K. Posner from Northern Illinois University and the University of Wisconsin-Madison followed 184 families with children in the third grade. Families were contacted again when their children were in the fifth grade. The study found that parents who held firm boundaries, yet were still able to implement kind and empathetic responses to their child's dilemmas, reported fewer behavior problems in the home and greater child responsibility in the fifth grade.[1]

I call this kind of reasoned, boundaried, and empathetic parenting firm-responsive parenting. Just so we're clear about what this is, a few examples of firm-responsive parenting strategies include:

1. Understanding your child and finding the correct balance of responsiveness and firmness. Responsiveness is empathic attunement, which acknowledges and validates out loud what your child is feeling and doing. Firmness is clearly knowing and implementing how you as the parent will deal with an issue, and then not wavering.
2. Understanding that immediate consequences for your child lead to a stronger relationship of behavior to consequence.

The father of a sixth grade boy who continued to call out in class, make jokes to be funny, and distract from the teacher's lesson asked how he should respond to his son. I suggested that since this boy passionately loves basketball, he needs to be told—without his father's angry temper—that each time his dad hears from the teacher that the boy disrupted class, the boy cannot go to his next basketball practice or game, whichever comes first. The boy's basketball coach was fully supportive and the boy's behavior improved radically.

3. Being crystal clear on specific expectations. Parents of a privileged eleventh-grade girl asked for advice about teaching their daughter to talk and behave respectfully to them. This girl was more than rude and hurtful. Although her grades were excellent and she had many friends, this daughter put her parents down and never acknowledged their birthdays or anniversary. I advised them to tell their daughter in a straightforward manner that they will no longer accept disrespectful talk and behavior. Not at all. If the daughter breached that rule, then she lost the fancy new car the family gave her for her sixteenth birthday for a day. It didn't take long before the girl did a complete 180.

These examples show that the firm boundaries you hold for your child pay off.

Shumow, Lowe Vandell, and Posner found that children who experience firm-responsive parenting strategies have more respect for themselves and others and show more responsibility. Some participants in the study even developed early leadership skills. One of the biggest benefits of implementing these strategies is that when parents follow through on clear, firm boundaries, the child does not get out of doing whatever it is that you expect of them. Instead, they respect the rules and comply. And, they respect you.

Another study, this one at the University of Hawaii at Manoa, studied substance abuse prevention among Hawaii's youth. While substance abuse may not be a problem for you or your child, Stephen's story shows that it can become a real risk for children of spaghetti parents.

In the study, more than half of the teens reported that their parents wouldn't discipline them if they were caught using alcohol, tobacco, or drugs, and as many as 44 percent said their parents did not monitor their whereabouts.[2] So even if you set boundaries and make an effort to know where your kids are, on average, roughly half of your child's friends have parents who do not. While this study was done in Hawaii, the numbers are typical across both geographic and economic lines. This means that no matter where you live, no matter what your income, almost half of your child's friends have the possibility of not being properly supervised or disciplined.

The study also found that kids who did not have specific expectations for behavior, who were not monitored, and who had overly severe or inconsistent discipline were at greater risk for substance abuse. And, the younger a child is when they first use alcohol, cigarettes, or marijuana, the higher the probability of continued use when they are older.

We sometimes forget what a scary world it is out there. That's why, for most children, you should begin discussing these issues in elementary school.

ARE YOU A SPAGHETTI PARENT?

As you have seen, there is so much more to spaghetti parents than first saying, "no," and then saying "yes." Some spaghetti parents, in fact, just say "yes" and most cannot set or enforce boundaries and do not know how to curb their son or daughter's disrespectful behavior.

So, how can you tell if you are wavering too much, or if your boundaries are not enough? Start by reading through the following questions:

1. Do you find yourself repeatedly excusing your child's behavior even though you have that "uh oh" feeling in the pit of your stomach?
2. When your child is disrespectful do you make excuses for her and say to yourself, "She's had a hard day at school," or "She's just going through a stage?"
3. When your child is upset, do you try to "wash away" the hurt with milk and cookies, rather than having some straight talk about what is going on in your child's life?
4. Do you find yourself begging and pleading for your child to do something she should already be doing?

5.   Do you have difficulty knowing how to talk to your child
      about his or her behavior, and so you often put off impor-
      tant conversations?

It is important to understand that many parents display elements of the
spaghetti parent. And, many parents would answer "yes" to at least one of
the questions on this list. That does not automatically make you a spaghetti
parent. But, if all (or most) of these items ring true for you on a regular basis,
then it is a clear sign that your parenting style is likely that of the spaghetti
parent.

ADULT CHILDREN OF SPAGHETTI PARENTS

While I care deeply about all families, I am especially concerned about
spaghetti parents and their children. I worry because, as you have seen,
some of these kids can turn to drugs, substance abuse, lying, stealing, and
other negative behaviors. Not all of them turn out this way, of course, but
some of them do.

The reason children of spaghetti parents can get into such big trouble
is that the boundaries they were shown as children were so unclear that
they have very little sense of when or where to stop themselves. These kids
often want more and more of whatever thrill they have found. And more
and more, they cannot deal with their feelings directly and instead leave
the responsibilities of life behind by using drugs and alcohol.

Remember that a boundary feels good to a child. It is both safe and
comforting to them. With a firm boundary in place, your son or daughter
knows that as soon as he or she goes over the line, there will be someone
there to pull them back. And trust me, your child will test the boundary
line, and that's good. Testing gives a child an even clearer sense of exactly
how much leeway they do or do not have.

When children without clear boundaries push against authority, each
time they are not reined in they will push a little harder and a little louder.
In time, kids without boundaries become risk takers and thrill seekers, and
they will look for bigger and deeper thrills to sustain them throughout their
life. The thrills can often reach dangerous levels, so it is doubly important
to set and keep boundaries, beginning when your child is quite young.

I mentioned that not all children of these parents turn to drugs, theft, and lies, and not all of them do. Some become weak, or meek, and cannot make decisions. These children can grow up to be well-meaning spaghetti parents themselves, and pass along indecisive and boundary-less parenting to their children—your grandchildren.

Some children of spaghetti parents become manipulative adults, due to all the practice they had in childhood. Other kids grow up confused. They don't know when someone means what they say. In these cases trust issues can be present. Some kids become insecure, because in childhood rules were not hard and fast. These children have difficulty as adults in knowing what they want. They have no direction and seem to flounder in everything that they do.

If this information has not convinced you that your child needs to have firm boundaries, then maybe our next scenario will.

The Benefits of Openness: A Case Study

Lauren is a spaghetti parent who is very well-meaning; she is also pretty, soft, and loving. But Lauren's mom was explosive and Lauren decided long ago that whenever she had children she would be the opposite of her own mother. That opportunity came when Lauren married a great guy named Gilbert and had two beautiful boys, Jackson and Larry.

Keeping her promise to herself, Lauren poured all the love she could into each boy. She was warm and nurturing without spoiling her sons. Even though she and Gilbert could have afforded to employ a full-time nanny, or to buy fancy computers, televisions, and phones for their boys, they didn't. Both Lauren and her husband wanted their children to learn to appreciate the value of things.

When the boys got old enough to challenge Lauren, at about age three, Lauren handled the situations well. But when her oldest son, Jackson, got to be seven he began to disrespect her, copying behavior he learned from kids he met at the playground and at school.

This time around Lauren didn't handle the challenges so well. She could not bear it when Jackson yelled at her and said things such as, "I hate you!" and "You're not a good mom!" Jackson's yelling and tone of voice reminded her of her own mother's explosive and hostile rejection, and this made Lauren very resentful.

It is normal for boys at this age to start to grow away from their mothers (and fathers) and test their boundaries. Lauren wanted to embrace this normal stage of growth but did not know how to handle Jackson's testing and pushing. When he said hateful things to her, Lauren did her best to turn her head and ignore him. But it didn't help.

Eventually Lauren would reach a saturation point with Jackson's pushing and disrespect and be unable to take it anymore. The problem was—as I mentioned earlier in this chapter—neither she nor Jackson knew where that point was. What they both did know was that when Lauren reached the magic line, she'd begin to scream words to the effect of, "I told you not to do that!" "You ungrateful child!" "You'd better stop it right now!" The words were always said with a mixture of anger and hysteria and just fueled Jackson's desire to test all the more.

Lauren wondered how her lovely son could be so mean to her when all she had ever done was love him. After all she did for him, she did not understand his antagonistic behavior. So, every time she turned her cheek, her anger and resentment built until, voila, she burst out in fury, just as her mother had.

The good news is that Lauren was a self-aware parent. She understood right away that she was in trouble, and entered therapy. When Lauren and Jackson first came to see me Jackson was disrespectful toward me. Like many spaghetti parents, Lauren became very angry with me when I corrected him. This was because she didn't want anyone to be "mean" to her son. But over time, I showed Lauren that there was another way. As she became more accepting, I gave her a few scripts she could use when Jackson began yanking her chains.

Instead of turning her head and ignoring Jackson, I taught Lauren to say, "I really want to hear what you have to tell me, but your tone is disrespectful. Show me how you can fix what you just said to me so we can move on." That way Jackson got a chance to say what he meant to say with a respectful tone and posture. Many kids will require a number of tries. They will say the right words but give you attitude in the delivery or say it while refusing to look directly at you. If that's the case, then you simply say, "Good try but I need you to say it like you mean it. Say it respectfully." Then keep repeating that until your child gets it right.

I like these words because they show no anger toward the child who is pushing against the boundaries, yet they also show that there is zero tolerance for the negative behavior. Additionally, the ball is put in the child's court. The child has the opportunity to choose the correct move, and the words steer him or her in the right direction. For this to be effective, though, the words have to be said in the same neutral tone every single time your son or daughter is disrespectful of you or the boundaries you set. Consistency is a must. This is your chance to teach your child that whenever she pushes too far, this is exactly the response she is going to get.

A twist on this strategy is also effective when your son tries to avoid correction, or dealing with the issue at hand, and physically walks away. In this case the well-meaning spaghetti parent has to physically bring their child back to Point A and not allow him to move on to the next activity until he fixes the disrespectful words that were said. This is hard, because the biggest conflict and biggest challenge for these parents is to learn to correct their child. The weak behavior of a spaghetti parent is deeply ingrained. There are so many years of repeating these patterns that it can be very difficult to change.

My work here, obviously, is with the parent. But no therapist can help unless a parent shows that window of openness that we discussed in many of the earlier chapters.

HELP FOR SPAGHETTI PARENTS

If you are a spaghetti parent, know that it can be hard to change. You want your son or daughter to like you. You want to indulge your child because you love him. But, as you've seen, setting firm boundaries is very important. Here are a few ideas that will help:

1. RECOGNIZE THAT YOU MAY NOT KNOW WHAT IS BEST

Spaghetti parents on the surface may seem wimpy, but inside they are as rigid as steel about what they think is best for their child. You must accept that no one person is always right, even when it comes to you and your child. Sometimes you get so close to a situation that you lose perspective, and this is what often happens with spaghetti parents.

2. GO TO THERAPY

Not to toot my own horn, but a skilled therapist can give you the perspective you so badly need. They can also help you understand the root cause of your inability to say no to your child, and give helpful ideas that are specific to you and your situation. Be sure to choose a therapist that you feel comfortable with. If you do not find the right one for you the first time, know that it is the match, and not the process. A word of caution, though. If a therapist does not agree with you all the time or if he points out areas in which you can improve, it doesn't necessarily mean the fit is not right. A good therapist will gently challenge you and ask for your openness in making changes for the better.

3. GET A SUPPORT SYSTEM IN PLACE

In addition to a therapist, it is helpful to get the support of those around you, particularly others who live in the same house with you and your child. It is also important for you to have one person—a spouse, friend, teacher, counselor, or pastor—who will listen openly. Trying to affect change on your own is nearly impossible; you need a partner in this, someone you can lean on when life with your child gets tough. And it will get harder before it gets better. That I can guarantee. As you rein in your child, he or she is going to push against those tighter boundaries and kick up a fuss when they don't move. If you don't buckle, before too long, life for everyone in the household will be vastly improved. Hang in there.

4. YOU ARE DOING THIS TO HELP YOUR CHILD

Remember that by setting firm boundaries you are not hurting your child. In fact, it is the complete opposite. The boundaries you set and hold will give your child coping skills so he or she can deal with disappointment later in life. Children need to know that things are not always going to go their way. Boundaries give them a safe place both to fall and pick themselves up again.

DR. FRAN'S TOP TIPS CHAPTER SIX

- Recognize that you may not always know what is best for your child.
- Acknowledge that you have a high propensity for caving in when your child protests, whines, begs, bargains, or cries.
- Once you commit to a position, do not change your mind.
- Adopt the belief that your child will not always like you. Sometimes he or she will be mad at you and reject you. This is a necessary part of claiming themselves as separate from you. Each of your children has individual wants and wishes. But while they live in your house they must abide by your boundaries.
- Find a companion who is available to you for comfort, guidance, and support. It is too difficult to change parenting habits alone.
- Do not give your child too much slack. The more slack in the rope, the harder it is to rein them in.
- Get comfortable with your child's protest. Your child needs to know that you accept, validate, and embrace him—flaws and all!
- Monitor your child's friends and their activities. Know where and with whom your child is with at all times.
- Deal directly with your child's feelings by talking with your child. Do not overindulge your child with gadgets and gifts to compensate for her struggles. Instead, equip her with coping skills by allowing her to feel her disappointments.
- Pay attention to your gut. Most parents have very good intuition if they would only follow it as a guide.
- Remember that to be a good parent you must be comfortable with two things: loving/nurturing your child and setting/holding boundaries. To love your child is only half the job. Children need boundaries, too.

CHAPTER SEVEN

CONTROLLING NEGATIVITY IN YOUR COMMUNICATION

No matter how non-judgmental and open we think we are, we all grow up with negative or critical messages that shape us. We all on some level categorize others in our minds. Many of us have strong uncomplimentary opinions and we sometimes, intentionally or not, communicate these thoughts and ideas to others. These messages, just like parenting styles, get handed down generation after generation, so if you are a negative or critical parent, know that your style and your messages will likely carry through to your grandchildren and beyond. What is unique about this style of parenting is that it breaks down into three types: the critical parent, the overly strict parent, and the rigid parent.

COMMON BONDS

I find it interesting that all three types of parents listed above often choose a profession that rewards people for being critical, such as attorney, security guard, police officer, or member of the armed forces. These are all professions that encourage admonishment of people for small infractions of the rules and involve telling people what to do. People who choose these occupations generally thrive on keeping people in line and assigning punishment when others stick a toe out to test the water. You can see why some who work in these occupations can have pent up aggression and can be confrontational.

Other shared attributes of the three sub-types include control and anxiety. All of these parents become very anxious when they lose control. Their automatic response is to become even more critical and harshly punitive, while the child either fights back fiercely or sinks into submissive depression. It becomes another vicious circle.

Those are the similarities, but there are differences between the sub-types, too. Let's take a moment to define each of them.

THE CRITICAL PARENT

The critical parent usually has a perfectionistic side. This mom or dad cannot bear to live a life with flaws or errors—in themselves, in their spouse, or in their children. Nothing ever is good enough. If a young girl comes out in a party dress hoping to be complimented by her critical dad, he instead might pick lint off her shoulder.

I have a special empathy for kids who have critical parents because my dad has a critical side to him. When I got my doctorate, which is something any father should have been proud of, rather than rejoice with me he slapped his bald forehead and said, "Now, if you could only marry a doctor." The fact that I had earned a doctorate of my own was not enough for him, and that (in a strange way) validated me. It showed me that for my father, nothing would ever be enough. From that moment on, I was able to be gentler with myself because I realized it was his issue, not mine.

The typical critical parent, like my dad, tends to criticize and control things that are extensions of themselves: spouses, children, employees, and possessions. And, in their criticism, they might praise others. "Why can't you be more like Russell's boy? He always gets good grades."

THE OVERLY STRICT PARENT

The overly strict parent, on the other hand, may not be critical at all. But they maintain a very tight hold on their child because they are afraid. Very afraid. The overly strict parent feels there is danger in people and places outside the home, in peer pressure, and also in a child's natural curiosity. A very strict curfew with severe consequences for being even a minute or two late is likely in place here. So is overly severe punishment for not doing chores properly, or not keeping a room spotless. This is because the parent believes any loosening of the ropes will cause their son or daughter to go straight down the road to sin. The fear these parents have is overwhelming. And, they are usually unaware of it.

I know an eight-year-old daughter of an overly strict mom. The daughter was invited to a sleep-over birthday party at the home of a family they knew quite well, but her mom said no, she could not go, because she and her husband do not allow their kids to sleep anywhere they are not present. Because her parents were afraid of what might happen, the little girl stayed home and sadly missed out on a prime opportunity for social bonding. This strict mom never considered that what "might" happen could be positive social interaction, friendship, and shared good times in the comfort of a nice home and the safety of responsible adults.

THE RIGID PARENT

Rigidity in a person is not at all healthy. A healthy person is flexible in their emotions as well as in their thinking; they are able to go with the flow, so to speak. Rigid parents often have an angry temper that flares whenever anyone presents an idea that is different from theirs. And when tempers flare, what happens next can get out of control. This parent also is afraid deep down that their way might not be the right way, but their way is all they know so they stick with it for better or for worse.

A rigid dad might, for example, become very angry when his daughter suggests that because she would like extra time to study for a test, she put off her weekly chore of dusting the living room until the following day, after the test has been taken. The rage that follows can then upset the daughter so much that she fails the test.

A Critical Dad: A Case Study

Laura, who was eleven, was the daughter of a critical and perfectionistic dad. Tony was an impeccable dresser and was supremely organized and neat in his appearance. His jeans were creased and ironed, his shoes were shined, no wrinkle would dare approach his starched shirt, and his sport jacket was quite expensive. It was obvious that Tony felt everyone around him should be just as neat and perfect as he was, and that he looked down on those who were not.

Laura, however, was one of those kids who had tactile sensitivity. This means that she just couldn't stand rough or stiff material, tags on clothing, or any style or cut of clothing that was too tight or that rubbed, pulled, or scratched. Because of this Laura did not like a lot of variety in her clothes. She knew what worked for her, what made her feel comfortable, and she'd just as soon stick with that, thank you very much.

What Laura usually wore was fleece sweat pants, a soft t-shirt, and a sweat jacket. That's what she was comfortable in, and it worked for her. In Tony's mind, however, those clothes were nowhere near appropriate for school. He thought Laura looked sloppy, too casual, and just a stone's throw away from wearing her pajamas. In addition to being very angry about this, Tony was mildly horrified that a daughter of his could present herself in public in such an unkempt state.

Miriam was Laura's mom and she just didn't know what to do. In addition to Tony's critically high standards clashing with Laura's tactile sensitivity, the issue was causing dissent in their marriage. So, I brought all three of them into my office. I tried to get Tony to first understand that Laura had heightened sensitivity and did not feel comfortable in "structured" clothing. Miriam sort of understood this but needed some help with the concept as well. Second, I explained that as long as the clothes were not sexually inappropriate, or weather inappropriate, as long as they were clean and in good repair, that trying to fight with Laura about what she was wearing was a losing battle.

I also helped Tony see that this problem that he had with his daughter was temporary. Sensitivities like Laura's are often outgrown, and most teens care a great deal about their appearance. Laura, at eleven, just wasn't there yet.

Fortunately, Tony was able to make sense of what I said and back off. I know how hard this was for him because critical people do not like to admit there is another way. When they do, anxiety (which is defined in the Dr. Fran dictionary as fear) creeps in and makes them very uncomfortable. That Tony was able to adjust so well was huge. And, as soon as he backed off, the entire family dynamic improved, including the marriage.

REBELLION AND ANXIETY

Criticism loves argument, and children of critical, overly strict, and rigid parents can often grow up to become very defensive adults. This is because they must constantly argue back to defend and protect themselves from attacks on their sense of self. After time, these attacks can penetrate. These kids also can have low self-esteem, become rebellious, and may suffer from depression. Whenever a warm connection in their relationship with their mom or dad is interrupted and broken by argument, these children experience a tinge of separation anxiety. The constant arguing makes it difficult for them to establish and maintain a positive bond with the critical parent.

Children of critical parents may also develop bossiness. They can become quite the boss of other children, and/or play the role of "cop" in the family or in school. Remember about passing along those parenting styles? Well, it can start to surface very early, even in the sandbox or on the playground. Then, because these kids are rigid, critical, and overly directive, it is hard for other children to be friends with them; they are never fully embraced by their peers. I don't think any of us want our son or daughter to be the child who sits alone in the lunchroom, but that's often the scenario for these children.

When Strict Is Too Strict: A Case Study

Mary was a lovely fourteen-year-old girl who begged and pleaded with her mom, Randi, and dad, Gary, to let her get her ears pierced. This is not an unusual request, particularly for a fourteen-year-old girl whose many friends were all wearing fashionable pierced earrings. But Randi had gotten her ears pierced when she was sixteen, and if that was the appropriate time for her, then she felt it was the appropriate time for her daughter.

As you can probably already tell, in this family Randi was the one who was overly strict. While Gary could also be strict at times, in this case he just felt it was a "girl" issue and went along with whatever his wife said, without thinking too much about it.

Mary first started asking for pierced ears when she was twelve—long before the family was in therapy with me. By this time a number of her friends had their ears pierced. After her requests were repeatedly shot down, Mary, who was now fourteen, developed a plan, and I thought it was a good one. Mary would have her ears pierced at a reputable store and use her own money that she had saved. The procedure was both affordable and sterile, and Mary promised to follow instructions for taking care of her piercings to the letter. But Randi still said no.

What Randi didn't realize was that in saying no, she was making her daughter feel both unattractive and "less" than her peers. She was also taking Mary out of the social aspect of admiring various pairs of earrings and going to the mall with her friends to purchase them. While sixteen may have been the normal time frame for a girl getting her ears pierced when Randi was young, and in the town Randi grew up in, it wasn't the norm for girls in Mary's day and location.

As you have probably figured out, I supported Mary in this. To help her, I sat with the three of them and had Randi and Gary listen as Mary explained how she felt sad and left out. When I didn't see much movement in the thinking of Mary's parents, we repeated the process. On the third try, Randi and Gary agreed to let Mary get her ears pierced.

Life often works best when there is a compromise, so I suggested that the big day be tied into a special event that would be memorable for everyone. I have to say that once Randi agreed, she went whole hog. She went shopping with Mary and together they chose a number of pairs of really cute earrings. And when Mary's next birthday rolled around, with her parent's permission, I also gave her a pair.

I love resolutions like this. Randi and Gary got to see that by being flexible and open to other options, we developed details to a solution that everyone was comfortable with.

THE OBESITY ISSUE

Did you know that the obesity epidemic is one of the country's most seri-ous health problems? According to "F as in Fat: How Obesity Policies Are Failing in America 2009," a report released by the Trust for America's Health and the Robert Wood Johnson Foundation, in thirty states, over 30 percent of the kids are obese or overweight. Only three states have childhood obesity rates lower than 25 percent, and Mississippi leads the nation in childhood obesity at more than 44.4 percent.[1]

I mention this because one of the many areas a parent can get "stuck" with their child is the area of food, eating, and diet. This is especially true of critical, overly strict, and rigid parents. Many of these parents criticize and argue about what their kids eat. If a parent tries to control what and how much his child eats, and the kid fights back, the parent will always lose. Eating then becomes a distorted way for the child to "get back" at his or her parent. In other, fewer, cases, the parents are negligent about edu-cating and setting boundaries with healthy eating. Either way it is impor-tant for parents to remember that what you do or do not put in your body is one of the few things in life that an individual can actually control. So, to acquire at least a little power, children of over-controlling parents often end up with eating disorders.

Dr. Kyung Rhee is a clinical instructor and research fellow at Boston University School of Medicine and the lead author of a study on parenting styles and the weight of children.[2] The study was most interested in com-paring authoritarian parents (strict disciplinarians) with authoritative par-ents (those parents who are respectful of a child's opinions and thoughts, while still maintaining boundaries). Two other parenting styles were also evaluated by the researchers: permissive (parents who are indulgent and don't discipline their children), and neglectful (parents who are emotion-ally uninvolved and don't set or keep boundaries or rules). Rhee and her colleagues evaluated data from 872 children, 11 percent of whom were overweight, defined as a body mass index greater than or equal to the ninety-fifth percentile for their age and gender. That translates to a lot of excess weight.

The study found that authoritarian—or strict, rigid, and critical—parenting was associated with the highest risk of children being overweight, with the risk being five times higher than for children of authoritative mothers. Interestingly enough, children of permissive and neglectful mothers were twice as likely to be overweight as children of authoritative mothers, so setting reasonable boundaries and sticking to them is absolutely critical if you want to encourage good eating habits.

Rhee said that authoritative—or good—parenting, has also been associated with better outcomes in academic achievement, better self-control, less depressive symptoms, and less risk-taking as teens. As you can see, the benefits are huge.

Back to the weight issue. If you don't understand how devastating obesity can be to a child's body, the results of another study will help you. Dr. Jack Yanovski, head of the unit on growth and obesity for the National Institute of Child Health and Human Development, found overweight children had a greater number of fractures and musculoskeletal discomfort.[3] His team reviewed medical charts from 227 overweight and 128 non-overweight children and teens enrolled in clinical studies at the National Institutes of Health from 1996 to 2004. They found that the incidence of fractures and musculoskeletal pain were both four times greater in overweight children.

Furthermore, Rick Stein, who is a research assistant professor in medicine at Washington University School of Medicine in St. Louis, added that authoritative parenting has been associated with many positive outcomes, including better glycemic control in diabetic children.[4] Stein suggested that parents maintain control but in a positive way. "Be sure to praise the positive," he said. "Catch them being good."

Rigidity: A Case Study

The most rigid parent I ever worked with was a mom named Sally. She made it very clear the first time I met her that she was only in my office because her oldest daughter's school required her to be. In fact, Sally so did not want to be there it was as if she came in dragging chains around her ankles, wrists, and neck.

Sally spent our entire first session trying to convince me she didn't need therapy. It didn't take me but a fraction of that hour to figure out that Sally's ideas and viewpoints were set deeply in stone. From her viewpoint, her way was the only way.

However, there was an obvious problem. Although each of Sally's four children was born normal and healthy, each had also been in therapy—because of Sally's rigid nature—and each had separate issues. One child had separation anxiety. Another floundered because she could not establish or sustain a warm connection with her mother. She could not read her mother's facial cues, because, like her viewpoints, Sally's face was made of stone. Yet another child had rigidity of her own. She was already modeling Sally's parenting style, and she was still in elementary school!

Sally's second child, her oldest daughter, Jean, was her favorite. I could tell this was so because while Sally almost always had a blank, emotionless expression on her face, the only times I saw her smile was when I caught her looking adoringly at Jean. But rather than catch a break, Jean received even more of Sally's focus and even higher rigid expectations. Because Jean was "special" to Sally, more was demanded. One of the biggest problems lay in the fact that Sally could not talk about her feelings and the anger she felt when Jean did not deliver what she expected. This happened frequently because what Sally expected was impossible.

For example, Sally not only expected Jean to get straight A's and be popular and sought after by her peers, she also expected Jean to be happy, compliant, well-adjusted, and agreeable all the time. Because Jean had no empathic adult available to help her talk and work through her feelings, Jean occasionally whined, sulked, and had angry outbursts at home. She also suffered from separation anxiety, which was rooted in the absence of a warm, sustained connection with her mother.

All of this resulted in Jean's building up anger and rage against her mom. While Jean couldn't act out against Sally, she did begin to beat up other kids on the school playground. That's why the school required Sally to be in my office.

I was disappointed to find that Jean's dad, Warren, was of little help. Though a successful entertainment executive, I have to say that Warren did not have a strong backbone with his family. If the theory that opposites attract is true, this was a match made in heaven.

Sally and I did not make much headway at first. We have talked of the window of openness that each parent has to have if they want to better their parenting skills, but in the beginning, Sally didn't have even the hint of a crack. She was so closed, so rigid, that even I couldn't read her. The sad part is that Sally could not see that her inability to open up, just a little, was negatively affecting all of her children.

Then, pressured by the school, Sally began to tentatively try a few of the things I suggested to her. When she came in one week and told me she had asked her children to all come up with their idea of fair consequences for breaking one of the many rules she enforced at home, I was thrilled! Sally was beginning to open up and leave her rigid ways behind. So day by day, week by week, I had the privilege of seeing Sally flower.

You know, no one is perfect, and there are always many different ways to deal with problems. But rigid parents have to dig a lot deeper to find them, and that can be scary and painful. Once Sally began to see results, her evolution escalated. Today, while Sally still has a tendency toward rigidity, she is so much improved that none of her children are in therapy and all are doing well socially and at school. Now, Sally can even laugh at herself when she falls back into a rigid response.

HELP ARRIVES

Many critical, overly strict and rigid parents feel they have to state rules and consequences with anger and stiffness in their voice, facial expression, and body posture if they are to be respected. But that is not the case. Not at all. The following are a few thoughts that will allow parents with each of these styles to relax:

IDEAS FOR THE CRITICAL PARENT

If you are a critical parent it is very important that you step back and take a moment to think before acting. Then, as best you can, put yourself in the shoes of your son or daughter. What is his or her perspective? What is he or she thinking and feeling right now? Make a real effort to understand your child's pain, confusion, sadness, or fear. This will help you develop empathy for your child.

Next, develop a sense of empathy for yourself. To do this, imagine how you would feel if your circumstances were exactly those of your child's. Take a minute or two to think about this, because it is the foundation for your change. Now transfer what you feel back to your child.

When you get to this point, it is time to act. Hopefully you are in a completely different place than you were a few minutes ago. This does not mean a conversation isn't appropriate. This does not mean a gentle correction shouldn't be made or that boundaries should not be firmly enforced. But the way you do this will hopefully be less critical and more positive, and will generate better results. Remember that line of openness, the importance of movement in your thinking. Go ahead and try it, just this once.

Developing empathy is all-important in understanding the impact of criticism on a child. If this is hard for you to do, simply say to yourself in a warm and loving tone, "It is tough to live in your skin. You are so hard on yourself, and you don't give yourself any room to fall. It is so hard to live wound up so tight and expecting so much of yourself. It's okay to be a little softer. In fact, it is good."

Then, in that frame of mind, again think of your lovely, lively son or daughter and say to yourself, "Can you imagine when you are so hard on Johnny how he feels?" Doing whatever you can to sympathize, empathize, and walk in your child's shoes—even for a moment—will give you an entirely new perspective, one that should be far more effective than your usual highly critical one.

IDEAS FOR THE OVERLY STRICT PARENT

Facts help here. Make a list of what you think the appropriate age is for your child to go to a sleep-over, the mall, a school dance, or to get ears pierced, a job, etcetera. Then, next to each item, have a field day with your imagination and write down all the things you think could happen, all the many things you are afraid of if your child goes ahead and does this activity.

Take a school dance, for instance. Many middle schools have them. Are you afraid your twelve-year-old daughter will drink alcohol there? Take drugs? Have sex? Or far worse, get date raped? Are you worried she will associate with "undesirable" kids? Learn swear words? If those really are your fears, then you have to worry about a lot more than just a school dance. What happens if she learns to dance, bonds with her friends, discovers she really does like fifties music, helps a chaperone carry snacks to the table, and has a great time? What happens if she takes her common sense and your good parenting to the dance with her? What happens if not one of your fears is even a remote possibility?

Know that you can take your fears away by finding out the facts. Who will chaperone? What kind of music will be played? How low will the lights really go? Once you have both the facts and your fears all written out, then you can look at it in black and white and finally make a good evaluation.

Understand that by preventing healthy milestones, such as the social aspect of a school dance, you do your child a huge disservice. Children, incrementally, need to have a little rope to make decisions and judgments about people and situations. And yes, they will make mistakes. Small mistakes because you have only, gently, given them a little rope. But if your son or daughter does not learn these lessons now, then there is the extreme likelihood that there will be a huge mistake, possibly a life-changing mistake, somewhere down the road. Better a little mistake now than a huge one later.

Be sure also to celebrate every step. Make your daughter's first dance memorable by buying her a new dress, and be sure to take a lot of photos of her before she goes.

IDEAS FOR THE RIGID PARENT

If you are a rigid parent, know that you will make more progress if you enlist the help of an ally—a counselor, pastor, or friend—who will help you walk this path of change. However, if your trusted friend or professional pushes too hard, you might retreat back into the safety of your rock-hard cave.

The best scenario is to find a good professional that you like and trust—someone who can validate your point of view and who will not judge you; someone who will share the journey with you and lighten your load. Then you can give yourself the freedom to open up and consider other ideas. Good alternatives to just about any situation are out there and they might benefit you and your child, so please consider them. But please don't try to do it alone. You deserve some help, so please allow this kindness toward yourself.

If you cannot, for whatever reason, find a counselor, therapist, or pastor, then every time you tell your child no, take time to stop and think of all the other responses (and the reasons for them) that you could give. Once you begin to see that there are several ways to accomplish a goal, then you are on your way!

A FINAL THOUGHT

Remember that I feel for you. I do feel your great discomfort and pain. I have walked this path with so many parents and I want to tell you that the vast majority of them have improved tremendously. And you can, too. You only have to try.

If I seem harder on parents in this chapter it is only because the stakes are higher, and because I care.

DR. FRAN'S TOP TIPS CHAPTER SEVEN

- Accept the fact that all of us grow up with messages of bias. Know where biases and judgments exist within you. Own it. Then you can decide whether you want to alter those beliefs.
- Take an honest look inside and notice if your anxiety rises when things are not in place, organized, or delivered on schedule. If you react by controlling you may be a perfectionist. Practice allowing your anxiety to rise and notice how much you can tolerate before taking control. Try raising the ceiling on your maximum tolerance level. Your goal is to be able to bear the anxiety that comes with imperfection.
- Do not ever compare or contrast your child to others. Measure your child by his or her own standards.
- Stay open-minded and flexible. Remember that rigidity is not healthy.
- Remind yourself that there is always more than one way to view and deal with a situation.

- If you are engaged in a power-struggle with your child, let go of the arm wrestle. She can only keep tugging if there is someone on the other end pulling in the opposite direction.
- Rules and boundaries must be stated with clarity, not anger. Be clear and concise, yet kind and empathic in your delivery.
- Know that for you, a critical person, life really is a little harder. Your expectations for yourself are greater than most. And the same is true for your child. Feel empathy for yourself so that you can feel empathy for your child.
- Stay open to listening to and hearing your son or daughter's feelings. You don't have to agree with your child's demands. But everyone wants to be heard, validated, and understood. So give that courtesy to your child.
- The strongest motivator for change is pain. Don't wait for something terrible to happen. Make improving your parent/child relationship and the lifelong happiness of your child your motivation.

CHAPTER EIGHT

MANAGING YOUR TEMPER

RAISING AWARENESS TO ANGRY FEELINGS SO YOUR TEMPER DOESN'T CREEP UP ON YOU

While critical parents do sometimes emit blasts of anger, they tend to express their anger on a predictable, daily basis. For them, anger is an ever-present emotion, so both the critical parent and the people around them become accustomed to the routine intensity. The parent who has huge unexpected outbursts of anger is quite different. This parent goes along in life quite pleasantly, often for long periods of time, until something triggers his or her anger and they suddenly explode. I call these moms and dads "explosive parents." Neither the parents nor the people around them can see this wall of rage coming, and everyone is taken by surprise. And that is the worst part of this scenario: the surprise element.

The explosion has a much deeper impact on a child when she doesn't see it coming.

In addition to angering suddenly, this parent also angers easily, blurting out of nowhere rage-filled comments such as, "Why did you do that?" "I told you a thousand times..." "Are you an idiot?" "Pay attention, you never listen to me!" And even more scary and upsetting than the words are the tone and facial expressions with which the words are delivered. They can shatter a child.

Most verbally explosive parents are just that, verbal. In rare cases the verbal explosion may turn into a physical outburst. This, however, usually does not happen unless the child turns oppositional and defiant or eggs the parent (and the anger) on.

While physical abuse does not happen with most explosive parents, researchers involved in the Fourth National Incidence Study of Child Abuse and Neglect, along with the U.S. Department of Health and Human Services and the National Center on Child Abuse and Neglect, have linked explosive parental behavior to many of the more serious cases of abuse in children between the ages of one and four.[1] It has been my experience that many explosive parents do not hit, but most physically abusive parents are explosive.

In toilet training, for example, parental stress and the inability to control emotions play a role in verbal abuse, but a trigger is required to set off the explosion. Soiled clothes and accidents frequently serve as this trigger. Some parents also have unrealistic expectations regarding bowel and bladder control for young children, and when their children are unable to live up to these standards, the parents explode in rage.

One of the things young children must learn is control over their bodies. I have treated a number of toddlers, along with their parents, who have gotten stuck in the crucial area of toilet training. What can occur is that the young son or daughter quickly learns it is extremely important to their parent that they stay dry and clean. If the child feels angry at the parent for attempting to control his body, the parent will lose this battle. Remember that your child is the boss over his body, and that angry children often hold their bowels. That's when repeated accidents can occur.

In an extreme case, I helped an eleven-year-old boy who had never been fully toilet trained. This was mostly because his father raged at him every time he soiled his pants. The boy was furious and could only retaliate by repeating the unwanted behavior. Once I helped Dad cool it and stop blasting his son with fury, the incidents of soiled pants disappeared.

An Explosive Outburst Ruins the Day: A Case Study

Let's look at my nine-year-old patient, Jonah, and his dad, Irv, as another example. Irv really was a good guy. He was a likeable, forty-ish professional who wanted to be a good parent. When he was growing up he did not have the kind of parents who took him to special events such as sporting games. Nor did they enforce his involvement in after-school activities. If Irv signed up for them and then later decided to skip out, well, that was okay. You can probably see that Irv's mom and dad were in the loosey-goosey range of parenting.

When I saw this father and son together, it was easy to understand that Irv loved Jonah. Very much. A while back Irv wanted to have a special day with his son, just the two of them, so he took Jonah to a ball game and then father and son went for ice cream afterward. The place they chose was one of those fancy parlors where you can design your own cone, and the cone Jonah made was a masterful creation. Because Irv was on a diet, he chose not to get any ice cream. Instead, he was happy to savor the pleasure on Jonah's face when he took his first lick of this wonderful treat. Then they walked out of the store.

Outside, Irv changed his mind about not having any ice cream and asked Jonah if he could have a bite of his cone. Jonah, who had just spent ten wonderful minutes choosing all the right ingredients said, "No, it's mine." Irv immediately exploded in anger. He grabbed the cone out of Jonah's hand in a whoosh of rage and threw it in the trash. It only took a second and happened so fast that at first Jonah wasn't sure what was going on.

At the same time Irv grabbed the cone, he let loose with a very public barrage of disparaging remarks toward Jonah. "You ungrateful brat! I took you to a baseball game and you won't give me a bite of your ice cream! If you don't share with me, then none for you!"

The interesting thing here is that it was Jonah's right to choose whether or not he wanted to share his ice cream. While there are many things children should be taught to share, food is not one of them. Unlike a pack of gum or M&M's, where each piece is individual, an ice cream cone should not have to be shared unless both people agree and are comfortable with it.

Also, food can feel territorial. If a child is given his portion, it's his. He should be asked, not expected, to share. If he refuses, his decision should be respected.

After twenty-four hours had gone by Irv realized, on his own, that he had messed up. Irv was feeling guilty about the incident and his wife, Jonah's mom, reinforced that. She had to live with his occasional explosions, too.

Jonah spent the first half hour of his session with me describing and illustrating his fantasy images of revenge on his dad. While I have to tell you that the pictures were not pretty, it is important to keep in mind that Jonah really is a good kid. After he got some of his frustrations out in his pictures, he explained to me that he was very hurt, angry, and embarrassed by the public explosion and berating that came out of nowhere. The good vibe of connectedness that father and son had shared throughout the day was gone. "Ruined," Jonah said.

I asked Jonah if I could bring his dad in to the session so we could talk about other actions and words Irv could have used, and I was happy, and a little surprised, when Jonah agreed. There was a lot of hurt and anger percolating in Jonah as he cried and spewed anger toward his father. I was glad to see that Irv tolerated Jonah's strong comments.

Together, we decided that instead of exploding in anger, Irv could have said to Jonah, "I get it. That's your special ice cream. Maybe some other time we can figure out a way to share, but today I'll get my own."

Actually, I was somewhat amazed at how easily Irv came around. It is not typical of explosive parents to feel guilt. But the fact that he did, and the idea that he could feel empathy for his child, is a real stepping stone for positive change. I am not a promoter of guilt induction in parents, but explosive parents need to understand the impact of their outbursts on their child. Sometimes it means injecting the parent with a little extra conscience or guilt. Because Jonah understood that his dad was truly sorry and wanted to change his reactions, Jonah eventually forgave him.

CHILDREN OF EXPLOSIVE PARENTS

The hardest thing about being a child of an explosive parent is being unable to anticipate when the outburst is coming. This puts these kids on a constant, wearing edge, and they never quite feel relaxed or comfortable. As a rule, these children have two ways to cope. One, the more common, is to become angry, explosive adults and repeat the behaviors they experienced from their parents. The second way is to become extremely timid and frightened, filled with self-doubt, and afraid to express themselves honestly and openly. Neither scenario is good.

As you have seen, the explosive parent often acts without thinking, and children of explosive parents do not learn effective coping skills for ordinary conflicts. They do not create a good ebb and flow in dialogue and action with their child. They do not sit down with their kids and talk out problems. Instead, these parents erupt in rage, often with unseen provocation. Explosive parents hold things inside so long that the only way the swirling emotion can be released is through this flurry of anger.

Let's say Susie brings home her report card with a C in math when she usually gets an A. Her father scolds and rages at her, so she does not learn by modeling how a person can express disappointment reasonably. She also does not understand that her father is disappointed or that he assumed she didn't try her best. You know, these are golden opportunities for a parent to model how to talk with a child about disappointment, worry, sadness, and anger without exploding.

Without the example set and experienced by the child, how can we expect Susie to grow up and know how to communicate feelings of her own? So many sons and daughters of parents who cannot control their tempers end up having relationship difficulties with their teachers, peers, and spouses. But, when handled calmly, disappointments and adversities are prime opportunities to teach your child by example the many healthy conflict-resolution skills that are necessary in life.

You know, every child wants what she wants. Right now. That's human nature. We all have seen the child in the grocery store who is screaming because she can't have a particular box of cereal, or because she isn't allowed to open a package of cookies immediately. Not getting something immediately is called delayed gratification, and some children have difficulty with delayed gratification throughout their adult lives. We have all seen the lady in the bank who pushes to the front of the line or the driver who speeds around the cars ahead of him. These adults both have trouble with delayed gratification.

Because explosive parents set limits through powerful anger, instead of using calm reason, they often do not set boundaries appropriately and have trouble enforcing them. To make matters worse, some children of explosive parents become sneaky and learn to hide the truth. These kids never know what will set their parent off, so, in the child's mind, the less the parent knows the less the chance for an explosion. As you might guess, this kind of behavior, carried into adulthood, does not bode well for relationships, either personally or professionally.

Sons and daughters of explosive parents are not only frightened of their mom or dad's extreme anger; they can also become frightened of their own volatile feelings. You know by now that normal anger is within the range of typical human emotion. Everyone feels angry sometimes and it is healthy to express and release that anger. If it is not released, the anger builds up inside. It has to go somewhere. Explosive parents and their children need to learn how to channel, regulate, and inhibit the impulse to explode, and also to appropriately release their anger. We'll talk about that later in this chapter. First, here are a few things I look for in the child of an explosive parent:

1. Timidity. The explosive child (and parent) might look timid, but do not let that fool you because it is not always the case. Many explosive children (and parents) know that exploding is a bad thing. They work very hard against it and often are perceived as quiet, gentle, nice people—then, surprise! An explosive daughter might be timid because she is afraid of her own anger, or her mom's.

2. Submissiveness. This is different from timidity. The timid child is tentative. The submissive child will do anything to avoid confrontation.

3.   Lack of verbal expression. This child may be afraid of expressing his or her true thoughts and feelings. This is because he or she fears that in doing so the explosive parent
will clamp down harder on them, and life will get even
worse.

All of these emotional stances, while different on the surface, are
under the umbrella of self-doubt. Self-doubt is the huge price paid by sons
and daughters of parents who cannot control their tempers. And it is all
because this child lives in a real, deep-seated fear that their mom or dad
will mishandle them once again. Whatever your kid did, there is no excuse
for this kind of behavior.

WHAT THE EXPERTS HAVE FOUND

Besides frightening your children and causing damaged relationships with
them, angry outbursts have been proven to shorten your life. A large study
at Johns Hopkins University followed 1,055 men, beginning just after
they finished their education, for an average of thirty-six years. It examined the risk of premature and total cardiovascular disease associated with
angry responses to stress. While most of the men were not parents when
the study began, most of them were by the time the study ended. Those
who reacted to stress with outbursts of anger had three times the normal
risk of developing premature heart disease. Additionally, those who said
they either expressed or concealed anger, or who became irritable or made
a habit of griping, were five times more likely than men who were calmer
to have an early heart attack, even if they didn't have a family history of
heart disease.[2]

While it has been clear to mental health professionals for many years
that anger damages relationships, until this study was published in 2002,
health problems associated with anger had not been medically proven.
Now medical professionals know that not only does anger hurt your relationships, it can also kill you.

What is especially interesting is that the highest level of anger was associated with the highest increase in risk of premature cardiovascular disease. When you get angry enough, your arteries squeeze tightly together.
Blood then pushes through an area filled with soft plaque and it can erode

the fatty substance to the point that it ruptures. This can lead to the formation of a blood clot. If one of these clots gets stuck in an artery that leads to your heart, well, you will have a heart attack. It's that simple.

Dr. Patricia Chang, who coordinated much of the Johns Hopkins research, said, "In this study, hot tempers predicted disease long before other traditional risk factors like diabetes and hypertension became apparent." And, "The most important thing angry young men can do is get professional help to manage their tempers, especially since previous studies have shown that those who already have heart disease get better with anger management."

In case you think this phenomenon is limited to men, in another study researchers at the University of North Carolina measured the anger levels of nearly thirteen thousand men and women and then tracked them for six years. This study found that both the men and the women who were most prone to anger were nearly three times as likely as the cool-headed subjects to have heart attacks.[3]

CHANGE FOR THE BETTER

The good news is that, as Dr. Chang said, professional assistance can help someone who explodes in anger. As I mentioned earlier in this chapter, I had one son in my office who was so angry and afraid of his dad's rage that he actually pooped in his pants when his dad screamed at him. But this dad loved his son, and when they first came to see me, he had no idea his angry explosions were so scary. Fortunately, this dad was horrified once he realized what he was doing to his child and he made great efforts to improve. He still has a tendency toward explosive anger, but by using the following techniques he is able to minimize his outbursts.

1. Learn to remove yourself from the situation as soon as you feel your anger building. Make an effort to notice when the angry feeling is coming. Then get away temporarily from whatever is causing the feeling. Leave immediately. A quick "cool down" the instant you feel your emotion rising is the best start to a calm resolution. Go take a walk or sit in a quiet room by yourself. Then think about calm, rational courses of action. When you have your plan in

place, then you can go back and discuss the incident head on, with your head on straight.

2.   Learn to deal with anger as you feel it in the moment. As I mentioned at the beginning of this chapter, explosive parents are people who save up their anger, store it until there is no more room inside, and bang, lash out at whomever is closest. It is important for this parent to learn to deal moment to moment with the anger. Understand what you are feeling and do not deny your angry feelings or push them aside. Remember that anger, in moderation, is healthy, as long as you do not damage those you love in expelling it.

3.   Teach your children to slow down. Get their attention and make eye contact when dealing with their behavior. One of the worst things that can happen is that a son or daughter can render a parent helpless. This occurs when the child ignores the parent, doesn't listen to them, or when the child becomes disrespectful and disses their mom or dad. All of these behaviors just add fuel to the parent's fire. If the child can be taught to acknowledge the parent, then together they can calmly discuss the reason for the mom or dad's anger and hopefully work out a quick and easy solution.

4.   Develop a clear plan for dealing with your child's infractions that includes non-explosive methods. If you have a plan in place, in those few seconds before the explosion when you feel the anger mounting, you can instead turn to the "plan" and react accordingly. This plan could, for example, include some of the following ideas.

- Talk to your child about what he is wanting, feeling, and doing. You could say to your son, for instance, "You didn't like that I told you what to do so you yelled at me instead of saying 'I don't like your idea, Dad.'"
- Tell your daughter that you need a cool-down time. Then you can return in five minutes to talk about what happened.
- If your child spoke disrespectfully to you, say, "Show me how you can fix what you just said to me so that we

can leave for the mall." Then delay your trip until she fixes what she just said.

- If your son hit you, threw something, or slammed a door, give him a short, stinging consequence that has meaning (for example, a short time out; or no use of the TV, computer, or cell phone for a few hours to a few days, depending on the age of the child and the severity of the infraction).

5. Talk with your son or daughter about what caused your anger. Remember that you always have the opportunity to go back later and deal with something calmly, but you can never erase the effects of an explosion. While *you* may quickly forget them, those incidents will remain with your child for his or her entire life. Remember, too, that these outbursts will eventually teach your child to either repeat the behavior or to become a timid person. No parent wants that for her child!

A Wonderful Case Study

Lynne was an explosive mom with a dark, difficult family history. She had an explosive dad and a harsh, critical mom. I am excited to tell you about her because Lynne's story shows just what can be accomplished when you are motivated and put your mind to it.

Lynne was married to Carl and they had two adorable daughters, Hailey, who was eight, and Darlene, who was five. Carl, though a very strict and proper person from England, was a warm and empathetic dad to his two girls. Carl was also great at making sound parental judgments. In other words, he was a good dad.

For her part, even before she married, Lynne made a conscious decision not to repeat the parenting style of her parents. To do this, she worked hard in her daughters' classrooms, walked her girls to school, picked them up every day, and tried hard to be a good mom. And she was. Most of the time.

By nature, Lynne's way of dealing with her tough background was to be practical and reasonable, rather than emotional and sensitive. Lynne had also read more parenting books than I had and put the best ideas into practice. But, while Darlene was a model child, little Hailey was born with a sensitive nature and constitution. Little things irritated and frustrated Hailey, and no matter how hard Lynne tried, her daughter set her off.

Hailey did a great job of activating Lynne's raw nerves, and Lynne frequently exploded. This was because Hailey's actions and behaviors reminded Lynne of tumultuous times when her parents yelled at her. So Lynne did the only thing she knew to do, and that was explode in a rage.

For instance, one day, after helping out in Darlene's classroom, Lynne stopped briefly to say hi to Hailey, who was playing on the recess yard. Hailey, who was filled with jealousy about her sister getting more attention, erupted into accusatory, angry screaming. "You can't leave! I need you to stay with me," Hailey cried.

Lynne was torn. Should she have left without saying hello to Hailey? Knowing that she was vulnerable to losing her cool, Lynne said in anger, "It's not your turn today," and left.

Hailey really needed an empathic response from her mom, but she did not get it. Instead, Lynne could have shared her ambivalent struggle and said, "I know it's hard to see Mom at school and then have to let go. I didn't know what would feel better to you: saying hello while I was here at school, or leaving and having you feel upset that I didn't say hi. Let's figure out a better way for Mommy to handle this next time I am at school in the middle of the day."

From Lynne's perspective, when Hailey angrily accused her of favoritism, it triggered the same rage-filled response that she felt when her father's harsh criticisms came down on her. Lynne became flooded with anger and attacked Hailey as a measure of self-protection. But Hailey was not Lynne's father. Lynne needed help separating the two in her reactions.

I have to mention that Lynne was very pretty, slim with long red hair, big blue eyes, and dimples. And, it petrified her daughters when this cute mom with delicate features and a normally sunny disposition suddenly turned into a terrifying monster. Out of nowhere, Lynne could go from the epitome of kindness to rage.

Like Irv, the dad who bungled the trip to the ice cream store, Lynne suffered from extreme bouts of guilt every time she flew off the handle. And at first, Lynne did not want to go into therapy. She saw it as a sign of weakness. She was trying so hard, doing all the right things; surely she should be able to get this right on her own. But ultimately, she could not. By the time she ended up in my office, Lynne was more than ready to accept any help I could give her.

I first met for eight to ten weeks with Lynne and Carl before I ever met Hailey and Darlene. During that time I came to understand the tremendous burden of serious troubles in the family Lynne came from. Without going into it too deeply, her harsh, critical, and explosive parents had produced a mixture of explosive and timid kids. The family dynamic was a disaster and one family member even committed suicide. Lynne did not want that to happen to her or to her girls, and I believe that was the basis for her strong work ethic in creating positive change for her own family.

In just a few weeks I could see that the change in Lynne and her family was almost miraculous. Lynne reported that when she felt her anger rise and bubble she used the tools I already listed for you. And, she would pull phrases that I gave her out of her back pocket as an additional antidote to her simmering rage. She said the words made her feel that she was no longer helpless. Here is one of those phrases: "Hailey, I see how super angry you are when you tell me, again, that when your sock seams are not straight the feeling bothers you. A lot! So give Mommy another chance. Say it respectfully so Mommy understands and can straighten your seams."

Hailey was a wiry, active child and loved to ride her scooter to school. This was fine with Lynne except for the fact that Hailey refused to wear her protective helmet if her classmates were around; she thought it made her look like a baby. Lynne was a stickler for safety and could not agree to Hailey's suggestion that she wear the helmet from the house to the block just before she got to school, and then take it off as she finished the ride to school. Hailey felt so strongly about this suggestion, in fact, that she had a meltdown when Lynne said no.

This behavior from her oldest daughter previously would have initiated an explosion in Lynne. But now Lynne was able to calmly negotiate a scenario where Hailey wore her helmet while she rode the scooter, and then took it off when she got off the scooter and walked it into the schoolyard. Together they came to this compromise that both were, if not happy about, comfortable with. The key was that Lynne did not get flustered, anxious, embarrassed in front of others, frustrated, or angry. She maintained her cool, and her calm contained and mellowed Hailey.

Lynne so wanted help for her explosive anger that she had a lot of openness to my ideas, and she soaked up my suggestions like a sponge. I am so happy that she did. Today theirs truly is a happy family. The kids are thriving, and Lynne and Carl's marriage is closer than ever before.

Explosive parents can change. This kind of parent can make life better for their entire family, stop terrifying family members, and remove the fear from the household. They just have to want that badly enough to make it a reality.

DR. FRAN'S TOP TIPS CHAPTER EIGHT

- Deal with your anger in the moment. The build-up and surprise factor is the scariest part for your child.
- When angry, remove yourself, take a short cool-down time, then return and deal with the situation directly and in a calm manner.

- Refrain from verbal putdowns, berating, or spewing hostilities to your child (or spouse). Make this a solemn commitment.
- As you recognize and accept anger as a natural, normal human emotion, accept it in your child. Invite your child to tell you about it openly.
- Talk about feelings with your child. Embrace anger as just another acceptable feeling.
- Set and hold boundaries matter of factly, rather than with a flurry of anger.
- Work on extending your tolerance for delayed gratification. Be patient. Your child will comply only if you are supportive and on their team.
- Teach your child to always tell you the truth. Assure him that you will work on not getting so angry because you love him and do not want to scare him.
- Know that you are a model for your children. Your child will think, "If Daddy explodes, why shouldn't I?"
- Be kind to yourself. Know this is a process, not a quick fix. Be sure to hold on to your motivation to raise happy, healthy, disciplined, loving children.

CHAPTER NINE

IT'S ABOUT YOUR CHILD, NOT YOU

The title of this chapter implies that parents who care about themselves do not put their children first. But the reality is that any parent who buys this book, or who is reading it, cares. The group of parents who are self-absorbed is small, but we have to take a hard look at them, as we are doing with all the other parenting types. This is especially true in understanding the parenting styles of your child's friends, or relatives your children may frequently be around.

In my practice, I see a self-absorbed parent just about every day. I metaphorically put my arm around each of them and cry with them as I gently lead these moms and dads toward better parenting. I have to say that I feel for each and every one of them. While I probably see more self-absorbed parents in Beverly Hills than average, I guarantee you that parents who are absorbed in themselves exist everywhere.

Just what constitutes a self-absorbed parent? Well, these moms and dads range from those who are engrossed in career building and are consumed with work and self-promotion, to those who lead a life of privilege and spend too much time in charity work, or are busy with hair appointments, physical trainers, shopping consultants, and the like. In any case, these parents do not spend enough quality time with their children, nor do they make their children feel that they are a priority.

In chapter 2, parents became so involved with the feelings of their son or daughter that the child's feelings become secondary. There is some of that operating here. Also, there are elements here of the mom or dad feeling their child is an extension of themselves. For example, how their son or daughter behaves is felt by the parent as a reflection of them. These moms and dads lose sight of what their child is feeling. In both of these situations there is a disconnect, because the parent is unaware of who his or her child is.

In case I have not made it clear, a disconnect is when a child feels that his or her mom or dad doesn't "get" their experience. And in fact it's true. It is a feeling of being misunderstood; there is no harmony, no connection. An example of this might be Stacy, a shy girl who cannot bear to look the family's neighbor in the eye. Stacy's mom is angry and embarrassed that Stacy cannot perform simple social tasks the same way other kids her age can. She views her daughter as an extension of herself and is frustrated with Stacy because she sees her behavior as a negative reflection on her parenting. As you can see, Stacy's mom is not empathic to Stacy's struggles. Instead, she pushes Stacy way out of her comfort zone to engage with people before she is ready.

Unlike other parenting styles, which tend to strongly favor either moms or dads, the number of self-absorbed parents is often split pretty evenly between the two.

Unrealistic Expectations: A Case Study

Yvonne was a young mom with good maternal instincts. In fact, she could have written a book on nurturing. She was a loving, caring mom to her daughter, Aileen, who was just seventeen months old.

Yvonne's husband, Sergio, was a different story, however. He over-identified with Aileen and was quite protective of her. Sergio was self-absorbed and critical of Yvonne for her daily missteps. And you know, we all have them. We forget to unload the laundry or maybe we didn't get to the bank before it closed. In Sergio's mind Yvonne could do better because as his wife, he perceived her to be an extension of him.

Both Yvonne and Sergio worked full-time jobs, and Sergio felt he had to create the perfect image of family life for the outside world to see. His goal, in fact, was to be the perfect professional man and the perfect dad, which we all know is just not possible.

During the day Aileen stayed with a warm and loving nanny. When her parents got home, Yvonne cooked dinner, set the table, and cleaned up afterward. During this time Sergio played with Aileen, and he would get upset with Yvonne for not doing the same.

When Yvonne and Sergio took Aileen to the park, if Yvonne glanced away from her daughter and her daughter fell, Sergio would berate her for her negligence. But you know what? Children fall. It's part of their growing and learning process. If children don't fall, how are they ever going to learn to stand? But in Sergio's self-absorbed world, his daughter couldn't fall. This is because, like Yvonne, Aileen was an extension of him. Hopefully you can see that Sergio was extremely self-absorbed. His world was all about him.

Yvonne took care of the home, but Sergio felt that in doing household chores she neglected Aileen. He really wanted Yvonne to be the "be all and end all" for their baby. All children need their moms, so there was truth in his feelings, but they don't need them to the extent he was asking. Nor was Yvonne deserving of the pressure he put on her to be the perfect wife and mother.

I met with this couple and quickly realized that like a lot of working moms, Yvonne's plate was full. We discussed her schedule and found that she could put off doing the dishes until Aileen was asleep and use the time between dinner and bed for playtime. Of course, Sergio had to understand that a few dirty dishes in the sink was not a failing on Yvonne's part. When we talked about scheduling, he did see that she could not both play with Aileen and do the dishes at the same time.

This new schedule also allowed Sergio some time after dinner to return business calls and emails. He also came to understand that it was okay if Aileen fell. It was okay if she occasionally cried. These activities had no bearing on him; instead they were good, normal, healthy signs of human development. As soon as he understood that, he backed off on his unrealistic expectations, and life in this household greatly improved.

As you might guess, the difficulties between Yvonne and Sergio were not just a matter of parenting. This couple had real relationship problems. In this case, I was able to help Aileen by treating her mom and dad without Aileen present. The end result was that this little girl benefited greatly from the improvement in her parents' marriage.

And, as Sergio gradually stepped away from his self-involvement and needs, he became more empathetic to the lives of his wife and child, and Yvonne found that she could relax. Now, she also loves the quality bonding time she gets with her daughter every day.

THE SYMPTOMS OF SELF-ABSORPTION

The interesting thing about Sergio is that, like many parents of this style, he had no idea he was too self-absorbed. He simply thought he had very high standards. So how do you tell the difference? There is a fine line, but I hope the following ideas will help you and other parents learn how to evaluate just where that line is.

1. Who and what is important to you? Self-absorbed parents are usually more concerned with themselves than with others. Ask yourself if you are concerned about your daughter's grades because she might miss out on learning important information, or because it is a blow to your ego that she only earned a C. Also ask yourself: What is important to those you love and care about? Imagine yourself living their life with their passions, challenges, and concerns. It is important that you begin to think outward, about others, as well as inward, about yourself.

2.   How do others view you? Take a brutally honest look at yourself even though it may be painful. To get an objective reading, choose several of your most trusted and truthful friends, and take a survey. Ask them to tell you how you come across. Let them know you are trying to be the best parent you can possibly be and you want to learn what you need to work on. But if you do this, you have to stay open to their comments. This can be difficult, especially if negative traits or characteristics are repeated in the comments. Then, instead of biting off more than you can handle, choose one area you want to work on first. If you are brave enough to try this you will be quite surprised at how quickly your parenting skills improve.

3.   How is your self-esteem? Typically, parents whose lives revolve around themselves have a constant need for attention, affirmation, and praise. Do you continually seek this kind of validation, or do you function just fine with the occasional compliment? If you typically need continuing validation, try paying yourself one nice compliment every morning and then spend the rest of the day complimenting those you love and care about. It all goes back to the concept of looking outward and being empathetic to others—in addition to you being empathetic with yourself.

4.   Do your dreams match up with reality? Self-absorbed parents often fantasize about attaining enormous success and power. Visualizing, even daydreaming, positive things is a good and healthy thing, but if this begins to penetrate your belief system and you start treating the fantasy as if it were reality, put your foot on the brakes. Instead, ask your family what they would like to see for themselves, then spend your mental energy building up their stature.

5.   Do you treat other people well? Relationships should be a give and take partnership, but self-absorbed parents have been known to use other people for personal gain. If you do something nice for someone, is it for their benefit . . . or

is it for yours (meaning is there an expectation attached)? Try asking your loved ones how you can make their lives easier, then, if the idea is realistic, seriously consider how you can best make that happen. In other words, be a giver rather than a taker.

6.   Do you expect special treatment? We all like to be treated well, but if you have a sense of entitlement and expectation of special service, that is not a healthy sign. This is especially true if "regular" treatment in a restaurant or retail store can ruin your day. As an alternative, reap pleasure in the reminder that we are all the same—we are all just people. In the big scheme of the world, we are each one of us a speck of dust. So take the "regular" table and enjoy (or tolerate) the feeling of being like everyone else.

7.   Do you find it hard to feel the pain of others? A lack of empathy is a classic sign of self-absorption. Is it in you to automatically think about the impact of your words and behavior on other people? If not, take time to visualize yourself walking in the shoes of someone you know. What are their challenges, their fears, their successes? What is life really like for this person and how can you best support them?

Climbing the Career Ladder: A Case Study

Every time I saw Adrian she looked as if she had gone through a wind tunnel. Her hair was messy, her clothes were wrinkled, and her make-up had drifted sideways. She was also always in a rush and was continually late, making a mad-dash entrance at the last possible moment.

Adrian juggled a demanding career as a lawyer for a huge entertainment conglomerate with parenting two young boys, Parker and William, ages nine and five. Adrian's husband, Preston, was a senior executive in the insurance industry and had an equally demanding workload. As a result of the demand on her both at work and at home, Adrian was exhausted. If I ever have seen a woman who needed two weeks in a lawn chair on the beach, it was Adrian.

Parker and William were both doing fine in school and each boy had lots of friends. But William was constantly restless and frequently demanded hugs from his mom. At home he often tugged on her clothing or wrapped himself around her legs. This constant quest for attention was a sign that William needed something from his mom that he was not getting.

As effective as Adrian was at work, her house was unkempt and her family ate frozen dinners on TV trays, or in bed; Adrian was too tired for anything else. What her boys desperately needed was for her to sit for a few minutes with each of them, giving her full attention, with no distractions. But Adrian was so validated by her professional accomplishments that at first she didn't see anything wrong with her life.

Do not think poorly of Adrian. She was just so unknowingly self-absorbed that she got her priorities mixed up. The good news is that at some point Adrian realized it wasn't right that her work deadlines were her absolute, number-one priority. She also realized that she needed a therapist to help readjust and realign her life.

In our sessions, I helped Preston and Adrian see the importance of each of them taking fifteen minutes every day individually with Parker and William to have uninterrupted time to talk and play. This small fifteen-minute chunk of time was all it took for William to settle down and feel more secure in his parents' love. When Adrian told William that every day at the same time they would have "special time," it became something he could count on. And when she delivered on her word, the benefits tripled. He thought about "special time," anticipated it, and it went down like chicken soup.

Remember that for your child, whose well-being needs to be your number one priority, this is a teeny, tiny bit of time. Adrian also reported that she felt refreshed and energized by her one-on-one time with her kids and because she was less tired, she met company deadlines more often and was more likely to be able to leave her work mindset at the office.

STATING THE OBVIOUS

The approach I took with Adrian and her husband will probably seem quite obvious to most of you, but for the self-absorbed parent who is so tied up in their own world of work and career advancement, sometimes the forest gets lost in the trees. I cannot stress how important "uninterrupted" time with your child is. Each child needs to know they are essential to their mom and dad, and if the parents are repeatedly interrupting their time with their child, the son or daughter will feel unimportant—and that's the last thing you want your child to feel!

Just like you, children have needs. In addition to food and shelter, your child needs love, guidance, support, play, attention, empathy, and bonding time. In short, your child needs you. If you do not meet your child's needs, then behavior problems can result. And as the next section shows, sometimes children of self-absorbed parents can develop a variety of problems as adults.

WHAT THE EXPERTS HAVE FOUND

Self-absorbed parents often make their children responsible for their own physical and emotional needs. These parents also often expect constant admiration and attention from their kids and can react with criticism and blame when these needs are not met.

As adults, some children of self-absorbed parents are overly attentive to the needs of others. Or, they can go the other way and withdraw when someone needs nurturing. Often, they lack self-esteem. It's normal for children to be needy, but parents whose worlds revolve around themselves can be more needy than their children. This can result in conflicting needs.

For example, a girl might need a ride to a soccer game, but her mom is so wrapped up in choosing an outfit to wear to the game that she misses the entire event. Parents should be there for their children. Not the other way around. Sadly, the end result in these situations is the same. Because the mom or dad has more power and is unable to empathize with the needs of the son or daughter, the child's needs go unmet.

An interesting twenty-two-year study by the Children, Youth and Family Consortium at the University of Minnesota traced the development of nearly four hundred people from age eight through age thirty.[1] The results of this study are especially interesting because they also factor in some of the other parenting styles we have discussed.

In the study, researchers identified several childhood factors that lead to self-absorption in adults. In short, the study found that children whose parents were overly critical, harsh, or authoritarian often turn into self-absorbed adults whose impulsiveness can lead to violence and substance abuse.

Alan Rappoport, Ph.D., a psychotherapist in San Francisco and Menlo Park, California, for more than twenty-five years, has written several articles about children of self-absorbed parents and agrees that they often feel overly responsible for other people. According to Rappoport, these children often assume that other people's needs are similar to those of their parents and feel compelled to meet them. Additionally, they can be unaware of their own feelings and needs and fade into the background in relationships.[2]

Because these kids have not been valued for themselves, and have been valued by their parents only to the extent that they meet their parents' needs, they are often insecure. These sons and daughters develop their self-concepts based on their parents' treatment of them, as do all children, and can have inaccurate ideas about who they are. For example, a child of a self-absorbed parent might be afraid that he is selfish, unloving, overly demanding, inhibited, or worthless. The same child might also have low self-esteem, work too hard to please others, defer to the views of others, and be depressed or anxious.

On the flip side, children of self-absorbed parents often end up being as insensitive to the needs of others as their parents were to their own. I know one family whose three boys are now in their late thirties and early forties. Both of the parents were self-absorbed and went out to business functions or charity dinners five of seven nights each week. Each of these now grown men have huge issues with responsibility and accountability, and each has a big sense of entitlement. This is because the parents were so busy in their own world that they left the raising of the boys to other people. No parent was ever there to teach these young men the value of hard work. I find it sad that the boys' father worked very hard but was so self-absorbed that he was never available to teach the same skills to his sons.

If you have a tendency toward self-absorption, I hope you can see how seriously this style of parenting can hurt your son or daughter.

THERE'S A LITTLE NARCISSISM IN ALL OF US

I have found that a very, very small number of parents actually fall under the umbrella of Narcissistic Personality Disorder. This personality is self-absorption on stimulants and includes a pervasive pattern of grandiosity, a huge need for admiration, and a total lack of empathy for others. This person will also be excessively preoccupied with issues of personal adequacy, power, and prestige . . . and is very self-centered.

I mention this because there is a little narcissism in all of us, and you know what? That's not all bad. Like it or not, we all care to some degree how good we look to the rest of the world. When compliments come our way, it is healthy to enjoy them, and if we occasionally get a little bit of extra attention, well, that's a good thing. The problems arise in parents who need an extra dose of all of this all the time. These are parents who put their needs before those of their child, and often it isn't even a conscious choice on their part. It's not a case of "my child or me"—most of these parents automatically put themselves first, without giving it any thought whatsoever.

THE IMPORTANCE OF PRIORITIES

There is a percentage of parents who instead of being overly busy with work are so wrapped up in personal trainers, shopping appointments, and lunches that their son or daughter feels secondary. In the eyes of these parents, it is important to look the best they possibly can, because isn't that how everyone feels? And they are having lunch with a friend who needs support during a messy divorce. What could possibly be more important than that?

Usually this mom or dad was raised in one of two ways:

1. They were not made a priority by their parents and as adults feel this deprivation as deeply as they did as children. This means that early on they did not consistently get the loving, attentive responses from parents that

every child deserves and is entitled to. These parents usually model the style that they experienced.

2.   Or, they were raised as "royalty" and told so many times
       that they were a "prince" or a "princess"—and treated as
       such—that they began to believe it.

Both of these situations can lead to self-absorption.

I have one mom who comes to see me who is amazingly busy every
day. On any given day, she might begin very early with her personal trainer
(who comes to her home). She then showers and changes into the fashionable outfit of the day before she drives to the salon where she has her hair,
nails, and make-up done. She then has lunch with a friend and heads
home to a private yoga lesson.

This mom's eight-year-old daughter might then be picked up by the
nanny and dropped off at home, only to find her mom chatting with a
lively group of ladies. When the daughter tentatively approaches her
mother to show her the picture she drew in art class that day, the mom im-
patiently shoos her away.

Disappointed, the little girl goes to her room because she feels like an
outsider in her mom's world. Her challenge is to somehow break into her
mother's circle, to be recognized, to some way be able to say, "Hey, I'm
here." This child desperately needs acknowledgement and attention from
her mom, but has no idea how to get it.

As you might guess, these moms (and dads) are very hard to grow up
with. They leave their sons and daughters always chasing what looks like a
fountain of nurturing. But the reality is that the nurturing is continually
interrupted so Mommy can go to her next appointment, and the child
then feels, "What about me? What about my feelings?"

These children often grow up with feelings of anger that are either
directed outward as a snappy, grumpy personality, or directed inward
and taken out on themselves. For example, each time a child gets shooed
away he or she feels a sting of sadness or depression. This feeling is
quickly chased by an angry resentment. The child knows that the parent
is *choosing* to be involved in other things. In the worst cases, the child
may end up being a self-cutter. These are kids who over and over describe longing for a feeling of being *alive,* which they get from the flow
of their own blood.

You may think, well, what kind of a mom behaves like that? The answer is: many more than you might think. Obviously, the mom in the scenario we just discussed had adequate financial means, didn't work, and had plenty of free time. But the average parent can create a similar climate for their son or daughter by using every non-working moment they can find to focus on themselves. And remember, this is usually done without the hint of a thought that they are slighting their child or spouse of time, bonding, and love. They are just so self-absorbed that they don't consider others.

THE GOOD NEWS!

The good news is that there is help for parents who want it. My goal is to get parents to understand that in the best of all worlds, the needs of a growing and developing child always takes precedence over their own needs.

One change self-absorbed parents can implement is to make a rule that during school hours (if all your children are in school) you are free to do whatever makes you feel good. But after school, your child needs you. You must be there for your son or daughter. This means all personal grooming, training, tanning, and charity appointments need to be made during school hours.

Understand, too, that the kind of adult your child evolves into depends on who is there to guide him. If you want your neighbor to have the most moral, ethical, religious, and character-building influence on your child, then shoo him over there every day after school. But if you want it to be you, then spend quality time with your children. I cannot over-stress the importance of this.

I understand that most moms and dads have to work to make ends meet. But this quality time with your child can happen every day even if you hold down a full-time job. Here are a few ideas that will help you make that happen:

1. Work hard at whatever you do, but when you are home, be home. Be available both physically and emotionally for your son or daughter. If you must work some from home, be sure to set aside at least fifteen uninterrupted minutes

every day to be with your child. If you are out of town, do the fifteen minutes by phone. Childhood goes by very fast, so make the eighteen-year commitment to be there for your kids. I am not asking that you give up all your interests forever, but during your children's formative years, you must be there to steer them correctly. Without you, they just will not get it right.

2.   Make a date with your child once a week. Just you and one child. Go out to dinner. Go for ice cream. Go to the park. Do something together. It's best if you can do this the same night every week. Put it on your calendar as a standing appointment. Kids thrive on routine and this gives them something to look forward to and be sure of. Unfortunately, I often see this plan work for a few weeks, then something comes up and the parents have to put it off, or postpone. Then life intervenes and this important time with the most important people in your life never resumes. Please don't let that happen.

3.   When talking to your son or daughter, look at them. This small act lets them know they have your undivided attention. Looking at someone during a conversation means they are important to you and it is amazing how much this will mean to your child. So the next time your daughter asks you a question, stop doing the dishes and turn around to look at her.

4.   Every time you do something for yourself, ask what you can also do for your child. Then go do it. Nothing is as great as the gift of your time, so if you spend two hours in the salon this week, then also commit to spending some one-on-one time with your son or daughter doing something fun.

5.   Get professional help. This is another of those parenting styles that can be greatly helped by the assistance of a trusted and neutral professional. This professional—whether it be a therapist, counselor, pastor, et cetera—can point out specific things you can do to become less self-absorbed and more helpful to your children and other family members.

DR. FRAN'S TOP TIPS CHAPTER NINE

- Take a hard, honest look at yourself. Admit if you are a self-absorbed parent. More than any previous chapter, this will require all of the openness you can muster.
- Ask yourself if you want your child to do something for them, or for you. Check your expectations of your child. If they are inappropriate, readjust.
- Make your child feel she is your number one priority.
- Give quality, uninterrupted time to your child on a regular basis.
- Always treat people the way you want to be treated. Remember, your kids are watching you.
- Get in the habit of considering the impact of your behavior on others. Think about it in the moment.
- When you are at home, be home.
- Give good, sustained eye contact when your child is talking to you and vice versa.
- Make the needs of your growing, developing child take precedence over everything else.

CHAPTER TEN

THE IMPORTANCE OF BONDING SOLIDLY WITH YOUR CHILD

Most of us take a step away from someone who walks up to us and gets too close. We do that because we are uncomfortable with the level of physical closeness. You know, each of us has an individual level of closeness to other people that we feel comfortable with. What is significant about the parents we will discuss in this chapter is that they cannot tolerate too much closeness or intimacy from anyone, including their children. But, unlike parenting styles discussed earlier, this detached style of parenting grows from an organic rather than a situational place. To an extent this reservation is innate; the parents really can't help it.

As you have discovered by now there is hope for all parents, and this is true for the detached parent—the mom or dad who does not bond solidly with their son or daughter—as well.

The majority of parents who do not bond well with their children are moms, and one of the biggest problems is that it is very hard for a mom who is detached to admit it to herself. It is hard to get her to "own" it.

Usually, a detached parent had a detached mom who missed injecting a vital piece of emotion because it was not in her to give. Please know that this is never intentional. Instead, it is a character limitation that is unavoidable and is in the fabric of the mom's being, likely because *her* mom related to her with the same detached quality. There's that generational handing down again.

Detached parenting is about the level of attachment between mom and baby. Remember when we discussed reading the baby's cues? Moms who have trouble reading an infant's cues likely had a mom who also had trouble reading cues. The concept here is similar.

There is a second type of detached parent that I call the "cell-phone parent" that we will discuss later in this chapter. These parents become detached from their children because they are so distracted with their cell phones, computers, PDAs, email, and the like that their children are pushed to the back of the line. This lack of attachment is situational and does not form early in a mom's development.

The important thing to know about attachment is that there is a process in play from the moment the baby is born. With a detached mom, early on there is a distance between her and her baby. Not to say that the baby is rejected. It is more of a stiffness, a reserve in the mom that the baby senses. This detached mom can probably only tolerate limited closeness and intimacy with other people, too. There usually is a noticeable lack of emotional connectedness to other family members, so the detachment goes far beyond her baby. It's something that is in the mom. But after repeated detached interactions, this element of disconnection becomes the baby's baseline, comfort level, and measuring stick for closeness from others.

I once saw a detached mom breastfeed her newborn baby by holding the infant in her lap at a distance. There was no closeness, no cradling, no caress. No visible sign of relationship and connection. This mom was there to provide food for her new son, and that's all she could give. The emotion was not in her to do more.

Many parents who cannot bond closely are smart enough to let others have a big hand in raising their children. This is especially important in the demanding first months of the baby's life. A grandmother or a loving, caring nanny can often provide the emotional intimacy that the mom cannot. I say this knowing full well that every detached mom loves her new baby. She just is not able to give or tolerate the deep level of close intimacy with the baby that the baby needs.

The reason this is so important is that babies who are not held closely, who are not loved and stroked and caressed as infants, often become disorganized toddlers and grow up to have symptoms like that of attention deficit hyperactivity disorder (ADHD).

You know, a baby's brain is very pliable in the first few months of life. Based on the emotional connectedness a child does or does not get during this time, the brain learns to fire in a certain way. Closeness and caring are calming, grounding, and centering to the young child. Toddlers who do not have that closeness can become more wound up than toddlers who do.

I have found that many detached parents are supreme achievers in business. Everyone has their strengths and weaknesses, and for the detached parent, intimacy is just not a strength. The challenge then becomes how to put intimacy in place for the baby. There are many ways this can be done, as long as the mom is open to the ideas.

It is so difficult for me to talk about this style of parenting, as I do not want you to think I am judging these moms. I am not. Even more important is the fact that I do not want you to judge them, either. Most parents who do not bond well with their children were not given necessary emotional and physical connectedness as infants, through no fault of their own. Plus, as you will see in the next section, studies have proven there is a measurable biological difference in attached and detached moms.

OXYTOCIN AND ATTACHMENT

Oxytocin is a neuropeptide that is closely linked to childbirth and breastfeeding, and a recent study shows that it has a biological role in bonding between mother and baby. The study was led by Lane Strathearn, M.B.B.S., an assistant professor of pediatrics at Baylor College of Medicine.[1]

I love this study because it shows that women raised with insecure attachment themselves are more likely to have difficulty forming secure attachments to their children. As I mentioned earlier in this chapter, infants who bond with a consistently responsive, attentive caregiver are able to form secure attachments. But separation from, or non-responsive interaction with, their primary caregiver can result in an insecure attachment, or even worse, no attachment. The study found that the quality of attachment formed in early childhood really does influence a person's relationships in adulthood.

In the study, researchers interviewed sixty-one first-time mothers during their third trimester of pregnancy and determined their attachment type and bonding experience with their own primary caregivers (usually their parents). Based on the interview, thirty women were chosen for the remainder of the study. Very important is the fact that based on the prenatal interview, half of the women chosen had a parent who was attached, and the other half were detached.

About seven months after giving birth, participants had their blood drawn to measure oxytocin levels before and after they played with their children. Then, eleven months after delivery, each participant had functional magnetic resonance imaging (fMRI) scans as she was shown photos of her baby's face and also an unknown baby's face. The photos showed the babies in various emotions ranging from sad to happy.

Researchers found that women who were attached produced significantly higher oxytocin levels after they played with their children than did women who had little or no attachment. In addition, the attached and detached mothers showed different patterns of brain response to the photos of their babies. The attached moms had more activation in the reward-processing regions of their brain when they saw both their child's smiling face and their sad face.

Detached moms had activation in the reward regions only when they saw their child's happy face. Their baby's sad face actually activated brain regions associated with feelings of unfairness, pain, and disgust. This meant the attached moms felt rewarded and motivated to interact with their babies regardless of whether the baby was happy or sad. The detached moms felt less motivated, especially toward a sad child.

Several previous studies, including a twenty-year study done in Minnesota,[2] indicated that the level of a person's attachment often remains consistent from childhood to adulthood, and that an adult's attachment or detachment is a reflection of his or her childhood bonding with parents. In this way, attachment is handed down in a family from one generation to the next. The differences in oxytocin release and brain activities between attached and detached moms suggest that a physiological "imprint" of a person's attachment type, which has been formed in early life, persists through adulthood and influences a mother's behavior toward her children.

Another important thing to know is that the transmission of attachment was also observed in this study, based on assessments of the babies at fourteen months of age. The study found that babies born to attached moms were more likely to have solid attachments themselves. And, they found that this early mother-baby relationship is the basis for attachment.

THE MANY CAUSES OF DETACHED PARENTING

Not all detached moms are lacking in emotion. Some detached moms are very warm, loving, caring, intimate people who are stopped dead in their tracks by postpartum depression. These moms may have loved and cared for other children, but with this birth, depression sets in and there is no emotion for them to give to their new baby. This is a perfect time for the grandma or nanny we talked about earlier in this chapter to step in and provide the baby with what its mother cannot.

Postpartum depression is especially sad because a newborn is gypped in his very first relationship, the one with his mom. The baby may grow up to feel that his mom is cold, intermittently connected, and in some cases, false. There might be a lack of hugs or a distance felt within the hugs, and in many ways, when this baby is a child, he may feel he is not of importance to his mother. He may also feel that his relationship with his mother is different from the one she shares with his siblings, and he may never really understand why that is.

Another cause of detached parenting is drinking or drugs. Very often the drugs in these scenarios are prescribed medications, such as narcotics and pain medications. In some people, those kinds of drugs have a flattening affect, and they can tone down a person's nurturing, empathetic, connected side.

I have treated a number of moms in my practice who are detached. While I initially believe they are detached because their own mother was detached, I am sometimes surprised when several sessions down the line the mom reveals that she has a drinking problem. Most of these women function on the surface very well. They are well-dressed, professional women who probably never would have admitted the problem had my line of questioning not stumbled across it. I have a typical pediatric psychology practice in that I see a little to a lot of every kind of issue that children and families face. Over the years, I have learned to consider the drinking and drug issue whenever I find a detached parent in my office.

While there are moms who drink, it is far more common to see this in dads. And yes, there are detached dads. Not all detached dads drink or abuse drugs, of course. Male babies of postpartum depressive moms who were unable to bring in other caregivers can sometimes become detached adults and dads. So can dads whose own moms were detached.

The Pain of Detachment: A Case Study

Bridget was a mom who started to see me when her son, Abraham, was a hyperactive toddler. He regularly bounced up and down on furniture, jumped on the bed, and was a sweet-natured boy who was just very hard to contain. Remember, if you do not give emotional closeness to a baby, the resulting toddler tends to wind up, rather than wind down.

This mom was very pretty, soft-looking, and aware. She knew something was not quite right with Abraham, and her husband, Bruce, supported her in this. I was so glad that one of the first things Bridget said to me was that whatever was wrong she wanted to do what was best for Abraham. There was an entire window of openness in this mom and that was the key to helping her son.

In talking with Bridget I discovered that her parents' marriage was in continual discord. Her own mother regularly took Vicodin to mask emotional pain, and from what Bridget told me of her early years, it is very likely that her mom was on the meds either when Bridget was born or shortly after. So, her own mother's reactions to her likely had an inconsistently attached quality.

Bridget could not pass on to Abraham an emotional closeness that she had never been given. Because of this particular discussion, as well as other conversations, it became clear to me that Bridget was not a securely attached mom. I also watched her interact with Abraham. I could see right away that Bridget loved her son. I also saw that she gave him all that she could—and it wasn't enough. But she was a mom who did her best and who wanted to make a change.

At the time Bridget first came to see me, Abraham was not quite two. Bridget had mentioned that she was quite close to her sister-in-law, Bruce's sister, Jane. Bruce, by the way, was a wonderful dad and when he was home, he was there for Abraham to help provide the emotional closeness the little boy was not getting from his mom. But Bruce worked long hours and often was not there. So after many hours of discussion that included helping Bridget accept her limitations and the need to embrace help, Bridget and Bruce asked Jane if she would consider coming over once a week to take Abraham out and give him what Bridget could not. Bless Jane, for she said she'd not only love to do it but she'd come twice a week.

I have to say that the only reason this plan worked is because Bridget supported it fully. She knew she could not give her son what he needed, so she did the right thing and allowed another woman to come in and give her son an additional experience of quality attachment. It takes a big person to do that, and I was so proud of this mom!

Over the years I saw this family professionally from time to time. In elementary school Abraham had trouble sitting in his chair and focusing, but because Aunt Janey was there to provide him with containment and closeness several times a week, Abraham was able to settle down. Aunt Janey also helped Abraham forge social relationships, and because of this he became a fun, well-liked little boy among his peers. Now, as a teen, he has a strong circle of friends and is doing quite well.

IT TAKES A VILLAGE

With detached parents, it often takes a village to raise a child. Abraham was so fortunate to have an entire family whose only goal was his best interest. There never was a point in this where he felt unloved, where he felt his mom did not care, or where Bridget felt Aunt Janey was overstepping her bounds. Everyone pulled together and Abraham is much better off for it.

This team effort very often works for detached parents. But they first have to admit that they, themselves, cannot provide all of the emotional closeness their children need. You might think, "That has to be so hard!" But in reality, to a detached parent it can be a relief. These parents often become stressed when they have to respond to their children's relentless demands for attention and closeness, and when they have to interact intimately with their children. They very often are pleased when another can do this for them.

None of us are perfect and none of us can be all things to everyone. However, to understand that a key, fundamental element in parenting is beyond you and then turn that part of parenting over to someone else says much about the openness of any detached parent.

SIGNS YOU ARE A DETACHED PARENT

So, how do you know if you are a detached parent? I mentioned before in this chapter that recognizing this in yourself is difficult to do. Here are a few signs that you might have elements of detached parenting in your style:

1. You feel pleasure and relief when you are not engaged with your child. Each and every day parents become spent and need a break. That is a normal and natural feeling. But this goes beyond the natural exasperation that every parent, from time to time, feels for his or her child. This is the repeated feeling that "I am far more comfortable sitting at my desk with my computer than I am with my child in my lap." Every parent wants to be a good one, so this is hard to admit.

2. You are not comfortable with close physical affection. If you know you are more comfortable with your child over *there*, rather than *here*, next to you, you may be detached. The next time you go out, take a look around and observe other parent/child relationships. How close do other moms hold their children? How far apart do they sit when they are eating or celebrating? What is the distance between them when they walk? Now compare and contrast

those observations with the distances between you and
your child.

3. Your affect doesn't change much when you are around
    your child. An attached mom will usually show pleasure
    when her child is close. A detached parent rarely shows
    displeasure, but her face will often be blank, hard to read.
    Facial expressions are critical because every child wants to
    know where he or she stands in the mind of the "other"
    (usually this means the mother). I don't know about you,
    but when it comes to my mom (and to other people I love
    and care about) I want to be right there in the front of her
    mind. The child of a detached parent may be confused be-
    cause she cannot elicit an emotional reaction from her
    mother.

Outside Help: A Case Study

Marlena thought of herself as a giver. She regularly contributed
her time and finances to a number of worthy causes, but the reality was that she did not know how to give to her three young
boys: Dillon, Dustin, and Elias.

I suspected Marlena had not fully bonded with her children the
first time I met her. I had spoken to Dillon in my office and when I
opened the door after our session, she said, "Come to Mommy and
give me a kiss." Not, "let me give you a kiss." The change in word-
ing is minor but the difference in meaning is everything.

I later learned that when Marlena was born, her mother had
a bad case of postpartum depression. There was no one else in the
family who could care for little Marlena and their financial resources did not allow her mom and dad to bring in another caregiver. Fortunately, Marlena and her husband, Frank, were
somewhat better off. Frank was a good dad, but was always away
on business and, through his absence, became distracted and
somewhat detached. His parental instincts were still, however,
more on target than Marlena's.

While they could not afford a full-time nanny, Frank and
Marlena made it a priority to find the resources to employ a very

warm, loving, and nurturing woman to come in when the boys were home from school in the afternoon, and on the occasional Saturday. Over many years this nanny became a stable, consistent, and available caregiver to the boys.

Dillon became especially close to the nanny and because of this, he grew up with much healthier values than his parents or his brothers. Dillon did not become a slave to work; he also began to care very much for the animals around him. This often happens when a child misses out on a close attachment with his mom as a baby and later has trouble developing attachments with people.

At the time I saw him, Dillon was in elementary school and had not developed good social skills with his peers. He often ate lunch by himself. But the nanny (and Dillon's growing menagerie of animals) was able to help with this. Animals often can unlock a child and there are a number of reputable centers across the country that offer animal-assisted therapies. While Dillon's parents did not go that route, they did understand that pets were important to Dillon and they supplied him with several. The nanny also had good instincts about setting and enforcing boundaries, and she was both loving and clear with Dillon.

Today Dillon is out of high school, and with his many peers he is just considered a little quirky. He is phenomenal with animals and has decided to pursue a career where he gets to work with them every day. In many ways, he is the healthiest one of his entire family, and while the nanny deserves a great deal of credit, most of it goes to Frank and Marlena. They were the ones who recognized that they could not give Dillon all that he needed and sacrificed to change that.

Keep in mind that detached parents do love their children very much; they just have difficulty showing it in ways that are important to young kids.

MORE ERIKSON

I have mentioned Erikson's Psycho-Social Stages of Human Development, in particular, the first stage, Hope: Trust vs. Mistrust.[3] I mention it again because it is of importance for parents who have difficulty bonding with their children. As you'll recall, the key event in this stage is providing the baby with food, sustenance, comfort, and affection. A child's relative understanding of the world and society comes from interacting with his or her parents. If the mom and dad expose their child to warmth, regularity, and dependable affection, the infant's view of the world will be one of trust.

According to Erikson, during feeding, the baby must form a trusting relationship with the parent or caregiver, otherwise a sense of mistrust will develop that can carry on throughout life. Erikson goes on to say that babies who are not trusting are also not securely attached to their mothers and are less cooperative and more aggressive in their interactions with their moms. As these infants grow older, they become less competent and sympathetic with peers. They also explore their environment with less enthusiasm and persistence. Often there is separation anxiety in the son or daughter, as he or she feels emotionally abandoned, lonely, or empty inside.

This is why the detached parent must consider the option of an alternative caregiver. As you have seen, even once or twice a week can make a huge difference. This does not mean that your child will cease to think of you as Mommy, or will cease to love you. Just as you might turn your child temporarily over to someone else so they can learn math or swimming, a warm and loving part-time caregiver can offer your child something that you cannot.

THE CELL PHONE PARENT

It is an unfortunate fact that in our society, most families must have two working parents to survive financially. That's probably why I see a lot of moms and dads in my practice who are overwhelmed with work. A lot of these parents are at the executive level in law or entertainment firms, or they are CPAs, or doctors, and through their busy work lives they have become swept away into a life of high achievement. This often starts with the high levels of performance that businesses require from employees today: Many hold people to nearly impossible standards.

In such a work environment, children often become second priority. The mom or dad somehow becomes a slave to their cell phone and laptop, to Skype and Twitter. This means that children often have to compete with electronics for mom or dad's attention.

When, for example, a parent interrupts a son's description of his day at school to answer a phone call, it feels to the child like an experience of detachment. He feels unimportant. In chapter 8 I told you about the boy whose dad took him for ice cream and the ice cream ended up in the trash. This is a lesser version of the same thing. When a positive connection, such as a wonderful conversation, becomes interrupted by an intrusion, such as an "important" phone call or email, it makes a son or daughter feel alone and lonely.

These cell phone parents need to carve out special time with their children even more than other parents. When you're together for special time, make a big, celebrated hoopla about the fact that Mom doesn't want to answer that phone call right now. She'd much rather see her son's painting and hear about his day. Accompany the words with eye contact, a warm hug, a smile, and a squeeze. When a child knows his mom or dad will ignore a call during their special time, it makes him feel very special, and isn't that what you want for your child? For him to know that the bonding time you share with him is important to you and that he truly is the most special person in your life?

WHAT YOU CAN DO

If you think you are a parent who is detached or who has not fully bonded with your child, know that you do have options. While the bonding time when your son or daughter was an infant has probably passed, there are other things you can do that will either bring you closer together or provide the nurturing love that you cannot give.

1. Recognize and admit that you have some detachment in your parenting style. This is the hardest part. But if you have read this chapter, you now understand that you are this way through no fault of your own. You also know that there are steps you can take that will improve the situation for your entire family. So, read on.

2. Enlist people you trust who can provide your child with what you cannot. Find an aunt, a grandparent, a cousin, a

nanny, or a neighbor who can pour love into your son or daughter. This does not have to happen every day, but it should happen at least once a week for a few hours.

3. Consult a child development specialist or a child psychologist. This person can be invaluable in giving you guidance, ideas, and suggestions. Then try them. Act on them. Some are bound to work for you and your family.

4. If your child is still small, join an infant/mommy or a toddler/mommy group. Watch the other moms. See how they interact with their young children. Then, as best you can, emulate what they do.

5. Have no shame. Know that you are not alone in this. There are plenty of other detached parents out there. You've learned by now that no parent is perfect. Bonding with your child just happens to be your particular challenge. As long as you are actively working to make the connection between you and your child stronger and ensuring his or her needs are met, you are doing fine.

6. Discover where your comfort zone is concerning closeness, then try to stretch it by inches. Celebrate teeny, tiny increments of success. Be sure you do not stretch yourself too far too fast. You should still feel a degree of comfort, and also feel yourself growing. And believe me, that is a great feeling!

7. Practice stretching your levels of intimacy with your spouse. The likelihood is that the level of discomfort that you feel with your child is the same level of discomfort that you feel in all intimate relationships. Your spouse will appreciate your effort, and your tries to achieve closeness will give you both some surprise benefits.

DR. FRAN'S TOP TIPS CHAPTER TEN

- Take an honest look within. Of all the parenting styles, this is by far the hardest one to own.
- Remember your child cannot feel pushed to the back of the line behind your cell phone, computer, or telephone.
- Know that children thrive and function best when well-attached to a warm, consistent caregiver. Trusting their world as a safe place is based on receiving regular, dependable responses.
- Observe your own comfort zone for closeness, both physical and emotional.
- Then try to stretch your comfort zone concerning closeness. Celebrate small increments toward success. Your goal is to grow so your child can benefit. And you will be rewarded, too!
- If it's too challenging to provide your demanding baby with all of the closeness he needs, enlist the help of a warm, responsive family member or caregiver. Remember, too, that it takes a village.
- Be kind to yourself. If you see that attaching to another is comfortable only at a distance, do not self-judge or self-punish.
- If your child is unfocused, filled with bouncing, high energy, and all over the place, do not leap to diagnosing things such as ADHD. Instead, examine the closeness of her relationship with you. If she is contained and calmed by closeness to a warm, supportive adult, she may be dealing with attachment issues.
- Consult a child specialist to get guidance, ideas, and support.

CHAPTER ELEVEN

WHEN ONE PARENT TRAVELS

Lots of people travel for work-related purposes, parents included. Salespeople, travel guides, people in the film and music industries, entrepreneurs, marketing and public relations professionals, import/export specialists, bankers, attorneys, speakers, consultants . . . the list goes on and on. Many other parents travel for non-work-related purposes. A mom might need to care for an aging or ailing parent in another state, or a dad could travel to house hunt for a pending move to another city.

Sometimes the travel revolves around the child and one parent. If your child is especially talented as an actor, musician, or athlete, it is possible that this son or daughter could leave the family home accompanied by one parent to train for extended periods of time.

Regardless of the reason for the travel, a child who is separated from one of her parents will miss whichever parent is not there. In fact, the more attached the child is to the missing parent, the more upset and upheaval there is. On the other hand, if a dad is almost always gone and there is little attachment between him and his children, then the problems the absence causes are less. So in a way if your child is having lots of difficulty with one of you traveling, that's a good sign. It means there is a strong attachment and that your son or daughter loves and misses the absent parent.

If you are a single parent who travels, keep in mind that whoever comes in to care for your children takes over the role of the stay-at-home parent, and this can cause some upheaval. There may be issues with setting boundaries, and your caregiver may be confronted with more opposition and neediness in your child because your child misses you. Or, if your son or daughter stays in another home while you are away, there may be a strangeness in the different surroundings, people, customs, and time schedules.

FROM THE CHILD'S PERSPECTIVE

Children thrive on routine. They feel secure in knowing the flow of each day. Saturday, for example, might be "visit the park day." Within this pattern of regularity, kids have normal ups and downs, just as adults do. But when one parent travels regularly, it adds turbulence to a child's life. Then, when the absent parent returns, the child has to adjust all over again to having both Mommy and Daddy there.

Sometimes the child is angry with the parent who left and lets that parent have it when they return. Depending on the timing of the trips, this cycle can be repeated week after week and cause numerous behavior issues. This situation is also very hard for the stay-at-home parent as the child often directs most of his or her upset their way and will drop that parent as soon as the "in-and-out parent" returns.

Be aware that if this pattern happens regularly, it can be quite upsetting to a child, particularly to a young child. No matter how "smoothly" the parents have this regular pattern of travel worked out, the child deeply misses the absent parent.

The Magic Shirt: A Case Study

Pauline and Thomas had been married for about five years, and while Pauline is a stay-at-home mom, Thomas traveled frequently in his job as a sales representative for a national company. When their son Garrett was three he began throwing temper tantrums whenever Thomas got ready for another two-week trip out of town. At first I thought Garrett was going through the age-appropriate phase of tantrums. But Garrett also began crying frequently, had sleep disruption, became easily angered, and was oppositional toward his mom. I knew then that Garrett was struggling with his dad's imminent departure.

I have to say that this was a very attached family—attached in all the good and strong and positive ways. Each member of this family loved each other, and Thomas especially loved and adored Garrett.

Garrett entered therapy with me for sleep issues and tantrums. In talking with Pauline, it was easy to see that Garrett's troubles revolved around his dad's trips. Garrett was not yet verbal enough to say "I miss my dad and I *hate* him for leaving me!" so he did the only other thing he knew to do: scream and yell and throw a fit. Garrett needed his mom and dad to contain his powerful rage and also talk with him about missing Daddy. Having someone narrate Garrett's sad and angry feelings out loud to Garrett was very calming to him.

There were several other ideas that also helped Pauline and Garrett while Thomas was traveling. When Garrett had a tantrum, Pauline would firmly hold Garrett facing away from her while she sat on the floor Indian style. This hold prevents you from getting scratched, pinched, or bitten. This is an effective technique for young children and gives them the containment, security, and safety they need when their emotions get the better of them.

Previously, Pauline had tried to distract Garrett with food, toys, or television. She had also tried to reason with him by talking to him. It was good that she was doing something to try to settle her son down, but none of those earlier ideas worked, either for him or for her. But the Indian-style sitting did work, even though Pauline is a tiny, gentle woman and at three, Garrett was all muscle-mass of large boy. She found, however, that Garrett settled down quite well when her arms and body were safely wrapped around him. Just be sure when you do this that you are not angry. That's when the technique can backfire and cause power struggles between you and your son or daughter.

When Pauline brought Garrett to my office, I got to see how he knocked over all the toys on my table. And, he not only knocked them off the table; he steamrolled over them and then refused to pick any of them up. This was a pattern of his that happened at home, too, especially when Thomas was away. This was one angry and sad little boy who really missed his dad.

I then showed Pauline how she could create more structure for Garrett. Every time he knocked something over, she was to say only once, "Show Mommy how you can pick up the train, or Mommy will help you." Pauline was to wait a silent count to two, then place her hand over his, and together they could pick the object back up. This simple action helped Garrett create organization in his disorganized life. It also gave him some power and control over his surroundings, and as his physical environment improved, so did his behavior.

As I got to know Pauline better, I realized there was a lot of stress in her marriage. Even though Garret was only three, he could sense the tension between his mom and dad, and that accelerated his turbulence. Pauline and Thomas fought a lot, and the stress of the angry behavior Garrett's mom and dad showed toward each other added fuel to Garrett's meltdowns. When I told Pauline that she and Thomas absolutely *could not* fight in front of Garrett, it helped. Neither she nor Thomas realized that their arguing had any affect on their son.

Another big help for Garrett was to sleep with an old, unwashed t-shirt of his dad's. The t-shirt smelled like Thomas and was a warm, comfy, physical, and intensely personal object that made Garrett feel very close to Thomas, even when he was thousands of miles away. This simple, transitional object helped little Garrett cope with his dad's frequent absences.

THE MILITARY DILEMMA

We all know that thousands of parents serve our country overseas, and many times their spouses and children stay here in the United States. But children of deployed parents have special worries because they not only have the stress and upheaval of their beloved mom or dad leaving the family home for period of a time, there are also real worries about the safety of the missing parent.

In 2007 a study conducted by the Boston School of Medicine and published in *Pediatrics and Adolescent Medicine* followed children on a U.S. Marine base. The study found that preschoolers who had one parent away at war were more likely to show aggression than other military children of similar age.[1]

Lead study researcher Dr. Molinda Chartrand is an active-duty pediatrician in the United States Air Force and said that incidents of children hitting, biting, and being hyperactive increased when a military parent was away. In addition, children who were three to five years old and had a parent who was deployed overseas had a higher rate of behavior problems than did the children whose parents were not deployed. About one in five of the older preschoolers with a parent at war also displayed troubling emotional or behavioral signs. The Marine parents had been away an average of about four months when the other parent was surveyed.

While children of absent military parents often do not have the in-and-out comings and goings of other parents who travel, lengthy separations of a year or more can bring on the same kinds of unwanted behaviors. It's good to remember that your son or daughter misses the absent parent and cannot always say that in so many words.

When Mommy Gets Sick: A Case Study

Peggy had four children: a daughter from her first marriage and two daughters and a son with Walt, her second, and current, husband. This blended family was getting along just fine until Peggy, age forty, was diagnosed with lymphoma. She was in and out of the hospital for four months and spent another four months recuperating at home.

All four of Peggy's children were very attached to her, and her illness was hard on them. This even though—or maybe because— she was a warm and fuzzy kind of mom who had trouble setting and keeping boundaries. Peggy was nice, loving, and nurturing, but ineffective in the rules and follow-through department.

Walt was an entrepreneur who worked from home and was available to the kids. He was a guy who was heavy on strictness and came down too hard on his delivery of punishments. In that way he balanced Peggy well, but you can imagine the problems these two styles of parenting caused, even before Peggy's illness came into play. Additionally, Walt adored his son, John, but was indifferent to his daughters, especially Peggy's oldest child, who was not biologically his.

When Peggy went into the hospital, Walt took household matters into his own hands. He pretty much let the girls, who were older, take care of themselves. This caused some of them to feel ignored in the short term, but because they had each other for company, they ended up okay. But it was a different story with John. Because John was clearly Walt's favorite, as sometimes happens, more was expected from John. To complicate matters, John felt closer to Peggy than to Walt.

With his mom in the hospital, John's life quickly became very difficult. One of the reasons was that Walt had this off-the-chart belief that his son needed intense physical exercise. Have I mentioned that John was just six? Walt took John on five-hour hikes and regularly had him do as many as forty-five laps in the pool. Poor John was an average first grader, not overweight, and quickly became exhausted and angry due to all the demands on him.

When I first saw John he had difficulty eating and sleeping, going to school, and making and maintaining friendships. His older sisters comforted him in their mother's absence, but it wasn't enough to overcome Walt's expectations. I read Walt the riot act, but he didn't listen. Walt loved John and John knew that. But Walt felt that love could also mean weakness. He was afraid of spoiling John and wanted to avoid that at all costs.

I was able to talk to Peggy and encouraged her to tell John positive things about his dad. And while Walt did not back off on the exercise, he did allow me to teach him how to talk to John about Peggy and her illness. I also encouraged Walt to let John call Peggy on the phone on the days she was strong enough for that. Visits were important too, on days she was presentable enough not to scare John and the girls. The visits, even though they were short, kept the mother/child connection going and the bond strong.

I also explained to Walt and Peggy that it was crucial that they be honest with all four of the children about Peggy's illness. Here are the words I gave them to say: "Mommy has a disease called lymphoma. The good news is that doctors have come up with new and strong medicines that *usually* get rid of lymphoma, but it can also *temporarily* cause Mommy's hair to fall out, make her tummy upset, and make her very tired."

When kids know the truth, it reduces their anxiety, they worry and fantasize less during their sick parent's temporary absence, and their behavior improves. But you cannot sugarcoat it. If there is a possibility that Mommy or Daddy might not make it, you cannot promise your son or daughter that they will.

MORE IDEAS FOR TALKING ABOUT ILLNESS

While it is good to be truthful about a parent's illness, it is also necessary to be concise, simple, and positive in your explanation. Let your son or daughter fill in the blanks with their questions. That way you will not tell them anything they are not ready to hear. Hopefully it will never come down to this, but if it does, it always is better if you can set up the discussion so that, instead of you, your child can be the first to say the words "death" or "die." Let them come to the idea gradually and process this concept in their own time.

You can also use "empathic reflecting." This means saying things such as "It is so hard when you miss your mom. I miss her too." This opens the line of discussion to include specific ways your son or daughter misses the absent parent. You may be very surprised at the kinds of things, both little and big, that your child misses. But once you know what your child misses most, you can take steps to fill the gaps as best you can. Saying, "I know this is not exactly how Mommy arranges the food on your plate. If you tell me what is out of place, I can do better next time," lets your child know that you validate his feelings and also that you are empathetic to them.

It is also important to encourage expression of anger. Words to the effect of "I bet you are mad that Daddy is not here for your school play. Mommy's here, but I bet you'd like Daddy to be here, too" also open the topic up for discussion and validate feelings.

THE WORST AGE OF ALL TO COME AND GO

While it is never ideal for a parent to be away for a long period of time, from around eighteen months until four years of age is the very worst time for a mom or a dad to be gone.

Dr. Margaret Mahler was a Hungarian physician who later became interested in psychiatry, especially the mother-infant relationship, and carefully documented the impact of early mother-child separations.[2] Mahler's theory states that child development takes place in phases, and that each phase has several subphases. The first phase, the Separation-Individuation phase, involves the development of limits and differentiation between the infant and the mother. Here, "individuation" refers to the development of the infant's ego, sense of identity, and cognitive abilities. This process is divided into sub-phases, each with its own onset, outcomes, and risks.

In the Rapprochement sub-phase (fifteen to twenty-four months) the infant becomes close to the mother. The child realizes that his physical mobility demonstrates separateness from his mother. The toddler may become tentative and want his mother to be in sight so that, through eye contact and action, he can explore his world. The risk is that the mother will misread this need and respond with impatience or unavailability. This can lead to an anxious fear of abandonment in the toddler. Disruptions in the basic process of separation-individuation can result in a disturbance in the ability to maintain a reliable sense of individual identity in adulthood.

In my private practice, I find that most adults who come to me for treatment are stuck in an unresolved area of the Rapprochement sub-phase. For instance, when a couple has a fight, the emotional distance and the disruption in the relationship caused by the fight might frighten one partner. They might tug on, cling to, or be overly possessive of the other. This could be a sign of poorly handled earlier separations from Mom. There are thousands of examples where unresolved separations can be triggered, but all can be helped in a good therapy experience.

While Dr. Mahler suggested the phase ends at twenty-four months, my own experience is that it can hang on until a child approaches four years of age. During this time there is a back-and-forth, rhythmic movement between separating from a parent and reattachment.

If, for example, a child of this age discovers a toy, she might go out into the world (or across a room) to get it. In the process, she picks up the toy, turns back to look at her mother, and registers what her mom's face shows (approval, fear, danger, irritation, celebration, et cetera). Then she brings the toy back to her mom to show it to her.

Understand that this is not about the toy; it is about the child asking, "If I go away to explore my world, will you stay securely here for me to come back to?" This is a normal stage of development, and it may be disrupted if a parent leaves frequently, particularly at the onset of this stage (at around eighteen months). Remember that a child of this age does not understand that their parent is coming back, and that can be very unsettling.

Also, children at this age have not yet developed a sense of time. For this reason, I am opposed to doing "time outs" in a room without a mommy or daddy during this stage because the young son or daughter is not clear that their mommy or daddy leaving the room is temporary. If you leave, there is a risk that your little boy or girl may experience a feeling of abandonment. We want our children to feel supported, flaws and all— even when they do not cooperate.

PROBLEMS WITH PARENTS WHO COME AND GO

There are five problems that I typically see in children who have one or more parents in and out of the home.

1. Sleep disruption. Sleep disruption is rooted in separation anxiety. Some kids might be wonderful sleepers when Dad is home, but when he is away, Mom wakes up to find her son in bed with her. Rule number one: It is never a good idea to invite your child into bed with you. There is no warmer, better place to be, but if you extend the invitation, you reinforce your child's dependency on your skin contact for soothing. I guarantee that you will regret the invitation each and every moment you try to get your child out of your bed. If your child needs your support in teaching himself to fall back to sleep, you can be a close, comforting, disengaged presence in a chair in your young child's room as he goes to sleep.

2. Clinginess. Some kids become more needy and clingy to the parent who remains behind. These are the kids who

grasp onto their parent's pant leg or throw their arms around Mom's waist whenever an uncertain situation presents itself. Providing lots of physical affection to your child will help. When your son or daughter grabs hold of you with neediness, offer reasonable extra support without reinforcing their dependency on you. For instance, if she clings to your leg, offer your hand for support, but discourage total dependency by not allowing her body to merge with yours. Always support and facilitate your child's self-reliance.

3. Poor grades and athletic performance. It is not unusual for an older child or a teen who is attached more to the absent parent than the one who stays to have their grades slip or to do poorly in athletic events. This is because your son or daughter cannot concentrate or focus as well on studying or the competition when the other parent is away. You can offer relief by being a great listener. Encourage your teen to talk about her frustration and missing her mom or dad. Serve yourself up as a homework helper, or offer to sit in the same room and work on your computer or read a book alongside your floundering teen. Your focus and concentration will help direct her attention.

4. Tantrums and meltdowns. These often increase when one parent leaves temporarily and again when he or she returns. On occasion, if there is stress in the marriage, you might see an improvement in behavior when one parent is gone. This happens because the tension is gone from the house when the mom and dad are not fighting. When there is an increase in tantrums, talk with your child about his anger and sadness when Mommy or Daddy goes away. Think empathy, empathy, empathy. Then, hold the line on your boundaries and continue to contain your child when he is out of control.

5. Oppositional behaviors. Sometimes the parent who remains home becomes lax in holding rules and boundaries when the other parent is away. The mom or dad who remains often feels guilty that their child is missing the other

parent. The parent at home may also be reluctant to con-
front a son or daughter about poor behavior without the
physical presence and support of the other parent. Then,
when Mom or Dad comes home, boom, the laws are back
in force again big time. This is very confusing for children
and can cause even more behavior disruptions because the
kids are not sure where the line or boundary is. The answer here is easier said than done, but your child and you
will reap the benefits. Keep boundaries, rules, rewards, and
consequences the same at all times. Remember that when
you loosen the reins, your child becomes unclear and
overly empowered, which is just the opposite of your goal.

HOW TO MAKE THE TRANSITION EASIER

In my office I regularly see a mom who heads up a large cable network.
She travels about 50 percent of the time, and the only reason this works
for her and her family is that her one child, her daughter Sadie, is equally
attached to her dad. This couple also communicates very well, both when
she is home and when she is traveling, and the mom also keeps in touch
with her daughter regularly when she is away. Sadie loves going to school,
performs well academically, and has many friends. Her dad arranges regular play dates for Sadie both at their house and at her friends' homes. Sadie
demonstrates no separation anxiety, and what we see instead is a natural
excitement when Mommy comes home.

There are a lot of activities you can implement to ease your child's
transition when a parent leaves and then returns. Some we have already
discussed but will go into more detail about here. Other ideas will be new
to you. These ideas, put into place effectively, can even become part of the
routine of the coming and going. That routine in itself can be soothing
and comforting to a child, particularly a young one.

1. Prepare your child in advance. Show them on a calendar
    when Daddy is going away and when Daddy is coming
    back. Your child can mark off each day that Daddy is gone
    and count how many days until Daddy returns. Be sure to
    explain the trip's purpose. You can also research informa-

tion about the destination together. Older kids can even make a school project and class presentation about the trip. This helps your child feel like they are a part of the travel and are more connected with the parent who is away.

2. Make audio or video recordings your daughter can use while you're away. If you are going to be gone three days, for instance, you could make three five-minute videos or podcasts that talk about your love for her and what you expect she may be doing that day.

3. Make a "thinking of you" box. You can make this box together, or make it as a special surprise for your son or daughter. Then fill the box with pictures, clippings, notes from you to her, and mementos that remind your child of good times you've spent together.

4. Make phone calls. Depending on the age of your son or daughter, one phone call a day from the absent parent will help your child feel connected. It helps even more if the call can come at the same time every day, or if the parent can say, "Tomorrow I have a meeting so I can't call you like I usually do just after you come home from school. Instead, I will call you at six o'clock, just before you have your dinner." It then becomes vitally important that the parent who is away calls at that time. It is also important that the call not come too close to a child's bedtime or before going to school, as those are more vulnerable times, especially for younger kids, and can trigger an increase in separation anxiety.

5. Supply photos. Young children especially like to keep a photo of the traveling parent next to their bed. If the photo is of the parent and child sharing a good time, even better. Through it, the young child is reassured that "while Mommy isn't here right now I can hold her close in my heart and mind."

6. Send an email or text message. An individual email or text sent just to an older son or daughter also helps ease the transition, as long as every child who is age appropriate for

texting also receives a message just for them. The same cookie-cutter words and messages sent to each child won't cut it. The emails do not have to be long, just targeted and sincere. The texts can be a simple "I love you. Can't wait to see you Friday night." This texted to an older child who has a cell phone makes them feel loved and special. A word of caution here: If you get in the habit and miss a day, your son or daughter will worry about you.

7. Have a conversation about the absent parent. If Mom is away helping her sister who just had a baby, you could discuss what she might be doing. You could say, "We're on our way to drop you off at school. I bet Mommy is giving your new baby cousin a bath and thinking of us." Or the parent at home could relay bits and pieces of news she has heard from the other parent. "Daddy is in Italy today, and this afternoon he went to a shoe store and bought some leather shoes. You can see them when he gets home tomorrow."

8. Hold on to the rules. While I know it puts an extra load on the parent who remains at home, keeping the rules, boundaries, and consequences exactly as they are when both parents are there reinforces stability and security for your child. It requires some backbone from the parent at home, and sometimes that needs to be reinforced by a phone call, email, or text from the parent who is away, but overall, it requires much less effort in the long run than the confusion of first being lax and then being strict.

9. Look at the calendar. Another great idea is to keep a calendar handy where everyone can see it. You could say to a son who is missing his dad, "Let's look at the calendar and count the days until Daddy gets back." Then let your son tick off another day and count how many more days there are until his father returns. If you do this the same time every day, it will become part of that safe, nurturing routine that children need so badly when someone they love is away. Even a child as young as two years of age can benefit from this.

10. Give your child something of the other parent's. As with Garrett, giving your son or daughter something of the parent who is away will help keep the connectedness going and ease fears and anxieties. It does not have to be a t-shirt or other piece of clothing, although the smell of clothing worn by the absent parent adds an extra layer of comfort. It could also be Dad's special baseball, or Mom's rag doll from when she was a child. Whatever it is, let your child know how special he or she is to you and that you are always thinking of them when you are away.

11. Keep routines the same. If you always get up at eight o'clock to get chores out of the way on Saturday morning, be sure to do the same when one parent is away. During chores, you can talk about Mommy being in Chicago or Daddy visiting his uncle, but keep the routine as much the same as possible. Your kids will transition so much better.

12. Make special time. Within your regular routines, the parent who is home should be sure to make special one-on-one time for each child. Fill all of your children individually with positive, uninterrupted attention as you hang out together. Be sure to ask about their day, which friend they sat with, what they had for lunch, how they did on their spelling test. You cannot be both a mommy and a daddy, but you can step it up a notch and be more available to your kids at a time when they need you most.

DR. FRAN'S TOP TIPS CHAPTER ELEVEN

- Expect disruption in your child's sleep, mood, or behavior during one parent's travel. Keep your eyes wide open for signs of upset.
- Know that the most challenging times will be those of transitions. The goodbyes and hellos are hardest.
- Invite your child to talk about his or her feelings. Include anger. Most parents want to bypass this one because it's

unpleasant for most of us to absorb and hold those powerful feelings.

- Maintain consistent routines, structure, boundaries, rewards, and consequences.
- Offer your child a transitional object, one that belongs to the absent parent.
- Don't be alarmed by behavior changes in your child. They are signs he is missing the mom or dad who is away.
- Use empathic narration. This is something I regularly teach all parents. It is the language of reflecting out loud to your child what he or she is feeling and wanting.
- Remember that how your child deals with separation is parallel to how they resolved the Rapprochement sub-phase of development in toddlerhood. Each separation is an opportunity for you to deal with separation better. Although it is stressful, it can repair something that was missed or mishandled earlier.
- Be patient with your child. She is struggling. She is not intentionally trying to aggravate you, but you are the one who is there. She has to expel her upset somewhere.
- Nurture yourself. Carve out regular time for you. Absences can be hard for parents, too. After all, we were toddlers once upon a time and may have leftover, unfinished areas of separation and attachment. I know I do!

CHAPTER TWELVE

HANDLING SPECIAL CIRCUMSTANCES

Many parents have personal challenges such as ADHD, cancer, heart disease, or paraplegia that can make it difficult for them to be everything that they want to be for their child. Some parents were born with these challenges, and for others the disability was acquired through trauma or an accident. In either case, the special circumstances these parents face are challenging, but this chapter should give you some great ideas about how to cope.

In all of our previous chapters, a main goal has been for you, the parent, to develop empathy for your child. If you are a parent with special circumstances, the goal is for you to develop empathy for yourself. If either you or your child's other parent has special individual challenges, you probably already know that it impacts your entire family.

You might ask why this book does not discuss parenting special needs children. That's a great question. First, there is already a lot of good information out there about how to do that. And second, this book is about you, dear mom and dad, and how you can be more self-aware. In this chapter I will make you aware of the hardships parental disabilities can have on your son or daughter. You will probably be very surprised at the different forms these hardships can take.

The Wheelchair Mom: A Case Study

Kailey was just one year old when her mom, Terri, was in a terrible car accident. The accident left Terri with little function in her lower limbs, and while she could walk very short distances with the aid of a walker, Terri found herself far more physically able when she was sitting in a wheelchair.

The accident also ended Terri's marriage to Kailey's dad, Les. After the divorce, Kailey spent 40 percent of her time with her dad, and the rest of the time was spent with her mom. When Kailey was younger, Terri's disability was not too much of an issue—having a mom in a wheelchair was all Kailey knew. Kailey did feel different from her friends, whose moms were not disabled, but aside from that, Kailey got good grades, reached normal milestones on time, and was well liked by her peers.

It helped that Terri was an intelligent, kind, caring person who was matter-of-fact about her circumstances. She was also an amazingly good provider for Kailey, despite her disability. But, at the age of twelve, almost thirteen, Kailey began to feel ashamed of her mother. Kailey was now embarrassed when her mom picked her up at school in their custom van with the wheelchair lift. She felt self-conscious about inviting friends over to her house or about going to parties where her mom would have to drop her off.

You know, when you are a girl Kailey's age, you are mortified by just about everything. Every single thing in life is an embarrassment, and when even one thing stands out as being different from that of your friends, you can perceive your world to be especially difficult. That's where Kailey was when I first met her.

It is important to recognize that every child needs to make a strong identification with a parent of the same sex. Boys need to identify with, aspire to, and want to be like their dad, and girls their mom. This becomes hard to do when a developing son or daughter feels their identification with the parent is profoundly limited. In other words, it would be hard for a pre-teen girl to want to be fully like her mom if her mom is disabled and in a wheelchair.

In Kailey's case, she could not make a full identification with her mom for several reasons. For instance, Kailey played soccer. As someone so involved in sports, it was almost impossible for her to relate to someone who was less mobile—like her mom. Kailey also wasn't sure if her mom could understand and empathize with her embarrassment in being different from the other girls. As a result, and because she did not want to hurt her mom's feelings, Kailey never articulated her discomfort. Also, psychologically, Kailey, and other children who have a parent with a disability, often think, "I do not want to be like that," and either subconsciously or actively push away from the full identification. In this way they end up unclear about who they are.

For this reason I was very glad that Terri chose a female therapist for Kailey. As an adult female, I was someone whom Kailey could identify with. I could help fill the gaps that Terri could not provide and in that way, our therapy sessions became female identity sessions.

I liked the fact that Terri, like many other moms and dads we have talked about, made it clear early in our sessions that she wanted what was best for Kailey. Her openness in this area was especially helpful when I explained to Terri that for a young girl to develop into a whole, complete young woman, she required a whole, complete adult female role model. This is in no way intended to say that Terri's disability made her less as a person, but it did make her different from the mothers of Kailey's friends. I know how hard this was for Terri to hear, but on some level she knew this before I said it. Once she was able to acknowledge this out loud, we could move forward in helping Kailey.

In addition to what Terri and I were doing for Kailey, Les years ago had married a very nice woman named Naomi. Naomi was a fabulous step-mom, and when Kailey was spending time with her dad, Terri could relax in the knowledge that Kailey was safe, supported, and well cared for. The only issues Terri had with Les and Naomi is that they were too loose regarding academic standards and their expectations of Kailey. But as we've found, no one is perfect, right?

Naomi was actually more nurturing than Terri, but luckily jealousy was not an issue for Terri, or for any of the family members, for that matter. That was a plus for Kailey, who took the best pieces of her mom, step-mom, and therapist and absorbed them into one strong female identification. Grandparents and aunts who can interact regularly can also be wonderful female models for children.

Kailey was able to achieve this identity only after she was encouraged and allowed to express her anger and sadness at having a mom who had a permanent disability. Like many children who have a parent who is disabled, Kailey had unspoken wishes of having a mom who could walk and dance and carry her through her childhood. Once that kind of open communication and honest discussion took place, Kailey was on her way to becoming a strong, well-rounded woman. Sometimes it really does take a village.

WHAT TO SAY WHEN THERE ARE NO WORDS

While Kailey's story ended up well, it took many months. Her initial reaction to understanding her mother's limitations was quite negative, and it was a long time before healing began. Part of the problem was that Kailey had a lot of guilt. She was physically able; her mom was not. Guilt is something most children of parents with special needs feel. They often also wish they could "fix" their parent, make them fully able. Unfortunately, life does not work that way. Kailey knew that. This fantasy of hers was a way to defend against feeling deep sadness and pain.

Words cannot express all of the feelings both you and your son or daughter need to say. But there are words that come close, and if you say them often enough, they can help. All three of Kailey's parents and I repeated statements to the effect of:

"It's hard to have a mom who is different from other moms."

"I can understand how you wish your mom could be like other moms so she could dance with you, swim with you, and walk you down the aisle at your wedding."

"You're a very lucky girl. Your mom loves you so much and wants the best for you so she lets you have close relationships with lots of other nice ladies."

"Your mom makes the best cookies!"

The idea behind these words is designed to accomplish four things:

1. Validate your son's or daughter's feelings. What your children feel is very real to them. Often they are not comfortable saying these things to you for fear they will hurt your feelings. If you can acknowledge and give permission for these feelings, it will reduce your children's anxiety and anger.

2. Acknowledge the losses. Whatever the disability, and for however long it lasts, there are going to be some things that you as a parent cannot do or be. Be sure to let your child acknowledge and embrace that. Have open discussions about it. That has to happen if your child is to accept you, flaws and all. These discussions are also critical to your son or daughter accepting him- or herself and their living circumstances.

3. Highlight the positive and the similarities. While it might not be possible for you to personally drive your son or daughter to school, it might be very easy for you to tell wonderful stories. Or, like Tommy's mom, you might be fun to play board games with. Or, like Sarah's dad you could be a great listener, tell funny jokes, and be a great Cub Scout leader. The more you can point out similarities to other parents and other families while still being open and honest about acknowledging the differences, the better off your entire family will be.

4. Enlist help. Enlisting or hiring help to fill in where things are needed will make life easier for your entire family. For example, a boy needs to throw a baseball around, and if a mom in a wheelchair cannot do that, she should hire a coach. Or, if driving is difficult, hire a responsible college

student to drive your daughter to ballet and art class. You can also arrange for carpools or pay another mom to take your daughter along.

MORE COMMON THAN YOU MIGHT EXPECT

You might think it is rare to find parents who have disabilities, but that is not the case at all. The National Center for Parents with Disabilities and Their Families reports that there are nearly nine million parents with disabilities in the United States. That's 15 percent of all American families.[1] Specifically, 15 percent of all families will have a parent with a disability before their child turns eighteen, as will 24 percent of single parents.

Single parents often do not have the in-home day-to-day support that a two-parent family has. Even though it is important for all parents to have an action plan for emergencies, particularly emergencies that might result in short- or long-term time away from regular activities, it is especially important for a single parent. A simple chart showing who is available to step in can be very helpful and can also be comforting to your child. Some disabilities are temporary and after a time the parent recovers all or most of their pre-disability functioning. Some disabilities, however, will be permanent, and more outside help will be needed. In either case, a plan is always a good thing to have.

Keep in mind that parents with special challenges come in all sizes, ages, shapes, ethnic backgrounds, and abilities. I mention this because there is a tendency to stereotype parents with special needs, when the reality is there are as many disabilities and variations within each special need as there are parents who have them.

SPECIAL PROBLEMS FOR SPECIAL NEEDS

The parent who has special needs often has burdens in addition to the many parenting difficulties we have already discussed throughout *The Self-Aware Parent*. The unemployment rate among disabled parents is higher than average, and many also feel isolated from their communities. These parents often feel frustrated, inadequate, or less than able-bodied parents. And, they may blame themselves needlessly for negative behaviors and other issues involving their son or daughter. Each situation is unique unto itself.

The Looking Glass's National Rehabilitation Research and Training Center on Families of Adults with Disabilities conducted a national survey of parents with disabilities, and the results are quite interesting:[2]

1.   Forty-four percent of parents with a disability reported that their disability affected their pregnancy and giving birth.

2.   Forty-three percent of parents with special circumstances said they needed assistance when playing with their children and a third needed help lifting or carrying their kids.

3.   Transportation affected more special needs parents than any other area. Seventy-nine percent said transportation was a problem that interfered with or prevented parent/child activities.

4.   About 30 percent of parents said they had trouble paying for childcare. Remember that many parents who have a disability are either out of work or on a reduced salary while on medical leave.

5.   Almost half of the parents said they could interact better with their sons and daughters if they had access to or could afford adaptive equipment for their particular needs.

6.   Only 57 percent of the parents said they had additional help for their parenting.

7.   Fifteen percent said others had attempted to take their children away and have them legally bound to a new custodial adult.

As you can see, the challenges are many. But, as you will soon find, how well a parent accepts him- or herself directly relates to how well a child adjusts and respects the parent.

Dad's Aching Back: A Case Study

Buddy was an involved dad who coached his son's baseball team and all three of his children's basketball teams. A former college athlete, Buddy was devastated when he ruptured a disc in his back at work and had a lengthy hospital stay, both before and after his surgery, which was not 100 percent successful. Afterward, Buddy lived in constant pain with his wife, Cheryl; son Richard, fifteen; and daughters Ginger and Kelly, seventeen and twelve.

Understand that each of us has an identity that makes us who we are. For Buddy, sports were an important part of his identity as a man and as a father, so his back injury was about far more than just his back. Buddy's downtime, recovery, and resulting disability assaulted his identity and shook him to his core. Without the ability to be mobile and active, Buddy felt less than a man and ineffective as a dad.

Fortunately, Buddy and Cheryl's marriage was solid and Buddy was able to accept comfort from his wife. Many men are not strong enough to do that. Buddy was also okay with the idea of assigning some of his sports involvement to Cheryl, because he truly did view her as an equal partner. But the kids felt his absence in their sports lives, and their behavior and physical and academic performance reflected this.

For this family, I did something I rarely do. I made a home visit. Several of them, actually. I did this because Buddy was laid up in bed and unable to come to my office, and because this family was so open to help and willing to change that I knew I had to meet them where they were.

I first met privately with the kids. This gave them the opportunity without their dad present to air their feelings about "why this happened to my dad." It also gave them the chance to ask "Why me?" and also to express their fear and anger over their dad's disability. They all had some anger at their dad, which is natural. Then comes the hard question of how you can be mad at someone who, through no fault of his or her own, is hurt. This open communication is so very important, and I encouraged Richard, Ginger, and Kelly to continue to share among themselves in the coming weeks and months.

I then met with Cheryl. Her openness and awareness was refreshing; I wish everyone had such a willing partner.

Buddy's session allowed him to cry and express the great deal of sadness and anger he had about his situation, and also to tell me everything that sports and athletics meant to him. Sports not only defined Buddy's identity and maleness to him, they also provided an outlet for his aggressive impulses (we all have those, whether we realize it or not), and he had a deep, pervading sadness that they had been taken away. Plus, he especially missed coaching his kids and going to all of their games.

On top of his personal sadness, Buddy felt guilt for not being able to be there for his children, as he had been before. And since there was no place for him to express his anger and release the tension that built up around his feelings, he found himself wound up and snapping at his family.

Buddy's feelings are typical of parents who have special needs. The anger, guilt, sadness, and tension are significant. Buddy, like other parents, had to learn new ways to let all of that go, and that included talking. That's why these independent meetings were so important. They were the perfect setup for a family meeting where real progress in awareness could be made.

During the family meeting everyone had a few minutes to say what they were feeling. The only rules were that they listen without interrupting, and while they could be honest, they could not talk in a hurtful manner toward any other member of the family. The kids spoke of how angry they were that this happened, and also how they now understood that their feelings were normal, understandable, and acceptable. Richard also mentioned that because the siblings all felt the same way, it had brought them closer. Buddy talked about how being allowed to express his negative feelings diminished them. The more he held his feelings inside, the more they festered and the worse he felt. Cheryl mentioned how the new policy of open communication around the house was keeping everyone on a more even keel.

This was all really good stuff, but more was needed. I asked Cheryl to videotape the kid's games. That way everyone could watch and discuss the games around Buddy's bed. Sharing a bag of popcorn made the experience even better.

I also asked if there was someone Buddy and Cheryl could enlist as a sports mentor to the kids until Buddy healed well enough to sit on the sidelines at the games. I was so happy when

Cheryl's brother, Nelson, stepped right in. He and Buddy had a positive, friendly relationship, and that helped a lot, but it took some time and work to ease Buddy into handing the job over to Nelson.

Eventually Buddy did recover enough to be more involved and he could go to the games, which he loved, but this family had to learn to live a "new normal." That they had learned to talk openly and found time to share their experiences with each other went a long way toward making this new life work cohesively.

The Importance of Communication: A Case Study

Jonas was twenty-two months old when he first came to my office. The reason he came to see me was that he had begun pulling his hair out. I took out the giant playhouse I have in my office, and he immediately went to the grandma doll I had in there and threw her out the window of the dollhouse. I eventually found out that the little boy's grandma lived with the family and shared a bedroom with him. His grandma had been diagnosed with cancer, went into the hospital for treatment, and was away for some time. During the course of her treatment her hair fell out and when she returned to the home, she was bald.

At twenty-two months, this poor little boy was not verbal enough to ask what had happened to his beloved Nanna, and no one thought to talk to him about it. His parents thought, "Well, he's not talking about it so we don't need to discuss Grandma's illness with him." In pulling out his hair, this toddler was saying two things. One, he was telling his parents that he was attached to, loved, and missed his grandmother and was angry that she disappeared without explanation. The second thing you already know. Yes, he mirrored what he saw. He loved his Nanna and she did not have any hair. I think you get the picture.

For three or four weeks, this little boy sat beside my playhouse and repeated over and over the gesture of tossing the grandma doll out the window. To help him I said simple phrases such as, "Jonas is mad at Grandma for going away," "Jonas misses Grandma," "I want my grandma!" Finally, the boy stopped throwing the grandma doll out the window, and our sessions became more about using simple, clear language that a twenty-two-month-old can understand. Then, when Grandma came home from the hospital, he stayed away from her for a while. This was because he was terrified she might abandon him again. He was also scared of the way she looked.

I helped Jonas slowly warm up to his grandma by doing the following three things, and his hair pulling eventually stopped.

First I told Jonas that Grandma got "cancer." I chose to use the word because Jonas overheard phone conversations and his mother's reactions. Then I told him her doctors wanted to get rid of the cancer, so Grandma had to go to the hospital for a time. The doctors used strong medicine and the medicine made Grandma's hair go bye-bye for a little while. Now Grandma's hair is growing back, but it is still short. Soon it will look the same as it did before. It is very hard to see Grandma this way ("confusing" is too big a word for Jonas to understand). Granted, all of this was too big for Jonas to understand, but he was able to get some of it, and, most important, he took in my affect and tone of gentle empathy for his experience. It helped Jonas that his mom was present for the sessions, and I saw that both Jonas and his mother benefited from my model of how to talk to this young child.

Second, I placed a giant piece of blank white paper with markers on my low table and invited Jonas and his mom to sit with me. I instructed Mom to make a picture of Jonas's bedroom because it helps young children to see a story as well as hear it. I asked Mom to make stick-figure drawings of Jonas, Mommy, Daddy, and Grandma in the house. Then I suggested that Mom draw a second picture that illustrated Jonas, Mommy, and Daddy in the house with Grandma's bed empty. On the side of the paper, Mom drew the hospital with Grandma inside waving at Jonas. Then she drew a fourth picture of all four reunited at home. Now Jonas had a book of his experience, *Grandma Went Away and Came Back,* which he could keep and return to for comfort and clarity.

When you talk with your son or daughter about matters like this, it is important that your tone of voice is matter-of-fact. No

matter if the disability is recent, ongoing, temporary, or permanent, this can be hard to do. That's because your voice is sure to
reveal your own worries, tension, and fear. But you must take
special care not pass any of these feelings along to your kids, especially for new situations.

Third, when Grandma was strong and well enough, I invited
her for a session with Jonas and Mom. Mom brought Jonas's
book and it helped everyone, especially Jonas, for me to talk
through the story *Grandma Went Away and Came Back* in the
presence of everyone. Grandma was then able to clearly narrate
what had happened to her so that Jonas could understand.

WORDS THAT WILL HELP

For parents with older and ongoing special needs, it might be that you
have never discussed your special challenges with your children. As they
grow they will want to know more, but may feel uncomfortable about asking. Or you might be facing a new surgery or a different medication or
therapy that they need to know about.

In either case you can say something like, "Your mommy is young and
strong. She plans to be here for many years to watch you grow up and lead
a successful life." You can also say. "This new medicine will make Daddy
more tired. He will be here to give you a hug and some cookies when you
get off the school bus. When he takes a nap, Mrs. Cohen from next door
will come over to play games with you and help you with your homework
until Mommy gets home."

Know that in situations like this, your child will worry about two
things. First they will worry about you. Then your son or daughter will
worry about him- or herself. They may think, "If this could happen to my
mom, can it happen to my dad or me?" You can ease their worries by
telling them who will take care of them, because their next thoughts will
be "Who will drive me to school, feed me, tuck me in, wash my clothes?"
That's why it is important to let your child know exactly what will happen
that concerns them, using age-appropriate words.

Another script that comes in handy is: "Let's talk about all the people
in your life who love and care about you. Besides Mommy and Daddy,

there's Grandma and Grandpa, Uncle Ed and Aunt Carla, Mr. and Mrs. Cohen, and Cousin Lucy." You can even make a game out of this and see how many people you and your child can come up with. It is very empowering for a child to discover on her own how many loving and caring people there are that she has a close relationship with and can count on.

The Mom Who Planned Ahead: A Case Study

You can't plan for disaster. Sometimes life hits you with a gale-force wind and bam, everything you know just turned sideways. But there are times when you can plan. Tina's hysterectomy was one of those times.

Tina had severe pain that accompanied her periods from the time she was a teen. Now the mom of three young children, she had tried all the treatments her physician could think of. None had worked, and she now had agreed to a complete hysterectomy. For years, Tina had gone to school functions doubled over in pain. She pushed herself to be all she could for her family, and at birthday parties she smiled through excruciating cramps. Plus, her troubles meant she often had to lie down frequently during the day. Tina was often crankier than she would have liked, and all of this, combined, was having a huge effect on her family.

Tina's doctor told her that a surgery as major as this one would lay her up for several months. She would not be able to drive for six weeks after the surgery and could not lift anything heavier than a small bag of flour for twelve weeks. Because her husband, Kevin, traveled, and her children were six, five, and one, Tina knew she would have to have full-time live-in help while she recuperated. Three months with three small children and a mostly absent husband was a long, long time.

The first thing she and Kevin did was arrange for her mother to come in and stay for a month before the surgery and for the three months after. Together she and the older children, Zoe and Michael, fixed up the spare bedroom for Grandma.

Then, because the hospital would only let her stay for several days after the surgery, Tina knew when she came home that her children would see her at her worst. I asked Tina to explain just the basics of this to Zoe and Michael, and here's what she said: "You know how Mommy's tummy hurts and she gets tired sometimes? Mommy is going to go to the hospital for a few days to have an operation that will fix the problem and make her a lot better. When Mommy comes home, at first Mommy will be even more tired and sore. She will sleep a lot and walk a little funny. But after a while, she will get better. Until that happens, Grandma will stay with us and do all the things for you that Mommy does."

Because toddlers under age three have not yet mastered pronouns such as "you," "I," or "we," I use the terms "Mommy" and "Daddy" when explaining things to them. I also sometimes use "Mommy" and "Daddy" with children who are a little older because it feels warmer and more personal, especially in situations that could be stressful.

This discussion opened the door for Michael and Zoe to ask questions. And they did! Who would feed Buster, the dog? How would Grandma know how to get to their school? Could they still have friends come for play dates? Would Mommy be well enough to come to Zoe's dance recital?

I have to say that Tina was a self-aware parent who really set this up well. In addition to opening the lines of communication and bringing her mother in early so she could learn all the day-to-day things Tina did for her family, Tina sat down with Michael and Zoe and helped them make a book that illustrated the ABCs of the entire upcoming experience. Here's a picture of Mommy and Daddy getting into the car to take Mommy to the hospital. Here's Zoe and Michael and baby Dylan and Grandma waving to Mommy. Here's Daddy cooking dinner. Here's Grandma and baby Dylan driving Zoe and Michael to school.

Step by step, Tina and Zoe and Michael either drew pictures or glued actual photos they took to illustrate each page. When all the pages for the "book" were done, Tina put them in a three-ring binder and put the binder on the low, reachable book shelf in the family room so anyone could look at it anytime they wanted to. She also told her children that when she got home, they could sit quietly at the foot of her bed and tell her about their day so she could stay connected to them.

Having easy access to the book they made gave Zoe and Michael a little bit of control during a situation when they had none. It also gave them reassurance that all would be taken care of; that everyone would be fed, bathed, and clothed; and that they would get where they were supposed to be when they were supposed to be there. Even though life in this household for the next four months was very different from what it usually was, Tina's thoughtful attention to detail made sure that her family eased into the transition as smoothly as possible.

This plan also eased Tina's guilt at not being able to do everything she usually did for her family. The process reassured her that all would be well. I also gave Tina a script to tell herself: "My children will be happiest and healthiest if I am happier and healthier. My job right now is to make that happen by taking care of me." These words eased Tina's anxiety and fears. She was aware that while three or four months of recovery was an eternity to her children, the surgery would really only mean days, or maybe a week, of absence. She could stay connected during the longer healing process at home. And, her needing special care was a very short time that would be followed by years of well-being and joy.

DR. FRAN'S TOP TIPS CHAPTER TWELVE

- Be empathic toward yourself.
- Always be honest with your child(ren).
- When explaining to your kids, less is more. Tell them the facts in clear, simple language.
- Answer all of their questions truthfully.
- Recognize that your condition and state (both physical and emotional) evoke feelings in your children.
- Invite and validate your child's expression of all the feelings he or she is experiencing.

- Find someone you can talk to. You need support and an outlet as much as your kids do.
- Enlist the help of caring, responsible people who can fill in the blanks for your child.
- If you can, prepare and plan ahead. Kids thrive on knowing what to expect. So do grown-ups!

CHAPTER THIRTEEN

WHAT TO DO WHEN THE CHEMISTRY DOESN'T MIX

I have a friend who for years was certain that she was adopted because she was so different from her mom. My friend had a 180-degree opposite personality from her mom. In addition, her dad was an outgoing extrovert and her brother was an introverted geek. You can imagine the intense frustration all these different personalities created in this family!

When the chemistry doesn't mix between you and your child, usually neither knows how to come together. This opposite-personality child can be a parent's nightmare, and personality differences often emerge during infancy. If your baby constantly cries and demands a response, and if you are a results-oriented doer, you may not be able to connect with this baby. If you have a shy, introverted baby and you are an "in-your-face" mom, you could overwhelm your infant and make a connection difficult. This opposite chemistry will progress into childhood unless something is done to turn it around.

As your child grows, he begins to feel that his parent "doesn't get" him, and he is not understood. It is as if you are on channel 8 when you need to be on channel 7 or 9. Of all the parenting types, parents of opposite-personality kids usually need the most help. But as bad as the interactions are, relationships with unmixed chemistries can be one of the easiest kinds to fix.

The most common opposite-personality types are introverted and extroverted, and we will spend most of our time during this chapter focusing on them. But there are other kinds of personality clashes, including emotional versus practical/intellectual, driven versus nonmotivated, solution-oriented versus process-oriented, risk taker versus cautious/tentative, and fast-tempo versus slow-tempo personalities. These differences can all cause significant discord within the family and you should be aware they exist.

With any personality difference, the first thing to realize is that you, the parent, should not be expected to change but rather to adjust and modify. You also need to accept the very real fact that your child is different from you. Children who are so different from their parents, and sometimes even the rest of their family, often grow up feeling as though they're not "good enough" and think they have to "change" to be loved and accepted. Every member of your family should be loved and valued through and through for who they are.

For example, yours might be a musical family. Everyone sings and plays an instrument . . . except your daughter, who happens to be a science genius. Even though she cannot sing or play a note, you need to embrace and encourage her skill with formulas, even though you may not understand it. This validation is critical in getting your daughter to support and motivate herself, and in allowing her simply to be her.

A Very Different Daughter: A Case Study

Lindsey and Dan had five children. The oldest was nine and the youngest had just turned a year. Both Lindsey and Dan were quiet, thoughtful people who fell under the introverted category of personality. They loved reading, studying, and working out numerical problems, and both were high-level computer programmers.

Interestingly enough, it looked as if all of their children were following suit. All except for their second daughter, seven-year-old Wendy, who was a loud, boisterous, attention-getting, inappropriate child. By the time I saw Wendy, who was referred to me by her school, she had had years to practice her loud, demanding voice. She was full of energy, as outgoing as the rest of her family was reserved, and was strong-willed, excitable, and very hard to rein in.

My first thought was that this might be a child with undiagnosed attention deficit hyperactivity disorder (ADHD). Tests were definitive and ruled the possibility out. This, then, was likely Wendy's personality, and her parents had no idea what to do with her.

Because Wendy's personality was so large, the other kids in this family shied away from her. Several of the youngest children were even somewhat afraid of her. She was too big, and all together she was too much for them to take.

The interesting thing here is that in another family, Wendy's antics might not seem all that different. She did things like stand on her head, or she made faces at the younger kids, stuck her fingers in her ears and waggled her tongue. Wendy skipped and shouted. When she threw a ball, she threw it hard. She made monkey noises, pretended she was an Indian, and danced around the house. The result was that this family of quiet, studious people was completely overwhelmed.

I told Dan and Lindsey that while Wendy had a big personality, part of her behavior at home and at school was to get attention. Five kids under the age of nine is a lot in any family, and Wendy felt she needed more attention. She needed people to look at her, to recognize her for her, individually, and not as one in a group of Dan and Lindsey's kids.

The truth was, Wendy felt like an outsider in her own family. She was bright enough to look around and see that everyone else was quiet—a group of thinkers rather than a talker like she was. Wendy needed to know that she belonged to this family even though she was different and her own unique person. Wendy needed one-on-one recognition from her mom and dad, but in addition, she needed to be reminded what was appropriate behavior and what was not. She also had to be held accountable when her actions hurt or inconvenienced other people.

Usually when you have one introverted parent, the other is on the extroverted side. It really is true that opposites attract. And that is good, because the balance in personalities brings depth to the marriage and family. That Dan and Lindsey were both introverts and four of their five children were also quiet, shy people is a little unusual. To complicate things, when Dan got angry, his was a quiet seething anger that festered. Lindsey rarely angered but frequently was exasperated and overwhelmed. She often let things go when she should have firmly put her foot down. I had several ideas for this family and was so pleased that when they implemented them, they worked.

As a general rule, all people, children and adults alike, want others to match and join them in their emotional state. If you are bouncing around in excitement over a big job promotion or a financial windfall, you want others to rejoice with you. That behavior makes you feel good. Lindsey and Dan had to learn that they could not expect Wendy to calm down and relate to them and to her siblings in a quiet way. Instead, they had to learn to step up their energy and come to her with a little more affect. Once the gap in personality styles was closer, then Wendy could learn to step down a little.

Wendy's mom and dad also had to learn that while quiet coloring, educational computer games, and organized hikes were great for the other kids, Wendy needed them to engage her by playing hide and seek or funny guessing games, and to enroll her in soccer, gymnastics, or basketball, where she could channel her endless energy to positive use.

Games where Lindsey and Dan could talk with Wendy and guide her to pull her back were especially important. For instance, I taught Lindsay and Dan to play stop and start games including red light/green light. On green light everyone runs, then someone calls red light and everyone freezes. This teaches a child to wind up and wind down. It's an excellent energy regulator. It helps kids to monitor their energy, accelerate, slow to a quick halt, and modulate their excitement. This allows kids to learn to keep the cap on their level of excitement and to avoid excitatory overflow, which is my term for aimless running and accelerating, the windup.

Correcting Wendy's inappropriate behavior in a calm, positive manner was also key. For instance, I taught Lindsey to say things such as: "You are standing too close to Mommy. Take a step back and give Mommy some space," and "That's an outside voice. We're inside now so let's use an inside voice that is quieter." Saying these phrases in a calm tone, over time, resonated with Wendy, and Lindsey found herself having to use the words less and less.

As you can see, Dan and Lindsey had to learn how to change their channel to meet Wendy's needs. One of Wendy's unvoiced concerns was that she felt lost inside this large family. When her older sister practiced the piano, Wendy became jealous at the attention her sister received. To "voice" her jealousy, Wendy ran around the house and made wild animal noises. Wendy had the potential to be a very likeable child, but she needed to be socialized and that could not happen without her parents adding more energy to their interactions with her, as well as being sure boundaries were clear and firm. They did all of this, and Wendy was doing well enough that I stopped seeing this family less than a year later. But that is not the end of this story.

I ran into Wendy a few months ago. She and her sister were at the park, and while Wendy was definitely her own person, her interactions with me were totally appropriate, as was the tone of her voice and her treatment of her sister. It took a lot of work from Lindsey and Dan, but the results were certainly worth it.

TRUE BIOLOGICAL DIFFERENCES

Not all opposite personalities involve clashes between introverts and extroverts, but a good number of them do. The term "introvert" was coined in the 1920s by psychologist Carl Jung.[1] Jung was one of the creators of modern depth psychology, which tries to initiate conversation with the unconscious that moves through each of us. He had deep appreciation of creative life and considered spirituality a central part of the human journey. Jung's method of interpretation of symbolic expression in dreams deepens our understanding of personal material. He used the term "introvert" to describe someone who is emotionally and physically worn out after being around people for a time. If you think of an introverted person that way, it makes sense that they not only prefer quiet activities but need them so they can recharge.

New research shows that an introvert's nervous system is wired in a different manner from that of an extrovert. Scans of extroverted children's brains show that their nervous systems are quite active, but introverts have more activity in the part of their nervous system that regulates rest and digestion. This means there is a true biological difference between these personality types.

Marti Olsen Laney, Psy.D., the neuroscience researcher and psychoanalyst who was the first to piece together this biological basis, agrees.[2] "An introvert won't feel replenished until he goes home and has some time to himself," she says.

This is because the dopamine our bodies produce, say, at an exciting soccer game, gives extroverted kids a pleasant boost, while it can overload an introverted child's circuits. Dr. Laney has said that as many as 30 percent of children are introverted, and this means they have an inborn need for quiet time to process what they take in.

A study in China has also confirmed that people who are shy or introverted may process their world differently from extroverts. The study was conducted by Stony Brook University, along with the Chinese Academy of Sciences.[3] Study results show differences in how introverts respond to stimuli. For example, some introverted children are slow to warm up to a situation but eventually join in, need little punishment, cry easily, and ask unusual questions or have especially deep thoughts.

Researchers involved with the Stony Brook University study also found evidence that the actual underlying difference between extroverts and introverts is in the brain's attention to details. The introverted child, a minority, chooses to observe longer than the extroverted child before acting. This is the equivalent of exploring with their brains instead of their limbs. Partially due to the Stony Brook study, biologists are beginning to agree that there can be equally successful opposite personalities.

Maybe because people who study human personality have not focused on genetics until recently, these personality styles have been overlooked. Researchers have already found that introverts are more bothered by noise and crowds, more affected by caffeine, and more easily startled. In that way, the introvert trait is somewhat about sensitivity. Current thought suggests that being an introvert is part of a "sensory processing sensitivity."[4] This means sensitivity to noise, pain, or caffeine could be a side effect of an inborn preference to pay more attention to experiences.

The end result to you, however, is that if you have an outgoing personality and your child is quieter (or vice versa), you are not going to change this. Instead, you have to learn to meet your child in the middle.

The Other End of the Spectrum: A Case Study

Eight-year-old Connor was the exact opposite of Wendy. He abhorred the spotlight and couldn't bear the thought of being in his class play. When he told his parents this, Mike and Christiana were not surprised. They had endured years of Connor's not wanting to have his picture taken or being so shy that he had trouble saying hello to people he knew, such as the postman and the librarian.

Because his parents were both outgoing people, they didn't know what to do when Connor clammed up. Christiana might say, for instance, "Say hello to Mr. Jones when he says hi to you, Connor." But Christiana didn't understand that her words only complicated the problem. By highlighting Connor's shyness, it put him in the spotlight and made him more embarrassed than if his mom hadn't said anything at all.

Now in the third grade, Connor cried to his teacher that he didn't want to be in the Thanksgiving play his class was putting on for the rest of the school and the parents. His teacher knew Connor was shy and had only assigned him a small part with one line, but at every rehearsal Connor fell silent. He could not muster up the courage to speak that one line out loud; it was far too overwhelming for him. In chapter 1 I mentioned selective mutism. Connor's reaction was a milder form of that, caused by his extreme discomfort in public situations. Connor, as you may have guessed, is a classic introvert.

When I initially met with this family, I observed that both Mike and Christiana pushed Connor farther than he was ready to go. This was to soothe their own embarrassment and need to have a child who was polite in public and could "perform" daily tasks in relating to people just as well as the other kids. But Connor wasn't ready for that, and their pushing only aggravated matters.

It was hard to get Mike and Christiana to accept Connor just as he was and not force him to do things he was not ready to do, such as be in the school play. They had to understand that being in even the smallest of spotlights was terrifying to Connor. For him, it was like being thrown into a pool of ice-cold water without knowing how to swim. But once his parents grasped this concept, they were happy to sit with Connor in the front row of the audience during the school play and say, "No problem, sweetie. You are not ready for the Thanksgiving play. We'll try again next year."

Notice that Mike and Christiana did not say, "*You will* be ready next year." Nor did they say, "You will be ready for the *Christmas* play." The first puts too much pressure on Connor to accept the spotlight and the second does not allow enough time for real change. The words you say and the subsequent actions requested of your child have to be comfortable for him. They also have to be said in such a manner that there is no invitation for resistance. Letting Connor know that he had a full year to prepare, and the idea that he then had a choice, was comfortable for him. Connor did not feel backed into a corner and had time to ponder how much of a spotlight he would be able to handle—and when he would be able to handle it.

I also taught Mike and Christiana that if Connor was not ready to respond to people, one of them can say, "I see you are not ready to answer Mr. Jones, so I will say hi to him on your behalf. Mr. Jones, one day soon Connor will be ready to say hi to you on his own." I also explained that saying this in a very casual, conversational, positive tone of voice is important in letting Connor know there is no pressure on him to move too far out of his comfort zone.

Connor's parents, at my request, also said to him, "Connor, you know best what it feels like to be in your skin. You know better than Mommy or Daddy what is comfortable for you.

And we want you to be comfortable, because that's what is most important."

These kinds of words and phrases gave Connor strategies he could use on his own. Instead of freezing in fear, he learned he could say, "Mom, I'm not ready to do that." In this way, Mike and Christiana taught Connor to register the specifics of how he felt and to self-advocate during each incidence of shyness and fear. And this family found how truly empowering that was for Connor when several months later he, on his own, walked up to their local librarian and asked for a specific book.

We have discussed research that shows that Connor will always be an introvert, just as his parents will always be outgoing. But by coming closer to Connor's style and helping him find his comfort zone, his extroverted parents were able to help Connor expand his personality in tiny little increments toward theirs. This family was one that, with a little knowledge, could and did meet each member emotionally. It was a harmonious joining of two personalities.

WHEN YOU AND YOUR CHILD ARE POLES APART

There are kids and parents, and then there are kids and parents. It is one thing to know and understand that you have a daughter who is a poet and a dreamer, while you love the order and precision of, say, accounting. But you will likely want to pull your hair out when your dreamy daughter is distracted by her internal thoughts and ignores your repeated comments and directives. Here are a few questions that will pinpoint your awareness of the differences between you.

1. Are you regularly irritated by your son or daughter, even when you realize that your child has not done anything very wrong? This may be a sign that you have not fully accepted that your child has a personality style that irritates and annoys you, or at least gets under your skin.

2. Do you feel that you want to connect with your child but cannot seem to find a way? If so, know that this feeling is different from the detached parent we talked about in

chapter 10. The detached parent does not know that they should want or need to be closer to their son or daughter. That you seek closeness is a good sign that with some effort you will eventually be able to achieve this goal.

3.   If you long to be more attached to your child, do you feel guilty that it has not happened? If so, rather than focus on the guilt, focus on the positive fact that you have been making an effort.

4.   Take a close look at yourself and decide what kind of personality you have. Do you have a strong will, or do you avoid confrontation? Are you outgoing, or do you prefer the quiet of home? No answer is right or wrong, but it is important that you know your style. I know that I am a very outgoing extrovert. I love a spotlight, and you know what? That's not so bad. My dad is the same way that I am, but my mom is quite shy. Early on she and I found common ground in her sense of humor. It was a place where my attention-getting childhood antics could find balance and rewards for good behavior.

5.   This is the last and most important question. Do you like your child? If you take an honest inward look and say no, then please think about getting professional help for you and your son or daughter. I know that there are a number of parents reading this book who *will* say no, so understand that you are not alone. You also should not think you are "less than" another parent if this is how you feel. But it is important to get professional help because your son or daughter is sure to pick up on your feelings. A trained therapist can also help you and your child find common ground and help you find the "likeability factor" that will allow the two of you to connect and create fun, shared experiences together.

THE JOINING PLACE

The personality styles we have been talking about so far have centered on introverts and extroverts. However, even more conflict-inducing than introversion and extroversion is the ongoing conflict between a strong-willed personality and a passive one. That truly is the biggest majority of clashes—a clash of wills. But there are hundreds of possibilities in personality combinations and clashes. If you look at all the variables in parenting styles that we have discussed so far, it will give you an idea of how many personality possibilities there could be. As an example, you might be a rigid, enmeshed parent who travels. Your daughter might be an unorganized and loosey-goosey person in her approach to homework and punctuality, and the two of you clash continually.

To make this relationship work, there must be a joining place, an area of interest that you both can share. With my mother and me it was humor. With you and your son maybe it is your love of football or nature. It might be the shared experiences you have in visiting Grandma every Sunday afternoon and your shared concerns for her health. It could be your tastes in music or a television show you both enjoy.

The important thing is that you find some interest or activity that you can either do together or discuss regularly. This one joining place can sometimes lead to others. It can also lead to a joining in the middle, meaning each of you adjusts a little to accommodate the other's style. Or, it can open the door to recognizing and learning to respect your differences. It can also teach each of you to accept the other for who he or she is. Each of you can learn to enjoy the activities the other is passionate about, but you cannot change who someone is at their core—unless they initiate the change themselves through growth, experience, and life events. If you keep all that in mind, you both will do much better together than you ever thought possible.

Denise the Menace: A Case Study

Denise was only four but her mom and dad, Claudia and Roy, already knew they had a challenge on their hands. Claudia was an outgoing, artistic architect who had difficulty in setting and keeping boundaries. Roy was an actuarial, a math whiz, who outside of his deep focus at work was vague, friendly, absentminded, and detached; and he had an angry temper that only rarely came out. This couple knew nothing about parenting an energetic, whirling dervish daughter who was so very different from them, so they let her run wild, thinking she would wear herself out.

What actually happened, with little in the way of supervision or boundaries, was that Denise became aggressive on the playground and in the classroom at her preschool. So I taught Claudia and Roy to contain Denise by sitting on the floor behind her and wrapping their arms around her. I worked with Claudia and Roy for several months and in the process grew increasingly puzzled with the lack of progress they were making with Denise. Not only was her behavior not getting any better, it was getting worse. Eventually she was expelled from her preschool.

Then Denise began coming to sessions and, while calm, said things such as, "I want to run away and live with another family." While this is not unusual to hear in an angry child, these words are rare when they come from a four-year-old who is not in the middle of a tantrum, so I paid special attention to them and to Denise.

After some trial and error, I realized that Roy and Claudia were doing everything I had asked them to do, but Roy was doing it forcefully and with anger, and Claudia was ambivalent so she inadvertently reinforced the negative behavior we were trying to get rid of. Turns out that our sessions had brought out unresolved feelings each parent had toward their own mom and dad.

For Claudia, they brought up deep fear she felt about her parents, who had divorced when Claudia was about the same age Denise was now. For Roy, some rage surfaced at his father, who died when he was ten, but who had mistreated him with hurtful, humiliating tactics. Neither Claudia nor Roy were aware of these issues before they came to see me regarding Denise, but as these issues surfaced, they began to unknowingly contain and control Denise with anger and ambivalence. Denise responded by becoming wilder and more out of control, hence the lack of progress.

In one key session, Claudia broke down and cried and apologized to Denise. Then Claudia and Roy hugged in a rare show of solidarity, and Denise cried, saying that she never ever wanted to run away. It was like watching the ending of an old MGM movie!

While therapists dream of a breakthrough like this, where every piece of the puzzle falls into place, it rarely happens. When it does, it can become a rich and rewarding experience for every-one involved. But the key is whether the family can sustain the togetherness and unification they have just found.

Sometimes a crisis has to happen for change to occur. What this family of very different personalities found in Denise's expul-sion, and her parents' unresolved anger at, and fear of, their own parents, is that they really did like and love each other. They also found common bonds in their shared love. Some might feel that that's not very much to build the foundation of a family on, but for this family, it was much more than enough.

BRINGING OPPOSITES TOGETHER

I know how hard it is to live with a mom or dad who is different from you, so here are some reminders that will help you help your opposite-personality son or daughter.

1.   Keep in mind that shyness is a personality trait and not a fault. The same goes for being an extrovert. This is what your child came in with, and who your child is. You can-not change that, so embrace them for their uniqueness, whatever it may be.

2.   There is no need to be apologetic. If someone comments about your child's shyness, you can say something to the effect of, "Yes, Kara takes time to feel comfortable." When others realize that you see your daughter's traits as positive, then your daughter will see them that way too. It is also important to keep the same strategy in mind for any trait your child displays. If Billy is a little rambunctious, instead of apologizing, say in a calm, positive manner, "I'm help-ing Billy learn to settle himself."

3.   Kids need parents they can trust and who discipline in a way that does not try to change their personality. With discipline, sometimes less is more, especially with an intro-verted child. Since they take so much to heart, simply talk-ing about an infraction may be enough to prevent future behavior. An outgoing wild child will likely need more of a

response to achieve the same effect. So instead of only talking about the infraction, perhaps taking away one evening of television would be appropriate. For all children, whatever consequence is given must be clear, enforced, and age and personality appropriate.

4. The more comfortable you are around people, the more appropriate your child will become. We so greatly underestimate the amount of time our children watch and learn from us. If they see us interact appropriately and with ease, they will eventually learn to model that too.

5. The harder you push, the more your child will run toward his or her personality type. For example, you can't pull a child out of being an introvert. It just will not happen. Instead, create a comfortable environment that lets her personality develop naturally.

6. Never label or categorize your child. Words such as shy, boisterous, quiet, or wild will make him feel that something is wrong with him, and will make him feel even more different from you than he already does.

7. Keep as much attention off your child as you can, until such time that she is comfortable with it. If you absolutely must show off introverted Beatrice's artwork to your mother-in-law, don't spring the request on little Bea without warning. Give her time to get used to the idea and for you to suggest alternatives if she is not comfortable with it. Maybe *you* can show off the artwork, or the artwork can be already displayed in your home. Or maybe nothing at all is said about Beatrice's artistic talents. For children who crave the spotlight, it might be appropriate to suggest that just one or two drawings be displayed and discussed. Remember that for these kids who are at the ends of the personality spectrum, you want to gently pull them toward the middle.

DR. FRAN'S TOP TIPS CHAPTER THIRTEEN

- First identify what your personality type is. Then identify your child's.
- Be brave. Admit to yourself if your chemistry doesn't mix with your child's.
- Keep your expectations realistic. Don't expect personalities to change. Expect modifications and adjustments.
- Know that just as you want to be acknowledged and fully accepted, so does your child.
- Meet your child where he or she is. Inch yourself toward the middle—somewhere between your comfort zone and your child's.
- Find your child's specialness and highlight it.
- Remember, your child is not aggravating you on purpose. This is who he or she is.
- Find your joining place in humor, sports, nature, music, art, et cetera.
- Do not push your introverted child, but do rein in your extroverted child.
- Manage your feelings of embarrassment.
- Be kind to your child, and be kind to yourself!

CHAPTER FOURTEEN

WIN-WIN PARENTING

The win-win parent is the parent who, despite normal day-to-day challenges, does their parenting job "good enough." Austrian-born American child psychologist Dr. Bruno Bettelheim first identified the "good enough mother." This mom (or dad) does a "good enough" job of tending to her child's basic daily physical *and* emotional needs.[1]

Like the good enough parent, the win-win parent is not a perfect parent, because there is no such thing. But the win-win parent does a good job. He or she does not get caught up in power struggles with their spouse or kids. This mom or dad does not engage in negotiations, bargaining, or deal-making, but instead balances nurturing and setting limits with follow-through. He or she also intentionally tunes in to the child, usually correctly reads verbal and nonverbal cues, creates an open pathway of communication, and understands that anger is a healthy expression.

Additionally, this win-win parent understands that separation is good and is a natural progression of the parent/child relationship, and shows their son or daughter that home is a secure, safe base in which to grow and thrive.

Sounds like a lot, doesn't it? It is, but you are probably much closer to this ideal than you think. Before you take the parent self-awareness assessment in chapter 15, which will help you pinpoint the different kinds of parenting styles that are unique to you, it is important to understand that a lot of parents do get it right.

For many chapters we have been talking about all the mistakes parents make, all the help they need, all the things parents do wrong. To balance that out we need to take a look at the parents who are very self-aware and do everything they can to guide their sons and daughters into becoming healthy, productive adults. Think about the best gift you could hand down to your grandchildren. This is it!

THE SECRETS TO WIN-WIN PARENTING

I see parents and children in my office every day, and the parents who do most things right have five things in common.

1. They are kind to their children. I put this first because of the five, this is by far the most important. If you are nice, speak with a kind tone, and have warm body language, you are already on your way to bonding with your child and making your son or daughter feel valued. What I especially like about this is that it is so easy to do. You do not need any special education or training, and it does not help to be wealthy or to have a nanny. All you have to do is be patient, listen with sincere interest when your child speaks, and empathize with his or her life struggles.

2. They spend "special time" every day with their kids. The parents who are doing the best job commit every day to a few minutes of uninterrupted quality time with each child. If yours is a two-parent household, it works best if both the mom and the dad can do this. It shows your kids that while you have to work to afford things such as your house, cars, and food, you really want to be a parent. You *want* to do this. In spending special time, your children know you enjoy talking to your son about soccer practice and helping your daughter choose a dance camp. You can even sit and enjoy ice cream together! Please make the time sacrifice so this can happen for your family. It will be well worth the few minutes away from your work environment, household chores, or evening television programs.

3. They never fight in front of their kids. If you have a dis-
    agreement with your spouse, your ex, or your mother, wait
    until your children are asleep (when you can disagree qui-
    etly), or they have gone to school or a friend's house. If
    you follow this rule, as all win-win parents do, you'll find
    that your children will be less anxious and have fewer
    episodes of worry. You will have created that safe haven of
    home that is so important for a child to thrive.

4. They do an excellent job of nurturing and boundary set-
    ting. Do not be afraid to say no. You can learn to say it
    kindly, but firmly. And when you say no, mean it. We've
    talked a lot about the effects that weak or unclear bound-
    aries can have on a child. Work to make this area a priority
    and you will see amazing results.

5. They ask for help when they need it. Everyone needs help
    now and then, especially parents. If you feel overwhelmed
    or out of your league, find reinforcements. Find the knowl-
    edge you need to make great decisions about your kids in
    the form of a supportive family member or a pastor, coun-
    selor, or therapist. Read books such as this one. Talk to
    other moms and dads, teachers, and educators. Someone
    has the answers and the help you need. Then implement
    your new approaches and watch your family thrive.

A Family That Got It Right: A Case Study

When I first saw Saul and Leona, their daughter Joni was nine
months old. During the course of therapy they also had a son,
Paul. Over the years I got to know Saul and Leona quite well and
I learned what made them such wonderful parents. It wasn't that
they were without struggles; they actually had more than their
share. It was that they really, *really* wanted to be good parents.
The love they gave to Joni and Paul was without bounds, but they
also were able to be parents who held the line when needed. This
is how, specifically, they did that.

First, both parents were very self-aware. Before getting married
each had embarked on individual counseling, and they received

couples counseling prior to taking their wedding vows. This meant that both Saul and Leona were not only aware of what issues pushed their buttons, but they also knew what pushed each other's buttons. Then they made a conscious effort not to push any buttons, their own or their spouse's. By the time Joni came along, this couple had developed a solid foundation in their marital relationship, even though they themselves were nowhere near perfect.

For example, both Saul and Leona came from families where expressions of anger were not encouraged. This meant they each had a tendency to hold their anger inside. It was hard for them, even years after leaving their parents' households, to understand they now had a safe place—their own home and family—where anger could be positively expressed. Over the years I knew them, Saul and Leona both struggled with this, and probably still do.

As for parenting, Leona was not dealing well with minor boundary issues. When Joni cried in the middle of the night, the first thing Leona wanted to do was shove a bottle in Joni's mouth. At nine months, Joni should have been sleeping through the night. If she woke up, she might not even have been hungry. Maybe she was seeking comfort and needed to learn to self-soothe. Once Leona understood that there were possibilities other than the fact that her daughter might be hungry, the problem resolved itself.

Leona was also very health conscious and tended to worry too much when her children occasionally did not eat healthily enough for her standards. But she learned to restrain herself from making negative comments. A hot dog at a ball game was not going to instantly cause clogged arteries. Leona also once in a while had trouble holding boundaries. She would sometimes give in and submit to her children's demands. The problem was that she would first say no, and when they would protest strongly, she would collapse with an angry snap. But with guidance, she got faster at calling herself on it and eventually stopped.

Saul, meanwhile, had very high standards and had to work not to keep them rigidly so. His children were both bright, talented individuals, and he had to learn that the rare B or even C on a report card was not cause for panic. For him, this was hard to do.

Saul and Leona both had great instincts, but they came to me regularly for years to prevent falling into bad habits. There were no major issues, but every few months they had questions and I would guide them. I got them through teething and toddling, the birth of their son Paul, separation, jealousy, the beginning of kindergarten, and a host of other typical milestones that families face every day. While these parents were not anywhere near wealthy, the well-being of their children was so important to them that they found the means for occasional expert advice.

One of the reasons Saul and Leona continued to come to see me is that both were very interested in continuing their exploration in self-awareness as parents. In this way, they were able to immerse themselves in each stage of parenting with their eyes wide open.

I realize this exact scenario will not work for all parents. Many of you are single parents. Many more have spouses who are unwilling to look within and change. You might be a step-parent or are dealing with your ex's new spouse. While you cannot change any of them, you can change yourself. You can be aware of who you are, what makes you mad, sad, anxious, and glad, and why this is so, and then communicate that to those around you. Maybe some of the others will fall in line, maybe not. But this approach will help you. It will also help your children.

And last, this couple was able to look at each of their children as the individuals they were. Joni loved gymnastics and earned good grades, but sometimes struggled with respectful behavior. Paul loved the spotlight and lived for his singing and dancing classes, but he did not perform as well academically and had to be motivated there.

As you can see, this was not a perfect family. But the parents were so self-aware and so tuned in to their children that they handled most bumps in the road extremely well.

THE BEST WORDS YOU CAN USE

Another reason Saul and Leona were so successful in their marriage and with their parenting is that the words they used motivated well, corrected without criticizing, and showed that they empathized while still staying firm.

SUPPORT

For example, to help push a child over a homework hump, you might smile, look at your struggling child, and say, "You are amazingly bright and I admire the way you stick to things when they challenge you. That's called determination." This is better than saying, "Study harder," or "You have to focus more," while you are busy picking up the house. Focus on your child and speak to him or her like a cheerleader, and in this way your son or daughter will not feel that you are nagging. Instead, they will feel encouraged. The difference in words, attitude, and tone is a very positive way to support your child, your spouse, or even yourself.

ANGER

You know that expression, validation, and acceptance of anger is good. The explosion of anger is not. You can help your child in this by saying words to the effect of: "I can see how angry you are at me right now. Maybe you can tell me about that, rather than hit your sister. I'm the kind of dad who wants to hear about your feelings, whatever they are." By giving your child a direct and positive venue in which to vent, you not only validate their feelings, you give them an opportunity to resolve the issue through communication and words.

BOUNDARIES

It can be so hard to enforce boundaries, but you know, if you give a little now, you will be asked to give more the next time. As my dad often said, you give a finger and they want the whole hand! However, there are ways to reward kids without loosening the rules. Let's say you have a rule about not watching TV on school mornings until after your daughter has finished her responsibilities of getting washed, dressed, and ready to go to school. If your daughter begs you for TV while dressing, you can say, "Mommy can see how you really want to watch TV now. Show Mommy how you can hurry up and get dressed and ready for school so you can have more TV time. The less begging and more dressing you do, the more TV time you have!"

These words allow your daughter to have what she wants without breaking your rule. It also motivates her to face her unpleasant responsibilities *first* and then enjoy her reward. This will reduce the number of times she pushes up against the boundary.

Remember that even though they push, children feel safe and secure in knowing where the boundary is and that it is firmly in place.

PRAISE

It is so important to be specific in your praise. I hear "Good job!" over and over, but you know what? Those pat words do not mean much to your child. They are so vague and overused that your child is not able to take anything positive away from them. There is absolutely no useful impact to those words. Here are a few alternative ideas:

> "I really like the way you politely ask your sister to pass the juice at the dinner table."

> "It was kind of you to open the door for your brother."

> "I see you are petting Spot gently and how much he likes that."

> "Your room looks wonderful with your toys put away neatly. I bet it is so much easier to find things now."

> "I loved how you spoke up so I could hear you."

It is important to be both specific and positive. If you are, you will see a big difference in how your child behaves. He will love your comments and work toward earning more of them, so be sure to notice the effort he is making in this direction. You will probably also notice your positive and specific comments coming back to you in the form of gratitude and appreciation. When kids feel appreciated they become appreciative people. You may find them expressing more words of thanks to you for your good deeds and generosity to them, and this goes a long way toward making parenting pleasant and a lot of fun!

MOTIVATION

So many parents that I see engage in yelling or nagging to motivate their child. The interesting thing is that rarely do these parents realize what they are saying, or how they are saying it.

"Get your homework done!" yelled in an angry tone is neither helpful nor effective. I think you can see that "Show me how you can finish your homework so we have extra time to walk around the block" is a better choice of words. In essence, good behavior should have a reward. That is motivation. "Help Mommy take the trash out and then we can have some lemonade."

Ultimately, we want your child's motivation to become the feeling of relief that comes with completion of a task. Motivation can also come from pleasing an important person—usually an authority figure like Mom, Dad, a teacher, a tutor, or Grandpa. Offering rewards that include a person-to-person connection, like taking a walk, sharing a delicious treat, or reading a book together, are much better for the development of your child's value system than using money, toys, or other material prizes.

Sometimes kids feel too overwhelmed to get through a task or a situation. Then words to the effect of, "What do you need from me to help you through your math assignment?" show your son that help is available. This doesn't mean you will do the homework for him but rather that together you can talk through the specific problem he is having. Maybe the solution is as simple as being sure his sister does not bug him, or allowing him to listen quietly to music while he is doing his homework. Some people actually do learn better that way.

Other solutions that you can come up with might include calling a homework hotline, if your school district has one, or encouraging him to do the best he can and ask the teacher for extra help. It might be he needs a tutor, or "homework helper," for a period of time or, and here we come to it again, a little reward. "When I see that you have finished your math, how about if we go out and shoot some hoops?"

For motivation to reach larger goals, you could say, "If you improve your C in science to a B on your next report card, I think we can go ahead with the karate lessons you have been wanting." Note that you are not nagging about the C. You are instead being supportive in motivating and encouraging your child to study harder. You should also ask how you can help your child reach that milestone. If the class will be studying astronomy, maybe a Saturday trip to a planetarium with a few of your child's friends would be both helpful and fun.

ACHIEVEMENTS AND SPECIAL MOMENTS

It used to be that families made a big deal out of ordinary milestones such as a daughter's first piano recital or a son's spelling bee. But that isn't always true in today's society. Just getting to today's piano recital is more likely to be a

hectic affair that involves washing clothes at the last minute, juggling transportation, and hoping the recital doesn't last too long so you can also get
your son to his baseball game on time. After the recital it is a mad dash to
the ball field, where you drop your son for the team warm-up and then go to
the grocery store in hopes that you get back before the first pitch is thrown.
Your daughter is still in her recital dress, and you are nervous and impatient.

You may not be aware of it, but this scenario can make your daughter
feel that her specialness is diminished or, worse, that she is an imposition
and her recital is an inconvenience. Let's stop and think for a second. Is
that really how you want her to feel? This is her first piano recital. A win-
win parent will celebrate this and all the other special moments in life with
all the hoopla they deserve. Let her moment shine without jumping so
quickly into the next.

"I am so looking forward to your recital! Where should we go to celebrate afterward?" will make your daughter feel special and important. So
will, "I am so proud of you. You have practiced long and hard for this!"

Words such as these are effective because they recognize the achievement and also make your child feel special. We all need to feel special
every now and then—especially when we have earned it. That's not narcissism. It's self-esteem!

Sometimes, however, the events do not go according to plan. Maybe
your child's team did not win the championship, or your daughter did not
get the lead in the school play. Part of life is dealing well with its ups and
downs, and it's a fact that you don't always get the spotlight when you deserve it.

As a win-win parent, you can positively support your son or daughter
through these disappointments too. Negative statements, such as "That
director didn't know what she was looking at when you auditioned," or "I
bet the girl who got the lead will make a mess of the part," are not at all
constructive. They only feed the bad feelings your daughter has and give
her the distorted idea that she is entitled to everything she tries out for.
They do not offer any positive or realistic ideas.

A positive statement, such as "I know you are disappointed you didn't
get the lead this time. You'll try again for a different play," said empathically,
is so much better. This takes pressure off your child to achieve when achievement is beyond his or her control. In essence, you, the win-win parent, are
telling your child that the director decided to give someone else a chance.

I see a number of girls and boys in my practice who are endowed with musical, dramatic, and athletic talent. I advise their parents to let them know that everyone wants a chance to sing the lead in *Annie,* particularly if their child just performed a lead role in *The Sound of Music.* The director wants each kid to experience both playing the lead and being in the chorus. That's part of being in a group. Same in a family. You cannot always allow the same one of your three children to choose the restaurant where you eat. Everyone takes a turn. Allow your children to experience the disappointment of losing. By doing this you will equip each child with coping skills.

These words and this attitude take the steam and potency of the disappointing loss away from your child. By letting your son or daughter know that this loss is not a big deal, you are also letting them know that you fully support their next try. This approach also lets your child know that they did not disappoint you by not getting the lead or winning the championship. Our children really do want to please us. They crave our approval so much more than we will ever know. It is good to let them know that you appreciate their efforts and that there will be other opportunities in life to achieve. Then let it go.

WIN-WINNING SOLO

Often, being a win-win parent means you are in a win-win marriage. A good working marital relationship where both partners give, take, listen intently when the other speaks, and respect their partner is important. But, as I have mentioned before, life does not always provide that opportunity.

There are many single parents out there who are doing an excellent job of raising their children. You could be one of them. I define "single" in several ways that go beyond the traditional meaning. In this book, a single parent is someone whose partner is frequently away for long periods of time (such as in the military families we talked about) or uninvolved. And, how single you are depends on whether your child's other parent is completely out of the picture, or if he or she is still a part of your child's life. Many single parents truly are doing it all by themselves.

When I think of single parents who did a great job, I think of a patient of mine named Marla. Marla's dad was an alcoholic, and she came from modest means. She had a lot of resentment toward her dad because he did not step up to the plate for her when she was younger, but Marla had a good ability to vent her anger appropriately. Marla was not a perfect parent by any stretch of the imagination and was under a lot of financial stress, but her son Jared, who was eight, never doubted that she loved him.

Every child needs to know, unequivocally, that their mom and dad love them. Single parents have to shower enough love and affection for both parents, and Marla was wonderful at this. She and Jared had regular snuggle time on the couch, where they burrowed into blankets and ate popcorn as they watched funny movies. This close snuggle time is different from inviting your child into your bed, as it does not involve sleeping, which a child should do on his or her own.

Marla was a naturally warm person and gave Jared many hugs throughout the day. She was also genuinely nice to him and let him know that she really wanted to spend time with him. He knew without a doubt that being his mom was the most important job to Marla.

Part of loving a job is being involved in it, and Marla gladly transported Jared to all of his sports and after-school activities and cheered him on from the grandstand in all of his competitions. Equally important, however, was that Marla designed their lives with lots of routine and structure. Rules were fair and age appropriate, and boundaries were clear and firm.

The most amazing part is that, like most single parents, Marla worked a full-time job. Her time with Jared was limited, but as you can see, she made the most of it. Jared is grown now, off at the college of his choice. He is a bright and eager young man who I know will soon make a positive mark on the world.

WINNING BY SEPARATING

Marla's goal as a parent was to raise Jared into a happy, independent, and productive adult, and she succeeded. I believe that all win-win parents share her goal. In addition to all of the challenges we have talked about so far, there is one final challenge for you. It is the challenge of separation. To be the best parent you can be, you must praise, celebrate, enjoy, and revel in every incremental step toward growth and independence that your child makes.

So many parents want to hold on to their child, and the reality is that doing so is not healthy—not for you, or for your son or daughter. To illustrate, I'll use one final patient family as an example.

Ava and Joel were sending their fourteen-year-old son, Moss, on a plane across the country to visit his grandparents. These days, children fly by themselves all the time, but this was the first time Ava and Joel felt Moss was old enough to attempt the journey. It was Ava and Joel who were having trouble separating, even though they knew it was time for this leap of independence to happen.

Instead of Ava and Joel projecting their worries and insecurities about the trip on to Moss, I suggested they walk with Moss to the gate with supportive smiles on their faces. (Parents of children who fly alone are usually still allowed to walk to the gate.) This mom, dad, and son also knew that Moss's grandparents would be waiting for him at the gate in the city where the plane landed. Moss had his cell phone with him, and his parents had put every precaution for his safety in place.

It was important that when Moss looked at his parents, all he saw was approval about his competence in their faces and body language. In this way, Ava and Joel gave Moss permission to separate from them just a little bit more.

Ava and Joel did well at this, as I knew they would. I had been seeing this family off and on for a long time, mostly for prevention and guidance, and I knew this couple was self-aware enough that they knew the importance of this journey. Over the years, Ava and Joel had become quite adept at masking their own insecurities about separation. For example, when Moss was younger and having trouble with a rough child on the playground, this mom and dad did a thorough job of teaching Moss to advocate for himself—even though they yearned to protectively step in themselves.

Once Moss knew to say to the classmate who was too rough "That's not right," or "You are not being kind," things got better. And if they hadn't, Moss at age seven felt comfortable enough to go to the teacher or other authority figure at school to explain the situation.

The win-win dad who fears his son will get hurt playing football still encourages his son to play, because deep down he knows his fears could inhibit his son's growth and independence. He also knows the coach will take good care of all the members of the team. The win-win mom cheers her daughter on as she leaves for college in another state, even though she secretly wishes her daughter would go to school locally so she would not have to move away, even temporarily. Win-win parents praise their son or daughter's differences in ideas and opinions and teach them to think for themselves. Independent thinking frees children.

Each new activity brings these families a step closer to the day when the younger generation leaves home to start lives of their own. But these moms and dads who allow their children to separate from them need not worry, for they will always be their children's parents. Adult children still need their parents, just in different ways. So relish these normal steps toward autonomy, and enjoy the thought that your children are happy, healthy, and pursuing their individual identities and dreams.

DR. FRAN'S TOP TIPS CHAPTER FOURTEEN

- Always be curious and open enough to look within and become more self-aware.
- Be kind and nice to your child(ren).
- Do not strive for perfection. Be "good enough."
- Don't get caught in power struggles.
- Never engage in negotiations, bargaining, or deal making.
- Balance nurturing, setting limits, and holding boundaries.
- Listen to your child(ren). Interpret both verbal and non-verbal cues.
- Encourage healthy expression of anger.
- Nurture and praise your child's incremental steps toward separation.
- Encourage your child's unique and individual ideas, thoughts, and opinions.
- Have special time with your kids every day.
- Shield your children from hearing Mom and Dad fight. Restrain the impulse and either find a private place or wait until after the kids are asleep.
- Ask questions of others if you don't know what to do.
- Have a weekly date night and daily talk time with your spouse/partner. The foundation of your family is built upon the bricks and mortar of your marital relationship.

- Build self-esteem by using words that support and motivate with empathic attunement, rather than criticize.
- Equip your child with coping skills to deal with disappointments. We cannot protect or prevent life's disappointments. The best we can do is equip our children with coping skills to deal with inevitable letdowns.

CHAPTER FIFTEEN

WHERE DO I FALL

AS A PARENT?

As you have probably discovered, few parents are exclusively one style or another. Most parents combine several styles of parenting, and now that you have learned what those styles are, it is time for you to define the different elements of parenting that make you exclusively you.

The following statements will let you know what your dominant style is and what other styles you have traces of in your parenting makeup. By thinking about and responding to the statements, and then adding up the score, you will become aware enough to take your own emotional temperature. This means you will be more conscious of your parenting strengths and weaknesses and, through this knowledge, can better your parenting skills.

While it will be very easy for you to whiz through the following statements, I suggest you find a quiet spot during a time when you are not distracted and give each question some serious thought. Take all the time you need. It is important to be honest with yourself, and that can take a bit of soul searching. Additionally, if you think back to the corresponding chapter, the families that were discussed, and what you learned about them and yourself, it will help you make an honest evaluation about yourself.

The scoring for all of the following statements is the same. If the statement is true for you:

Always = 4 points
Often = 3 points
Sometimes = 2 points
Rarely = 1 point
Never = 0 points

The *lowest* score out of the following thirteen areas is your dominant form of parenting. Your sub-styles of parenting will be your second-, third-, and possibly fourth-lowest scores.

Note that a few of the later chapters might not apply to every parent. However, it is good to do a self-assessment on the statements in those chapters that do apply to you. It is a great learning experience.

Now, let's get started!

PERSONALITY ASSESSMENT CHECKLISTS

CHAPTER 2: SEPARATING YOUR CHILD FROM YOU
Summary: Chapter 2 discussed enmeshed parents who have difficulty separating themselves from their child.

____I give myself permission to not be consistently successful at the beginning of a new stage of my child's separation from me.

____I am able to separate my own feelings from those of my child.

____I keep my fears, worries, and anxieties away from my child.

____I never share adult or other inappropriate issues with my child.

____I praise every increment of my child's movement away from me.

____I listen to my child and act based on what he or she is feeling, rather than on my own feelings.

____I teach my child to advocate for him- or herself.

____I encourage peer relationships for my child and for myself.

____I do not break down or "lose it" in front of my child.

____When I find the process of separation too painful, I enlist the help of my partner/spouse, or another trusted adult, to assist my child and me.

_____I know who I am, separate and beyond being my child's parent.
_____**My Score**

Scoring: 0–10 points: You are an enmeshed parent. Rereading chapter 2 will be especially helpful to you.

11–20 points: You are somewhat enmeshed and can benefit from working on specific areas of separation that are troublesome for you.

21–30 points: You have a slight tendency to be enmeshed. If you are aware of your tendency, you will do well.

31–40 points: You are not at all enmeshed. You have a good handle on separation and praise your child for each step toward his or her independence.

CHAPTER 3: MANAGING YOUR PARENTAL WORRIES AND CONCERNS

Summary: Chapter 3 discussed parents who worry too much.

_____I separate which worries are mine and which are my child's.
_____I don't worry about germs my child might come into contact with.
_____I do not react before anything has gone wrong.
_____I don't obsess over my child's performance in academics or sports.
_____I do not "over-control" those around me as a way to manage my worries.
_____I do not project my fears and worries onto my child.
_____I can create an inner dialogue to calm and settle myself.
_____I find facts and use concrete information to settle my worries.
_____I have support from someone whom I trust.
_____I accept that I will have failures mixed in with my successes.
_____**My Score**

Scoring: 0–10 points: You are a worried parent. Rereading chapter 3 will be especially helpful to you.

11–20 points: You are somewhat worried and can benefit from working on specific areas of worry and anxiety that are troublesome for you.

21–30 points: You have a slight tendency to worry. If you are aware of this, you will do well.

31–40 points: You have a good handle on appropriate worry and anxiety.

CHAPTER 4: LET YOUR CHILD EXPERIENCE THE WORLD ON HER OWN

Summary: Chapter 4 discussed the parent who hovers so much their child fails to learn needed life skills.

——I believe obstacles and disappointments in my child's life are chances to learn and grow.

——I encourage my child to make mistakes and deal with challenges on her own.

——I can separate my issues from my child's issues.

——I teach my child age-appropriate life skills, such as washing clothes, doing chores, and taking the bus.

——I know my child can function well without me.

——I am emotionally self-sufficient as a model for my child. I demonstrate how to manage my own feelings, including anxiety.

——I respect that each person does things their own way.

——I am involved in my child's activities, but not overly so.

——I praise every increment toward my child's independence.

——I am able to give my child space.

——**My Score**

Scoring: 0–10 points: You are a helicopter parent. Rereading chapter 4 will be especially helpful to you.

11–20 points: You often hover, and will benefit from working on individual areas of separation that are worrisome for you.

21–30 points: You have a slight tendency to hover. Catch and correct yourself when you can.

31–40 points: You have a good awareness of age-appropriate separation. Congratulations!

CHAPTER 5: DEALING WITH YOUR PARENTAL DOUBT

Summary: Chapter 5 discussed those parents who doubt themselves and are unsure.

——I ask for help when I need it.

____I partner with a nonjudgmental, supportive, understanding person.

____I do not have trouble making decisions.

____I strive for consistency in my decision making.

____I realize I will have successes and failures in parenting.

____Making a decision does not cause my anxiety to temporarily rise.

____I am okay if my child becomes angry with me about a decision I made.

____I inform myself before I make a decision.

____Once I commit to a decision, I stick to it.

____I give myself permission to occasionally make a decision-making mistake.

____**My Score**

Scoring: 0–10 points: You are unsure of yourself. Rereading chapter 5 will help you become more definite in all that you do.

11–20 points: You often doubt yourself and will benefit from making small decisions and sticking to them.

21–30 points: You have a slight tendency to be unsure. Note this and lean toward holding the line firmly.

31–40 points: You are a decisive and confident parent!

CHAPTER 6: THE SPAGHETTI PARENT: LEARNING THE VALUE OF SAYING NO

Summary: Chapter 6 discussed parents who are inconsistent.

____I do not cave in when my child protests, whines, begs, bargains, or cries.

____I can say no to my child when I need to.

____I recognize that I do not always know what is best for my child.

____I understand that my child will not always like me.

____I trust my parental instincts.

____I have someone who is available to me for comfort, guidance, and support.

____My child is very clear about my expectations of her.

____I rein my child in before things get out of hand.

____I know where and with whom my child is at all times.

____I deal directly with my child's feelings by talking with him.

____**My Score**

Scoring: 0–10 points: You are a spaghetti parent who has trouble setting consistent boundaries and sticking to them. Rereading chapter 6 will help you learn how to do this.

11–20 points: You frequently are inconsistent and will benefit from being firmer about your parenting decisions.

21–30 points: You occasionally forget to set and hold consistent boundaries but are doing well overall.

31–40 points: You are a clear, firm, and loving mom or dad who is strong enough to say no and mean it.

CHAPTER 7: CONTROLLING NEGATIVITY IN YOUR COMMUNICATION

Summary: Chapter 7 discussed the parent who tends to be negative and critical.

____I know exactly where my biases exist and work to be more accepting.

____My anxiety does not rise when things do not go exactly according to plan.

____I never compare my child to others.

____I am open-minded and flexible.

____I have a positive outlet for my natural anger and aggression.

____I do not engage in power struggles with my child.

____I do not expect my child to be perfect.

____I state rules and boundaries with clarity and not anger.

____I feel empathy for myself as well as for my child.

____I am open to the validity of my child's feelings and am available to listen.

____**My Score**

Scoring: 0–10 points: You are usually too critical of yourself and your children. Rereading chapter 7 will help you be more accepting of realistic expectations.

11–20 points: You have a tendency to be critical and negative when things do not go smoothly. Be aware of this and you will do better!

21–30 points: Once in a while you are too hard on yourself and your family. But in general, you do well here.

31–40 points: You are a positive person who is understanding of human imperfections. Well done!

CHAPTER 8: MANAGING YOUR TEMPER—RAISING AWARENESS TO ANGRY FEELINGS SO YOUR TEMPER DOESN'T CREEP UP ON YOU

Summary: Chapter 8 discussed parents who explode in anger.

____When I am angry, I take a short cool-down and then deal with the situation calmly.

____I never use verbal putdowns or spew hostilities to my child (or spouse).

____I recognize and accept anger as a natural, normal human emotion.

____I talk about feelings, including angry feelings, with my child.

____I never get so angry that I hit my child in rage.

____I have a good tolerance for delayed gratification.

____I have a planned course of action for when I get angry.

____I do not store up anger. Instead I have a healthy outlet for it.

____I teach my child to always tell me the truth about their feelings.

____I understand that I am a "feelings" role model for my children.

____**My Score**

Scoring: 0–10 points: You often have angry feelings that can result in angry eruptions. Rereading chapter 8 will help you develop good coping skills.

11–20 points: You can sometimes explode in anger, especially when you are tired or stressed. Awareness is key.

21–30 points: Sometimes you can explode; but it is a rare occasion.

31–40 points: You have a good grip on your angry feelings and can model this in a healthy way to your child.

CHAPTER 9: IT'S ABOUT YOUR CHILD, NOT YOU

Summary: Chapter 9 was about parents who are self-involved.

____The needs of my child take precedence over everything else.

____I give quality, uninterrupted time to my child on a regular basis.

____I make my child feel she is my number-one priority.

____I can easily empathize with my child and others.

____I treat others well and also teach my child to do this.

____I look my child in the eye when I talk to her.

___I accept compliments graciously but do not need them for validation.

___I do not expect special treatment from others just because I am me.

___Whenever possible, I make personal appointments when my child is in school.

___I actively consider the impact of my behavior on other people.

___**My Score**

Scoring: 0–10 points: You have been known to put your needs ahead of the needs of others. Rereading chapter 9 will help you define your specific areas of challenge.

11–20 points: You can "forget" the needs of your child. Put yourself in their shoes, and the frequency of this will diminish.

21–30 points: Occasionally you can be a little self-absorbed. Talk to your kids to get a reality check!

31–40 points: You have a healthy respect and empathetic feel for others—your children included.

CHAPTER 10: THE IMPORTANCE OF BONDING SOLIDLY WITH YOUR CHILD

Summary: Chapter 10 discussed parents who are detached or have trouble bonding.

___I feel deep pleasure and contentment being with my child.

___My child comes first, before my phone or computer.

___I want to increase my level of closeness with my child.

___I am either a warm, consistent caregiver, or I provide one for my child.

___My child knows he comes first with me.

___I do not beat myself up over my ability to bond, no matter what my success level.

___I value and appreciate other adults who have warm relationships with my child.

___My face shows pleasure when I am with my child.

___I know what my comfort zone is for physical and emotional closeness.

_____ If I have difficulty bonding or attaching, I will consult a child specialist.
_____ **My Score**

Scoring: 0–10 points: Bonding and attachment can be tough for you. Reread chapter 10 to reinforce helpful ideas.
11–20 points: You struggle some with attachment. Actively work to bring your relationship with your child closer.
21–30 points: Once in a while you can be distant. Your new awareness of this will help prevent it in the future.
31–40 points: You have a wonderfully close attachment to your child and have developed an excellent bond.

CHAPTER 11: WHEN ONE PARENT TRAVELS
Summary: Chapter 11 involved parents who travel.

_____ I prepare my child in advance for a trip I or his other parent will take.
_____ I make more time for "special time" when the other parent is away.
_____ I look for disruptions in my child's sleep, mood, and behavior when one parent travels.
_____ I encourage my child to talk about his feelings and the parent who is away.
_____ I maintain regular routines, boundaries, rewards, and consequences.
_____ I have learned to use empathic narration.
_____ When I am away, I give my child something special of mine.
_____ I check in regularly with my child when I am away, or I see that the other parent does.
_____ I am attentive and patient with my child, especially when her other parent is away.
_____ I carve out time for me.
_____ **My Score**

Scoring: 0–10 points: Your child struggles when you or his other parent is absent. Review chapter 11 and implement the ideas there. This will help your child cope.

11–20 points: You can do more to ease the transition of parental travel for your child. Plan the absence in more detail so your child has an easier time.

21–30 points: Overall, you are doing well here. Consider doing more to make your child feel less lonely and more special while you or your partner is away.

31–40 points: You have prepared your child well and held the lines during the transition!

CHAPTER 12: HANDLING SPECIAL CIRCUMSTANCES
Summary: Chapter 12 dealt with parents with disabilities or who have other special circumstances.

____I have learned to be empathic toward myself.

____I am honest with my child.

____I do not play the victim around my child.

____I have acknowledged and accepted what I have lost.

____I tell my child the facts in clear, simple language, and let her ask questions.

____I understand that my health evokes strong feelings in my child.

____I validate the expression of everything my child is feeling and experiencing.

____I highlight positive similarities between myself and able-bodied parents.

____I have someone I talk to who lends support.

____I have the help of loving, responsible people who assist me in caring for my child.

____**My Score**

Scoring: 0–10 points: You have difficulty handling your special challenges. Revisit chapter 12 for ideas that will help your child. Then find resources that will help you.

11–20 points: You are struggling to stay balanced, but you are probably doing better than you think. Continue to make your child feel validated and loved and to accept help when needed.

21–30 points: In spite of challenges, you are doing quite well. Remember to keep open communication between yourself and your child, and discuss her feelings often.

31–40 points: Congratulations on succeeding when others might have given up!

CHAPTER 13: WHAT TO DO WHEN THE CHEMISTRY DOESN'T MIX

Summary: Chapter 13 involved parents who clash with, and who have an opposite personality from, their child.

____I understand I should adjust my personality dial up or down, rather than change it completely.

____I do not get annoyed with my child.

____I accept the reality that my child is very different from me.

____I feel very connected to my child in spite of our different personalities.

____I do not attach labels to my child.

____I encourage, rather than push, my child toward social norms.

____I don't react with anger, even when my child upsets me.

____My child and I both love at least one same thing.

____I seek activities for my child that are best suited to her personality and not mine.

____I love my child for who he is, rather than for what I'd like him to be.

____**My Score**

Scoring: 0–10 points: You and your child are poles apart. Reread chapter 13, then take a deep breath and dig in. Life can, and will, get better.

11–20 points: There are many differences between you and your child. Increase your acceptance of this, and him, and keep nudging.

21–30 points: You and your child may be very different people, but you have a healthy and positive outlook.

31–40 points: Even though it is hard to do, you fully embrace the many differences between you and your child and encourage her uniqueness.

CHAPTER 14: WIN-WIN PARENTING

Summary: Chapter 14 championed parents who got it right, despite rocky waters.

____I often engage in negotiations, bargaining, or deal making.

___I get caught up in power struggles with my kids.

___It is hard for me to balance nurturing and setting limits with holding boundaries firm.

___I miss opportunities to tune in to my child.

___I forget to celebrate the healthy steps and achievements of separation.

___I am nice to my child, but it often is an effort for me.

___It is difficult for me to make uninterrupted special time every day with my child.

___I fight with loved ones in front of my child.

___I do not ask for help when I need it and sometimes do not accept help when is offered.

___I forget to put myself in my child's shoes and empathize with her.

___**My Score**

Scoring: 0–10 points: You are a truly self-aware parent!

11–20 points: You are so very close! A few tweaks here and there and you've got it.

21–30 points: You get some things very right. Work to improve other areas and notice the positive change in your family.

31–40 points: You find it difficult to put all the pieces in place. Review chapter 14 to better understand how the "win-win" families made it work.

THE FINAL TALLY

Now that you are more aware of your specific parenting style, I hear you asking what you should do with the information, and that is a great question. Being aware of your specific weaknesses will help you develop a plan to overcome them. After all, it's hard to improve when you don't know what needs improving.

Now that you know, for instance, that you really don't take enough cool-down time when you are angry, or that you could do a better job of scheduling your personal appointments when your child is in school or at another activity, you can implement positive change.

In the next, and final, chapter, we will take your newfound awareness to a higher level with specific ways you can check your emotional awareness from moment to moment. Plus, I will show you how to make great parental decisions and act effectively on both your positive and negative feelings.

DR. FRAN'S TOP TIPS CHAPTER FIFTEEN

- Remember that in taking the self-assessment evaluations it is of utmost importance that you be painfully honest with yourself.
- All through this book I ask you to be kind and gentle with yourself. In this chapter I want you to be truthful, even if it hurts.
- You never have to show your self-evaluation to anyone else. It is for *you* to know so you can continue to evolve and grow as a parent.
- Take your time to give some of the statements careful thought. You might want to sleep on it before you write down your answers.
- Once you see your scores, don't beat yourself up. Remember no perfect parent exists. Everyone has an issue somewhere, or even in a few areas. The less you self-judge, the faster you can pick yourself up and start working on your challenging spots.
- You can be the best parent you wish to be. I am here right beside you. Good luck!

CHAPTER SIXTEEN

APPLYING THE KNOWLEDGE

THE PROCESS OF CHANGE

There is an art to self-awareness and self-exploration. To be effective, there is an internal tempo that has to speed up and an external tempo that has to slow down. When dealing with your child, you need to speed up your thinking process. You must ask yourself first what *you* are feeling, then what your *child* is feeling. It is a rapid back and forth in your mind of registering feelings within you and within your child. Your accelerated thinking process slows down your external talking. This puts a fresh spin on the old saying, "Think before you speak."

Everyone has an objective underneath his or her words and behavior, including your child. There is an ongoing probability that your child will occasionally push their objective to the forefront of a situation, and that's when events can get out of hand. As a self-aware parent, you have to be one step ahead of your child so you can understand and empathize with their experience. But, you must have two things before you can achieve this: mental space so you can think and the honesty to respond to the question "What do I feel, right now in this moment?"

Knowing how you feel in any given moment gives you the freedom to choose how you will respond to your child and his or her words and actions. Without this awareness, most parents react automatically, without thinking, making it more likely that they will repeat the behaviors of their own parents. That's when behaviors often escalate, rather than settle down. As you have seen, not all of these behaviors are positive.

But you are a self-aware parent. You have options! You are aware of your parenting style, and probably also of the styles of your parents and partner. Now you can learn to take a detailed and ongoing assessment of your internal temperature and find out how to talk yourself through any situation. For example, if your child is scared, your internal assessment and dialogue might go something like this:

> *My daughter is scared. What do I feel?*
>
> *I am panicky, anxious, frozen, flooded with ideas, and I can't choose what to say or do. I am running a thousand miles an hour inside myself.*
>
> *What I feel is not nearly as important as what my child feels.*
>
> *I see that her fear is subsiding. She got turned around on the playground. We could not find each other. We both were scared, but she does not need to see my fear.*
>
> *I need to show her she is safe.*
>
> *I can slow my outer tempo and relax my body, my expression. I can smile warmly and hold her close. I will take a big breath to help her settle, then I will dry her tears. Maybe we should go for ice cream.*

Note that what you feel is not anything you need to communicate to your daughter. It is very important, however, that you are able to define your feelings *quickly*, so you can adjust how and what you communicate to your child.

You do not want your child to see your anxious and panicky feelings on your face or in your body. Because you are aware of this, you adjust your tone of voice, facial expressions, body language, and words to whatever your child needs to see and hear. In this way you can choose what messages you want to communicate to your child, and choices give you power over any situation.

Remember that in your internal tempo there is a back-and-forth movement in the way you register and regulate your feelings. Emotions change from moment to moment. Every time you or your child say something or do something, you must again take the temperature of your internal tempo, and then readjust your next steps and responses.

Your thoughts might be to the effect of: How am I feeling right now? How is my daughter feeling? What should I do next to help my child? As you can see, there is an art to this and it does take some real practice. But once you master this technique, you can also put it to use in your relationship with your spouse and in relationships with friends, coworkers, and other family members. So it is worth the effort to practice until it comes naturally and instinctively.

Then there is the fact that if you don't develop this art of internal dialogue, you will inevitably respond to situations in the ways your parents did, or in ways you really wish you hadn't. Remember, too, that all children want the same thing. They want to be seen, heard, and validated. By checking in with your feelings from moment to moment, you can determine in every situation how to best meet the needs of your child.

The following four scenarios are very different, but as we see how these parents take their internal temperatures and register their thoughts and feelings, you will learn how you need to think, assess, and act in order to regain control of a tough situation.

THE GROCERY STORE MELTDOWN

We've all seen it. Most of us have been there. A young child begins shrieking because she can't have a specific box of cereal *right now!* Not only is it embarrassing, but it makes parents feel helpless and out of control.

Let's suppose you are a mom who is shopping at a grocery store with your three-year-old daughter, who wants a cookie. You say, "The cookies are for after dinner. You can have one then. Here are some fish crackers you can have now." Because you are a self-aware parent, as soon as your daughter's screams begin, you start to think this through for the first time in a very specific way.

I feel helpless. I am being publicly humiliated. I have a quick rage that is building toward my daughter. I am overwhelmed, exhausted. I feel guilty for saying no. I feel shaky and full of panic.

Keep in mind that all this thought has to happen and be defined in an instant. Your evaluation of your feelings also has to happen silently. The chaser is that what your daughter needs right now is to feel understood, but how do you get there? Here's where your next thoughts might go:

This is a learning opportunity. I can begin empathic attunement out loud.

"Mommy sees how really mad you are right now and sees how much you want the cookies. It is so hard to wait until after dinner."

Unfortunately, your daughter's shrieking continues.

I need to give one statement that she is to stop, or we will leave our groceries right here and go to the car. I hope she stops. I need the groceries for dinner tonight.

Okay, I gave the warning statement and she is still shrieking. In fact, it is getting worse. We're leaving. I am so embarrassed. I want to run away to a desert island. I am full of self-doubt. I don't know if I can contain her out-of-control angry meltdown. It's really big. All these people probably think I am abusing my little girl.

At the car, your daughter's fury escalates. She can't believe you had the nerve to actually carry her out of the store! You are still frustrated and angry, but you are fully aware of your feelings and do not show this to her. You do this by being sure not to squeeze her hand too tightly and by maintaining an even voice and neutral facial expression. This is the art, balancing *your* behavior with containing your child's behavior. Measuring, empathic narrating, and balancing from moment to moment is an important continual update of your feelings and actions.

When I recognize that I am angry, it takes the heat down a couple of notches. That's an interesting thing to discover. My daughter is

*settling. Could it be a reaction to my lower intensity? Finally.
Now her rage-filled cries have the sound of mournful sadness because she did not get her cookies and she did not succeed in over-
powering me.*

*Now I feel sad for her because she is hurting. I hurt, too, and I
feel guilty. Did I do the right thing? I am learning that when my
daughter cries sad tears my heart breaks, and I am vulnerable to giving in to her in those moments. Wow, that's a useful discovery.*

Can you see that in this scenario you have a tendency to be unsure?
But by being aware of your feelings, you are able to be definitive and
strong, yet compassionate toward your little girl. Awareness of your feelings frees you to come up with a plan, and the responses of your daughter
to the plan determine your next move.

*She's completely cried out now. I feel drained. It all was so intense. I'll
offer her the one-time chance to go back into the grocery store and try
again.*

*"Let's try one more time. If it's too hard for you today, then we'll
go home and try again tomorrow."*

Notice that you, the mom, did not say, "That's it, we are going
home." Instead, you maximized the learning opportunity by allowing
your child one chance to behave. This method is a great motivator because if she does well, she gets to stay in the fun store and you buy the
groceries. Then after dinner she has her cookie. In this if/then scenario,
your daughter learns that *if* she loses control, *then* she loses the privilege
of going to the grocery store. But if she behaves, then she has the privilege of staying at the grocery store. Either way, she gets her after-dinner
cookie.

Remember that you must always deliver what you promise. If you
have no cookies at home, offer another treat after dinner because you do
not take away *more* than the privilege of being in the store. If you and your
daughter go back into the store and if she cannot show appropriate public
behavior, then you also have to make good on your other statement, go
home, and try again the next day.

THE PLAY DATE

Here's another example. Your seven-year-old son has a friend over, but when the friend's mother comes for a short visit with you before taking her son home, your child has a tantrum because he does not want the play date to end.

"I want more time to play with Johnny," your son yells. "I hate you. I want another mom." Of course, this is all shouted with rage toward you in front of the other mom. To make it worse, your son runs into his room and slams the door hard enough to make the house shake. Whew. Your internal dialogue might go something like this:

I am so angry with my son. His behavior reflects back on me. I am embarrassed. What is that other mom thinking right now? I bet Johnny will never want to come over to play again. My son will never have any play dates again. I must stop his behavior but I am not sure I am up for the job. My son must not be allowed to disrespect me in public, in private, certainly not in front of other parents. I can't believe he acted like this. What do I do now?

I should say something to Johnny and his mom. I am still so angry with my child. I know he is upset that he can't have more of what he wants and has trouble stopping himself. But he went over the line and said terrible things. Johnny's mom looks awkward and uncomfortable. I bet she wishes she did not witness our little scene. She looks like she feels bad for me. She's not saying anything so she probably doesn't know what to say. I wonder if she is judging me? I must act now.

You, the self-aware parent, decide correctly that your son's needs take precedence over the needs of your visitors, and you say as you show them to the door, "I'm so sorry our play date has to end abruptly and this way." But when you go to your son's room, you feel your anger rising again.

I want to say, "How can you do this to me?" even though I know my son's behavior has nothing to do with me. He is just immature about handling limits on something he wants more of. I need to take a deep breath, measure my internal temperature. I am still angry, but not uncontrollably so. I know I can manage my feelings and actions no matter what happens next. I have to say something to him, but he can't know how rattled I am.

"I see how you got really mad when we had to stop your fun time with Johnny. When you get really mad you can say some pretty strong words. That's your way of letting me know you are so very angry. One day soon you'll be able to tell me right to my face that you are super mad at me for having to end the play date. I'm the kind of mom who really wants to hear you tell me about your feelings. But, I can't let you say disrespectful things or slam doors. If this happens again, I'm going to ask you to show me you can fix what you said to me, even in front of your friend.

With these words you empathically narrate your child's emotional and behavioral experience. To spare his public shame, you prepare him for the fact that while you didn't ask him to fix what he said to you this time, next time you will.

You know your seven-year-old is too old and too big to hold in the containing way that works for younger kids (where the parent holds the child from behind while sitting Indian style on the floor). It also risks humiliating him, so you invite your son to talk about what happened.

I feel my anger zooming down. Now I am worried about my son. He gets so angry. I can think more clearly than I could a few moments ago. Let's see how we can turn this into a positive learning experience.

"I sent Johnny and his mom home. You know if you get angry like that, any play date has to end right away. I am sorry you weren't able to say goodbye. Maybe next time you will be able to thank your friend for coming over and tell him good bye."

I hope there is a next time.

"I also heard you slam the door. That's not allowed in our house. I need you to show me how you can open and close the door gently."

Is this enough consequence for now? I think so. My son looks devastated. I can see that he is sad about the way the way his time with his friend ended abruptly and how he behaved.

WHAT NOT TO DO

This was one angry mom. A previous response might have been to yell at her son or give him weeks of no electronic privileges. But this mom, like you, is self-aware, so she didn't. This mom was able to take her emotion out of the scene and give her son exactly what he needed. As you can see by reading her internal thoughts, it wasn't easy for her, but she did it because it was the right thing to do for her son.

Part of being self-aware is learning to trust your instincts. It is knowing when enough is enough and when it is too much. It is learning to use what you are feeling for the betterment of your child. In this case, you, the self-aware mom, knew that additional punishment would make your son feel bad about himself and resentful toward you. You did enough.

If the son in this scenario had not gotten up and opened and closed the door gently when asked, if instead he had slammed the door again, then you could help him by putting your hand over his and helping him open and close the door gently. But he has to do it on his own before he can leave his room. Note, too, that this is not a time out and he is not "grounded" to his room. You didn't put him there. He ran there for refuge. He is free to leave *after* he complies by opening and closing the door gently.

THE "BAD" GRADES

Let's now say you are a single dad with a bright thirteen-year-old son. He could easily be on the honor roll at school, but because he is unmotivated and undisciplined, and because he'd rather have fun with his friends than study, he recently has been earning Cs and Ds. Sports are also very important to him. You think to yourself:

> *I feel a seething resentment toward my son. I work very hard to afford a good school and plenty of extras for him and he is so unappreciative. He's lazy and selfish. I am also mad at myself because I know my son is not purposefully defying me. This behavior has been building for some time and I have let it go on far too long. I should have taught him better life skills when he was younger.*

You are a dad who before might have been an explosive spaghetti parent. You would have let boundaries slide and then exploded in anger after your seething feelings got too big. Now, as an evolved self-aware dad, you are taking ownership of an area you are deficient in: boundaries. You also have developed empathy for your son and realize his poor grades and lackadaisical attitude are not all his fault. Because of this you do not become a battleship of accusation, as you would have before.

> *I feel upset with myself for not setting and holding boundaries better. I can improve, but my son won't like it. I have to get past the fact that for a while he won't like me. This is really hard for me but I have to have this conversation.*
>
> *"Son, I know you can do better on these grades. So temporarily, until you bring your grades up, all your after-school and weekend sports activities have to stop. Today. I know this means you will be off the team for the season, but your grades are more important. Your sports are a privilege I want to give you, but only if you can keep up your schoolwork and get better grades on your next report card."*
>
> *I see how furious he is with me. I can't expect him to have a normal conversation right now. He needs time to process this. He will try to bargain with me, but I have to stand firm. I feel sad for him because I brought us to this point. But I feel good, too, because I took a positive step to turn a bad situation around.*

You, the dad, made an excellent decision here. Because sports mean so much to your son, he probably will buckle down and bring his grades up. And, because you are so empathetic toward him, he will eventually stop resenting you for enforcing the boundary on this and in other areas of his life. That you gave a long-term goal is also good. Report cards come out infrequently, so this gives your son the opportunity to get in the habit of studying, rather than study for a week or two and earn his sports reward quickly.

Note, too, that this scenario did not involve an immediate crisis. This had been a long-standing problem that was going to take time to turn around. This dad took time to think it through, went in knowing his tendencies, and was able to overcome them on behalf of his son. Well done!

THE CAR KEYS

For our last scenario we have a mom and a dad of a sixteen-year-old high school junior who stayed out past her curfew. You might think that parents of an older teen like this would be done with their self-exploration, but I have found that that is not always the case. In my practice I see many parents of older kids, young adults, and adult children who are only beginning the path of self-awareness. As I always say, it doesn't matter if you are late to the party, what does matter is that you are here now. And I'm glad you're here!

In our scenario, your older teen daughter was only thirty minutes late, but you and her other parent waited up. You were worried and angry that she not only defied her curfew but did not call to say she was going to be late.

> Dad: I am so tense and angry. I want to read her the riot act. How did she get to be so disrespectful? Doesn't she know how worried her mother is?
>
> Mom: He is so angry. I am worried he will have a heart attack or a stroke. What if she is hurt, is in a ditch, or the hospital? Will someone call us? Who will let us know?

When your daughter comes home at midnight, she says she is tired and will talk about it with you in the morning.

> Dad: I need to talk to her right now! Her behavior is unacceptable. But I do not have a handle on my anger. If we talk now I will say things I regret.
>
> Mom: My relief that she is safe is overwhelming. We can't allow her to do this again, but I am so emotional right now all I can do is cry. Plus, I can see that she is tired. We won't accomplish anything if we talk now. None of us is in any mental frame to find a positive resolution.

You both made excellent choices here in not speaking to your daughter immediately. In the morning you and your spouse talk to your daughter, but you don't do the best job of it.

> Dad: I am intimidated by my daughter. How weird is that? She is so smart and vibrant, but she is revealing a manipulative side.

How could she be part of me? We have to talk to her, though. We have to get to the bottom of her disrespect. I am not as calm as I would like to be. I feel so angry I could yell at her, but I know that will not accomplish anything.

Mom: *I am too tentative with her. I do not have a strong personality like she and my husband do. And I am afraid of my daughter's rebellious nature. I hope whatever we say does not provoke that in her. She is so like her dad. Her anger scares me. I feel shaky inside, but I have to be firm.*

Daughter: *"I haven't had my coffee yet and I know what you are going to say. You already told me."*

Dad: *I hate the way she brushes us off. I feel hate for her slick avoidance of the issues. She's my daughter. How can I feel hate for her? I don't hate her. I just don't like her very much right now. I still love her though. More than I can say. What should we do?*

Mom: *This isn't going well. I need to say something. "But honey, we have to talk about an appropriate consequence."*

Daughter: *"I've already had the lecture. Many times."*

Dad: *"It's Saturday. You blew your curfew last night so you will not be allowed to go out tonight." That wasn't great. We together should have come to that. Should have talked it through. I can't let her see my indecision. But I said it so I have to stand by this.*

Your daughter is angry. She gets dressed and when neither of you is looking, slips the car keys off the counter and takes her mom's car. She not only drives off for the day, she drives off with a sense of entitlement.

Dad: *I know she is saying "I'm sixteen; you can't tell me what to do." She is such a spoiled brat. What have we done to create such a monster? I must put a stop to this. I feel I have no authority with her.*

Mom: *I hate this shaky feeling I get when things go wrong. She took my car without permission. That's stealing! I feel used and ineffectual. Should we call the police? Will that get her attention? But then she will have a record. That might hurt her college admissions. Is this worth that? I don't think so. I am finally angry. Very angry.*

Together you decide to wait it out. When your daughter comes home around dinnertime, she walks into the house, replaces the keys on the counter, and goes into her room without saying a word.

> *Dad: I'd love to barge in on her and scream at her. What is she think-ing? What am I thinking? I have to get a handle on what is going on in my head. I have to let go of this fury. It is not pro-ductive. I need to take a few deep breaths. Okay. My wife and I have to structure a scenario with firm boundaries that she can-not wiggle out of.*

When you enter her room together she yells at you to leave. "I've had a hard day," she says. In response, you calmly pick up her purse, retrieve her wallet, and remove her driver's license.

> *Mom: I want to shake some sense into her, but I have to be gentle so as not to provoke her. But I also have to be firm. "You stole my car. If you take my car again and drive it without your driver's license, we will call the police and let them know. When you are stopped, we will not rescue you."*
>
> *Dad: This is my little girl. My heart is breaking. I do not want her to have to deal with legal issues, but if she has to I know it is be-cause she has brought it on herself. I feel sad for all of us.*

I love this scenario because it shows that just because parents are self-aware, it does not mean you won't make mistakes. Expect that. It will happen. As with the parents here, you always have a chance to go back and try again. This calm resolution of quietly removing her driver's license and requiring this daughter to go through the inconvenience of either catching rides from friends or not attending an event was a perfect solution. When her license was eventually returned and she regained driving privileges, this daughter knew what the full consequence would be should she ignore her curfew again.

IN CLOSING

We have covered a lot of territory in the last sixteen chapters, and you have come a long way in understanding yourself as a parent. In closing, I'd like you to remember three things:

- In every decision, the needs of your child come first.
- It is important that you stay continually aware of your thoughts, feelings, and tendencies.
- Give yourself the freedom to make mistakes.

Parenting is both the biggest challenge and the biggest reward you will ever have. I know you will do well. If you have questions or comments, I invite you to visit me online at www.DrFranWalfish.com. I am so excited about your new parenting adventures, and to each of you I send my sincere support, affection, and warmest wishes.

DR. FRAN'S TOP TIPS CHAPTER SIXTEEN

- Speed up your internal thinking tempo and slow down your external behavioral tempo.
- Register what you are feeling and what your child is feeling from moment to moment.
- Always empathize with your child and yourself.
- Evaluate and keep your personal feelings and thoughts private until you have adjusted them. Then you can say what you want to say in the way you want your child to hear it.
- Narrate out loud what your child wants, feels, and is doing.
- Manage your negative feelings, including shame, humiliation, rage, and embarrassment.
- Always make what is best for your child come first.
- Consequences must have meaning to your child and be implemented immediately.
- Timing is essential. You are honing your thinking and behavioral tempos.
- The more self-awareness you have, the greater your options are to parent well.
- Expect mistakes. No one is perfect.
- Practice, practice, practice.

NOTES

CHAPTER 1

1. David Kerr et al., "A Prospective Three Generational Study of Fathers' Constructive Parenting: Influences from Family of Origin, Adolescent Adjustment, and Offspring Temperament," *Developmental Psychology* 45 (September 2009): 1257–1275. Quotes from Kerr on ensuing pages are from the same source.
2. H. C. Steinhausen and C. Juzi, "Elective Mutism: An Analysis of 100 Cases," *Journal of the American Academy of Child & Adolescent Psychiatry* 35, no. 5 (1996): 606–614.

CHAPTER 2

1. John T. Walkup et al., "Fluvoxamine for the Treatment of Anxiety Disorders in Children and Adolescents," *The New England Journal of Medicine* 344, no. 17 (April 26, 2001): 1279–1285, available at http://content.nejm.org/cgi/reprint/344/17/1279.pdf.

CHAPTER 3

1. Erica M. Jackson and Rod K. Dishman, "Cardiorespiratory Fitness and Laboratory Stress: A Meta-regression Analysis," *Psychophysiology* 43, no. 1 (January 2006): 57–72.
2. Dr. Petra Arck, "Stress-Induced Neurogenic Inflammation in Murine Skin Skews Dendritic Cells Towards Maturation and Migration: Key Role of Intercellular Adhesion Molecule–1/Leukocyte Function-Associated Antigen Interactions," *American Journal of Pathology* 173 (October 28, 2008): 1379–1388.
3. Ibid.
4. David W. Brown et al., "Adverse Childhood Experiences and the Risk of Premature Mortality," *American Journal of Preventive Medicine* 37, no. 5 (November 2009): 389–396, available at http://www.ajpm-online.net.

5. Elissa S. Epel et al., "Accelerated Telomere Shortening in Response to Life Stress," *Proceedings for the National Academy of Sciences* 101, no. 49 (December 2004): 17312–17315, available at http://www.pnas.org/content/101/49/17312.full?sid=8a354869-b23f–4e22–8935-dd5381ff6c3b.
6. United States Department of Health and Human Services, National Center for Health Statistics, "The Marriage Measures Guide to State Level Statistics," 2008, available at http://aspe.hhs.gov/hsp/08/marriagemeasures/report.pdf.
7. Judicial Council of California, "2004 Court Statistics Report," available at http://www.courtinfo.ca.gov/reference/documents/csr2004.pdf.

CHAPTER 4

1. Foster W. Cline, M.D., and Jim Fay, *Parenting with Love and Logic: Teaching Children Responsibility* (Colorado Springs, CO: Piñon Press, 1990).
2. David Wood et al., "Impact of Family Relocation on Children's Growth, Development, School Function, and Behavior," *Journal of the American Medical Association* 270 (September 1993): 1334–1338.
3. Ibid.
4. Eva Pomerantz and Qian Wang, "The Role of Parental Control in Children's Development in Western and East Asian Countries," *Current Directions in Psychological Science* 18, no. 5 (October 2009): 285–289.
5. Quoted in Kay Randall, "Mom Needs an 'A': Hovering, Hyper-Involved Parents the Topic of Landmark Study," The University of Texas at Austin online feature, March 26–April 2, 2007, available at http://www.utexas.edu/features/2007/helicopter/index.html.
6. Quoted in Paul R. Kopenkoskey, "Are You a 'Helicopter' Parent?" *Grand Rapids Living,* January 4, 2010, available at http://www.mlive.com/living/grand-rapids/index.ssf/2010/01/are_you_a_helicopter_parent.html.

CHAPTER 5

1. Martha Stout, *The Sociopath Next Door* (New York: Broadway Books, 2005).
2. D. Shaffer et al., "The NIMH Diagnostic Interview Schedule for Children Version 2.3 (DISC–2.3): Description, Acceptability, Prevalence Rates and Performance in the MECA Study," *Journal of the American Academy of Child and Adolescent Psychiatry* 35, no. 7 (1996): 865–77.
3. M. M. Weissman et al., "Depressed Adolescents Grown Up," *Journal of the American Medical Association* 281 (1999): 1701–1713.
4. Erik H. Erikson, *Childhood and Society* (New York: Norton, 1950); Erik H. Erikson, *Identity and the Life Cycle* (New York: International Universities Press, 1959); Erik H. Erikson, *Identity, Youth and Crisis* (New York: Norton, 1968); and Richard Stevens, *Erik Erikson: An Introduction* (New York: St. Martin's Press, 1983).

5. Herbert L. Mirels, Paul Greblo, and Janet B. Dean, "Judgmental Self-Doubt: Beliefs about One's Judgmental Prowess," *Personality and Individual Differences* 33, no. 5 (October 5, 2002): 741–758.

CHAPTER 6

1. Lee Shumow, Deborah Lowe Vandell, and Jill K. Posner, "Harsh, Firm, and Permissive Parenting in Low-Income Families: Relations to Children's Academic Achievement and Behavioral Adjustment," *Journal of Family Issues* 19, no. 5 (1998): 483–507.
2. "Leeward Coast Community Profile, Wa'ianae-Nänäkuli: State Incentive Grant for Substance Abuse Prevention among Hawaii's Youth," 2001, Center on the Family, College of Tropical Agriculture and Human Resources, University of Hawai'i at Mänoa, available at www.uhfamily.hawaii.edu/publications/ SIG/CRPP/leeward.pdf.

CHAPTER 7

1. "F as in Fat: How Obesity Policies Are Failing in America 2009," Trust for America's Health, Robert Wood Johnson Foundation, July 2009, available at www.healthyamericans.org/reports/obesity2009/.
2. Kyung E. Rhee et al., "Parenting Styles and Overweight Status in First Grade," *Pediatrics* 117 (June 2006): 2047–2054, available at http://pediatrics.aap publications.org/cgi/reprint/117/6/2047.
3. Erica D. Taylor et al., "Orthopedic Complications of Overweight in Children and Adolescents," *Pediatrics* 117 (June 2006): 2167–2174, available at http:// pediatrics.aappublications.org/cgi/reprint/117/6/2167.
4. "Strict Parenting Can Produce Overweight Kids," DisneyFamily.com, available at http://family.go.com/parenting/article-mm–77922-strict-parenting-can-produce-overweight-kids-t/.

CHAPTER 8

1. Andrea J. Sedlak et al., "Abuse, Neglect, Adoption & Foster Care Research National Incidence Study of Child Abuse and Neglect (NIS–4), 2004–2009," U.S. Department of Health and Human Services, Administration for Children and Families. Office of Planning, Research and Evaluation. Westat (2008), available at http://www.acf.hhs.gov/programs/opre/abuse_neglect/natl_incid/index.htm.
2. Patricia P. Chang et al., "Anger in Young Men and Subsequent Premature Cardiovascular Disease: The Precursors Study," *Archives of Internal Medicine* 162 (2002): 901–906.
3. Ramachandran S. Vasan et al., "Assessment of Frequency of Progression to Hypertension in Non-Hypertensive Participants in the Framingham Heart Study: A Cohort Study," *The Lancet* 358, no. 9294 (2001): 1682–1686.

CHAPTER 9

1. Eric Dubow, L. Rowell Huesmann, and Leonard D. Eron, "Childhood Correlates of Adult Ego Development," *Child Development* 58, no. 3 (June 1987): 859–869.

2. Alan Rappoport, "Co-Narcissism: How We Accommodate to Narcissistic Parents," available at http://www.alanrappoport.com/pdf/Co-Narcissism Article.pdf.

CHAPTER 10

1. Lane Strathearn et al., "Adult Attachment Predicts Maternal Brain and Oxytocin Response to Infant Cues," *Neuropsychopharmacology* 34 (December 2009): 2655–2666, available at http://www.nature.com/npp/journal/v34/n13/full/npp2009103a.html.

2. Everett Waters et al., "Attachment Security in Infancy and Early Adulthood: A Twenty-Year Longitudinal Study," *Child Development* 71, no. 3 (May/June 2000): 684–689.

3. Erik H. Erikson, *Childhood and Society* (New York: Norton, 1950); Erik H. Erikson, *Identity and the Life Cycle* (New York: International Universities Press, 1959); Erik H. Erikson, *Identity, Youth and Crisis* (New York: Norton, 1968); Richard Stevens, *Erik Erikson: An Introduction* (New York: St. Martin's Press, 1983).

CHAPTER 11

1. Molinda M. Chartrand et al., "Effect of Parents' Wartime Deployment on the Behavior of Young Children in Military Families," *Archive of Pediatric Adolescent Medicine* 162, no. 11 (2008):1009–1014, available at http://archpedi.ama-assn.org/cgi/content/full/162/11/1009?maxtoshow=&hits=10&RESULTFORMAT=&fulltext=deployed+parents+military&searchid=1&FIRSTINDEX=0&resourcetype=HWCIT.

2. Margaret S. Mahler, Fred Pine, and Anni Bergman, *The Psychological Birth of the Human Infant: Symbiosis and Individuation* (New York: Basic Books, 1973).

CHAPTER 12

1. *Ability Magazine,* May 2010, available at http://www.abilitymagazine.com/news_NCPD.html.

2. National Center for Parents with Disabilities and Their Families, Project Number: H133A080034, led by Megan Kirshbaum, PhD; Paul Preston, PhD; Leslie J. Caplan, PhD, Project Officer.

CHAPTER 13

1. "The Jung Page," http://www.cgjungpage.org/index.php?option=com_content&task=view&id=743&Itemid=54.

2. Elizabeth Larsen, "Raising an Introvert in an Extrovert World," *Child* 20, no. 3 (May 2005): 139–144.

3. Arthur Aron et al., "Temperament Trait of Sensory Processing Sensitivity Moderates Cultural Differences in Neural Response," *Social Cognitive and Affective Neuroscience* 5 (April 2010): 219–226, available at http://scan.oxford journals.org/content/early/2010/04/13/scan.nsq028.abstract.

4. Elaine N. Aron and Arthur Aron, "Sensory-Processing Sensitivity and Its Relation to Introversion and Emotionality," *Journal of Personality and Social Psychology* 73, no. 2 (1997): 345–368.

CHAPTER 14

1. Dr. Bruno Bettelheim, *A Good Enough Parent* (New York: Simon & Schuster, 1987).

INDEX